Securing Urban Heritage

Securing Urban Heritage considers the impact of securitization on access to urban heritage sites. Demonstrating that symbolic spaces such as these have increasingly become the location of choice for the practice and performance of contemporary politics in the last decade, the book shows how this has led to the securitization of urban public space. Highlighting specific changes that have been made, such as the installation of closed-circuit television or the limitation of access to certain streets, plazas, and buildings, the book analyses the impact of different approaches to securitization.

Claiming that access to heritage sites is a precursor to an informed and thorough understanding of heritage, the editors and contributors to this volume argue that new forms of securing urban heritage, including community involvement and digitalization, offer possibilities for the protection and use of urban heritage. Looking more closely at the versatile relationship between access and securitization in this context, the book provides a theoretical framework for the relationship between urban heritage and securitization. Comparing case studies from cities in Angola, Bulgaria, Eritrea, France, Germany, Hungary, Italy, Japan, Latvia, Mexico, Norway, Russia, Suriname, Sweden, Turkey, UK, and the US, the book reveals some of the key mechanisms that are used to regulate access to heritage sites around the world.

Providing much-needed insight into the diverse challenges of securitization for access and urban heritage, *Securing Urban Heritage* should be essential reading for academics, students, and practitioners from the fields of heritage and urban studies, architecture, art history, conservation, urban planning, and urban geography.

Heike Oevermann is a postdoctoral researcher and lecturer in interdisciplinary urban and heritage studies at the Georg Simmel Center for Metropolitan Studies, Humboldt Universität zu Berlin in Germany.

Eszter Gantner is a postdoctoral researcher with a focus on urban history and heritage studies at the Herder Institute for Historical Research on East Central Europe in Marburg, Germany.

Routledge Studies in Heritage

10 **Marie Antoinette at Petit Trianon**
Heritage Interpretation and Visitor Perceptions
Denise Major-Barron

11 **Heritage after Conflict**
Northern Ireland
Edited by Elizabeth Crooke and Tom Maguire

12 **Historicizing Heritage and Emotions**
The Affective Histories of Blood, Stone and Land
Edited by Alicia Marchant

·13 **Underwater Cultural Heritage**
Ethical Concepts and Practical Challenges
Elena Perez-Alvaro

14 **Cultural Heritage, Ageing, Disability and Identity**
Practice, and the Development of Inclusive Capital
Simon Hayhoe

15 **Securing Urban Heritage**
Agents, Access, and Securitization
Heike Oevermann & Eszter Gantner

16 **Visitor Encounters with the Great Barrier Reef**
Aesthetics, Heritage, and the Senses
Celmara Pocock

www.routledge.com/Routledge-Studies-in-Heritage/book-series/RSIHER

Securing Urban Heritage
Agents, Access, and Securitization

Edited by Heike Oevermann and
Eszter Gantner

LONDON AND NEW YORK

First published 2020
by Routledge
2 Park Square, Milton Park, Abingdon, Oxon OX14 4RN

and by Routledge
52 Vanderbilt Avenue, New York, NY 10017

Routledge is an imprint of the Taylor & Francis Group, an informa business

© 2020 selection and editorial matter, Heike Oevermann and Eszter Gantner;
individual chapters, the contributors

The right of Heike Oevermann and Eszter Gantner to be identified as the authors
of the editorial material, and of the authors for their individual chapters, has
been asserted in accordance with sections 77 and 78 of the Copyright, Designs
and Patents Act 1988.

All rights reserved. No part of this book may be reprinted or reproduced or utilised
in any form or by any electronic, mechanical, or other means, now known or
hereafter invented, including photocopying and recording, or in any information
storage or retrieval system, without permission in writing from the publishers.

Trademark notice: Product or corporate names may be trademarks or registered trademarks,
and are used only for identification and explanation without intent to infringe.

British Library Cataloguing-in-Publication Data
A catalogue record for this book is available from the British Library

Library of Congress Cataloging-in-Publication Data
A catalog record has been requested for this book

ISBN: 978-0-367-14843-0 (hbk)
ISBN: 978-0-429-05355-9 (ebk)

Typeset in Sabon
by Newgen Publishing UK

Contents

List of figures	vii
Notes on contributors	ix
Acknowledgements	xii
Introduction	1
ESZTER GANTNER AND HEIKE OEVERMANN	

PART I
Agents and forms of agency — 11

1 Community involvement in times of social insecurity — 13
CHRISTOPHE FOULTIER

2 Participatory matters: access, migration, and heritage in
Berlin museums — 31
KATARZYNA PUZON

3 Agents, access, and cultural policies of sharing in
Kyoto City and Osaka — 47
OLIMPIA NIGLIO

4 Urban heritage, communities, and environmental
sustainability — 62
DENNIS RODWELL

PART II
Technology, heritage, and access — 81

5 Securitization through digitalization and visualization — 83
PIOTR KUROCZYŃSKI

vi *Contents*

6 Documenting modernity 98
TORBEN KIEPKE AND HANS-RUDOLF MEIER

7 Urban nuclear reactors and the security theatre: the
making of atomic heritage in Chicago, Moscow,
and Stockholm 111
ANNA STORM, FREDRIK KROHN ANDERSSON,
AND EGLÉ RINDZEVIČIÛTÉ

PART III
Securing urban heritage in time and space 131

8 Fences and defences: matters of security in City Park,
Budapest 133
JULI SZÉKELY

9 Rewriting history: interpreting heritage in Saint
Petersburg and Istanbul 153
AYSE N. EREK AND ESZTER GANTNER

10 Disregarding youth proposals: intangible heritage,
securitization, and soccer fan groups in México 171
RICARDO DUARTE BAJAÑA

11 (Re)activated heritage: negotiating socialist history
in the urban space of Luanda 188
NADINE SIEGERT

Conclusion 206
HEIKE OEVERMANN AND ESZTER GANTNER

Index 212

Figures

1.1	Public places and high-rise housing estate in the district of Franc-Moisin-Bel-Air.	17
2.1	The refugee protest camp at the O-Platz.	39
2.2	Participants of the Reclaim Your Space team holding their posters.	41
3.1	Picture of historical Gion Matsuri, Kyoto.	52
3.2	Picture of present-day Gion Matsuri, Kyoto.	53
3.3	Kitakagaya Creative Village, Osaka during a cultural event.	57
4.1	Venice, inscribed on the UNESCO World Heritage List in 1987. The resident population has more than halved since the early 1970s.	64
4.2	Paramaribo, Suriname, inscribed in the UNESCO World Heritage List in 2002, and monumentalized for its Dutch colonial heritage.	66
4.3	Madryn Street, part of the Welsh Streets in the Toxteth district of Liverpool. The Beatles' drummer, Ringo Starr (Sir Richard Starkey) was born at 9 Madryn Street.	69
4.4	Chimney Pot Park, Salford, Greater Manchester. The plan-form inversion of the houses has the symbolic objective of turning people's perceptions of non-elite industrial urban heritage upside down.	75
5.1	Visualization for the competition "Post-Castle" submitted by Arthur Sarnitz.	90
5.2	3D Wikipedia: Using online text to automatically label and navigate reconstructed geometry.	93
6.1	Demolition of the Ahornblatt/Maple Leaf, Berlin.	99
7.1	In 1947, only five years after the first successful experiment worldwide to control nuclear energy, a bronze plaque was installed to commemorate the event and to indicate its location on the University of Chicago campus.	117
7.2	The neoclassical architecture of the F-1 reactor building with surrounding woods emphasize the exclusive working and living environments for nuclear physicists and engineers in Moscow during the Soviet period.	119

viii *List of figures*

7.3	In the early 1980s, the R1 reactor was removed from its underground location on KTH campus, and the cavern decontaminated of radioactivity. The hole in the ground and the numbered grid from measuring radioactivity in the ceiling serve as reminders of what is no longer there.	123
8.1	Hacking the advertisement of the Liget Budapest Project.	134
8.2	Construction site on the grounds of the Liget Budapest Project.	145
9.1	Trams at Nevsky Prospekt.	157
9.2	Emek Cinema building.	163
9.3	Roma Garden.	165
10.1	Members of La Banda del Rojo in the Nemesio Diez stadium.	179
10.2	Patrol police blocking the parade of La Banda del Rojo.	183
11.1	Mural at the Military Hospital in Luanda. Original version painted by Teresa Gama in 1978.	197
11.2	Memorial Agostinho Neto, Luanda.	199

Contributors

Ricardo Duarte Bajaña earned his PhD in social anthropology at the Ibero-American University, Mexico City, and holds an MSc in bioethics from Universidad el Bosque, Bogotá, Colombia. He specializes in communication and education at Universidad Central (Bogotá) and physical education at Universidad Pedagógica Nacional de Colombia (Bogotá). He has participated in studies related to socio-cultural processes within groups of soccer fans, female prisoners, and neighbourhood communities.

Ayse N. Erek, PhD, is an associate professor at the Faculty of Art and Design, Kadir Has University, Istanbul, Turkey, where she serves as director of the Design Research Graduate Program, focusing on methods and formats of transdisciplinary research on issues concerning theories and practices of contemporary art and design.

Christophe Foultier, PhD, is a postdoctoral fellow at Linköping University, Sweden. He holds a master's degree in urban planning and a PhD in international migration and ethnicity. His doctoral thesis, *Regimes of Hospitality: Urban Citizenship between Participation and Securitization— The Case of the Multiethnic French Banlieue*, analyses how urban strategies generate intersecting processes of participation and security.

Eszter Gantner is a postdoctoral researcher with a focus on urban history and heritage studies at the Herder Institute for Historical Research on East Central Europe in Marburg, Germany.

Torben Kiepke, PhD, studied architecture and conservation of monuments/preservation in Berlin and Venice. From 2005 to 2012 he taught in the Department of Preservation and Architectural Design at the Technical University of Dresden. In 2013, he concluded his dissertation on the architectural redesign of facades in Berlin during the 1920s. From 2013 to 2018 he was a lecturer and researcher at the Bauhaus-Universität Weimar, where he was involved in the project "Which Monuments— Which Modernism?" that compared methods of selecting and listing late-modern architecture in Europe. Since 2018 he has worked as an architect and researcher for the German Archaeological Institute.

x *Notes on contributors*

Fredrik Krohn Andersson, PhD, is Senior Lecturer in Art History and Heritage Studies at the Department of Culture and Aesthetics, Stockholm University. His research interests include critical architectural historiography as well as the heritagization of nuclear power plants and Cold War–built structures.

Piotr Kuroczyński, PhD, is an architect specializing in the field of digital 3D reconstruction, documentation, and visualization of cultural heritage. Since 2017 he has been Professor for Computer Science and Visualization in Architecture at the Hochschule Mainz—University of Applied Sciences Mainz.

Hans-Rudolf Meier, PhD, holds the chair in the Preservation of Historical Monuments and Sites and the History of Architecture at the Faculty of Architecture, Bauhaus-Universität Weimar. He graduated in history of art and medieval archaeology, and researches and publishes in fields including the history and theory of preservation, urban heritage, history of medieval and modern architecture, and history of archaeology.

Olimpia Niglio, PhD, is an architect and is Associate Professor of History and Architectural Restoration and foreign researcher at Japan's Kyoto University Graduate School of Human and Environmental Studies. Since 2002 she has been a professor at the University of Pisa, and is a professor at Universidad de Bogotá Jorge Tadeo Lozano (Colombia). She is an International Council on Monuments and Sites Italia member and an international academic member of the City Planning Institute of Japan in Tokyo.

Heike Oevermann is a postdoctoral researcher and lecturer in interdisciplinary urban and heritage studies at the Georg Simmel Center for Metropolitan Studies, Humboldt Universität zu Berlin in Germany.

Katarzyna Puzon, PhD, is an anthropologist and a postdoctoral research fellow at the Centre for Anthropological Research on Museums and Heritage (CARMAH) at Humboldt Universität zu Berlin. She conducts ethnographic research in Germany and Lebanon; her research interests lie in cities, and at the intersection of heritage, memory, and mobility. Her recent publications include "Saving Beirut: Heritage and the City" in the *International Journal of Heritage Studies* (2017).

Eglė Rindzevičiūtė, PhD, is Associate Professor of Criminology and Sociology at Kingston University, London. She is the author of *The Power of Systems: How Policy Sciences Opened up the Cold War World* (Cornell University Press, 2016) and co-editor of *The Struggle for the Long-Term in Transnational Science and Politics: Forging the Future* (Routledge, 2015), with Professor Jenny Andersson.

Notes on contributors xi

Dennis Rodwell, MA, DipArch(Cantab), DipFrench(Open), RIBA, FRIAS, FSA Scot, FRSA, IHBC, is an architect-planner. He works internationally in the field of cultural heritage, focused on the promotion and achievement of best practice in the management of historic sites and cities of all dates and periods up to and including the present day. Previously a principal in private practice as a conservation architect, he has also served in local government posts as a conservation officer, urban designer, project manager, and principal planner, and successfully promoted the rescue of a number of historic buildings at risk.

Nadine Siegert, PhD, is a researcher, curator, and publisher with a focus on modern and contemporary arts of the Global South. She is currently Deputy Director of Iwalewahaus, University of Bayreuth, Germany (www.iwalewa.uni-bayreuth.de), and a member of the research project "Revolution 3.0" at the Bayreuth Academy of Advanced African Studies. She received her doctoral degree from the Bayreuth International Graduate School of African Studies, in which she explored "(Re)mapping Luanda", through nostalgic and utopian aesthetic strategies in contemporary art in Angola (LIT).

Anna Storm holds a PhD in the History of Technology at the Royal Institute of Technology (KTH), and is Associate Professor in Human Geography at Stockholm University. She is the author of "*Post-Industrial Landscape Scars*" (Palgrave Macmillan, 2014) which was shortlisted for the 2015 Turku Book Award.

Juli Székely, PhD, is currently a post-doc research fellow at ELTE (Department of Sociology) in Budapest. She received her master's degrees in Hungarian literature and art history at the Eötvös Loránd University in Budapest, and later in sociology at the Central European University. She did her PhD studies in sociology at CEU, during which she was also a research fellow at Humboldt Universität zu Berlin. Her research interests lie primarily in the relationship of art and city, with a special emphasis on public art, (in) tangible heritage and memory politics in urban space.

Acknowledgements

The Alexander von Humboldt Stiftung funded a three-year international cooperation on "Claiming Public Space," which allowed us to run several international workshops and discussions as well as to publish this book. We thank the Alexander von Humboldt Stiftung for funding, and the Georg Simmel Center for Metropolitan Studies at Humboldt Universität zu Berlin for hosting this project. Furthermore, we would like to thank all authors and institutions for contributing, as well as our team and Routledge for their assistance in realizing this publication.

Introduction

Eszter Gantner and Heike Oevermann

Recognizing the importance of access to and use of heritage sites, this book discusses the concept of securitization in the field of heritage. Considering today's rapidly changing social, political, and technological environments, the book examines how securitization challenges access to urban heritage sites. We invited authors studying this question across a range of geographical and disciplinary contexts: case studies from Japan, Mexico, and Russia, as well as international comparisons, map the variety of local cultural and social practices. The interdisciplinary approach of the book helps to deepen understanding of the multiple facets of the influence of securitization on urban heritage sites.

Understanding securitization and heritage

In 1877 the English artist, writer, and socialist activist William Morris published his manifesto on the protection of ancient buildings. Following John Ruskin's argumentation, Morris reasoned that such sites needed to be *protected* for the future: "Thus, and thus only can we protect our ancient buildings, and hand them down instructive and venerable to those that come after us" (Society for the Protection of Ancient Buildings [SPAB], 1877, p. 2). At that time, Morris used the term *protection*. However, a year later, in an article published in *The Times*, he used the term *preservation* to argue against any kind of destruction of ancient buildings, which he presented as a duty towards future generations (Morris, 1878). Thus, at this point emerges the question of whether there is any difference in the application of the terms *preserve* and *protect*: Did Morris use them synonymously? What kinds of added meanings did these terms possess at that time?

According to the *Oxford Language Dictionary* (Simpson & Weiner, 1989, p. 677) the word *protect* originates from the Latin expression *protegere*, meaning to defend or guard from injury or danger; to preserve intact; and was used first in this sense in 1526. Moreover, it also encompasses the meaning *to keep safe*. However, the process of 'keeping safe' had also been described by the term *secure/secured*. According to the dictionary definition, the term *secure* includes making something secure; "to render safe, protect

2   Eszter Gantner and Heike Oevermann

or shelter from, guard against some particular danger" (ibid., p. 852). In this sense, the expression *secure* was already used in 1634 by John Milton in his first drama, *Comus* (ibid., p. 618).

This very short overview provides a glimpse of how the terms *protect*, *secure*, and *preserve*—expressions commonly used in the field of contemporary heritage studies—had overlapping meanings in the 19th century. Therefore, we argue that the terms *protect* and *preserve*, as in the quotation by Morris, also include the meaning of securing these sites for coming generations. Thus, the expression *secure*, which is currently used in both the media and the scholarly literature, is reduced to (physical) threats through decay, changes, including also terrorist attacks (Cambridge English Dictionary, 2018), and has always been an integral part of the heritage discourses. Therefore, for Morris and his associates in the Society for the Protection of Ancient Buildings, to *secure the heritage sites* meant that they also added a temporal dimension to the act of protection: The task, therefore, became to secure sites inherited from the past, for the benefit of the future. Thus, Morris changed the focus of the heritage movement's activities, from the past to the future: "Alas for those, who are to come after us, whom we shall have robbed of works of art which it was our duty to hand down to them uninjured and unimpaired" (Morris, 1878, p. 6). Moreover, Morris— with his ground-breaking approach of widening the temporal scale of heritage protection—also strengthened its existing *spatial approach*, pointing out their unity, as securing both the spatial and tangible structure of a site is crucial for its long-term security.

However, Choay (2001) points out that John Ruskin (the '*master*' of William Morris) and Morris focussed on a memorial approach when referring to urban heritage. Urban heritage corresponds to the ancient city. Its fabric is understood as the essence of the city and so—following Ruskin and Morris—should not be altered because this urban fabric roots its inhabitants in space and time. The pre-industrial city "remains conducive to the exercise of memory and piety, without specifying or distinguishing the respective statuses of those who inhabit them from those who only pass through them" (Choay, 2001, p. 122). It was the Italian conservationist Giovanni Giovannoni (1873–1944) who integrated *museum-value* with *use-value* through preservation of the urban fabric. Going beyond this, he linked the preservation of ancient urban ensembles—the past—with the currency of ongoing developments and the daily life of city dwellers in the present and future (Choay, 2001, pp. 136–137). Giovannoni thereby established an approach that brought into play agents, access, and preservation.

Today, the UNESCO Convention Concerning the Protection of the World Cultural and Natural Heritage (1972) notes that cultural heritage is threatened by decay as well as by social and economic changes. Therefore, the convention defines the "duty of ensuring the identification, protection, conservation, presentation and transmission to future generations of the cultural and natural heritage" (UNESCO, 1972, Art. 4) for each state party.

This aim is confirmed in Article 7 of the most recent operational guidelines for implementing the World Heritage Convention (UNESCO, 2017).

Following this path, we suggest that securitization in relation to urban heritage sites includes a more complex meaning, as suggested by current social scientific narratives (Balzacq, 2015; Mavelli, 2017). By doing so, we assume that securitization in relation to urban heritage is multifaceted, incorporating spatial, temporal, and social factors. We will discuss whether and how this is reflected in the findings of the case studies.

The temporal and anthropological dimension of heritage corresponds to Laurajane Smith's (2006) idea of heritage as a cultural process. Smith understands heritage as a cultural process including such elements as experience, identity, memory, remembrance, and performance. She points out the dissonance that often unfolds when diverse agents create heritage through interpretations. Her reference to urban studies and the discourse on place as socially constructed helps us, on the one hand, to also understand the process of heritage production and, on the other hand, supports the perception of an urban heritage site as a unity of tangible and intangible characteristics: tangible because of its material dimension and geo- and topographical settings, and intangible because of its social constructiveness according to cultural meanings. In other words: "it is a place where things happen, but importantly this doing has particular meaning because of the place" (Smith, 2006, p. 76).

Smith's understanding includes addressing the variety of agents—she includes in her definition those individuals, institutes, and organizations that take part in the production in their own right. Nevertheless, urban research has already recognized that new agents are involved in shaping and reshaping the urban landscape (Carmona, 2010), described as the multiplication of agents (Kaschuba, 2016). This process is not only characteristic of urban development, but is also happening in the heritage sector. This multitude of actors makes varied and often contradictory claims for reshaping the use of heritage sites while at the same time also influencing access to them.

The concept of historic urban landscape (HUL) makes it even more evident that urban heritage and its conservation are rooted in public access: Bandarin and van Oers (2012, p. vii) speak of the 'public's fascination' with representations of history, personal and collective memory, and the spirit of places. Urban heritage today is not only understood as landscape, and as part of sustainable urban development, but also as an assemblage of social practices (Smith, 2006; Labadi & Logan, 2016). This holistic approach includes a multiplicity of agents forming part of urban heritage conservation and development. Tunbridge and Ashworth's (1996) concept of 'dissonant heritage' makes clear that access to heritage is not a given, but instead part of a process of claiming and interpreting heritage. Here, conflicts arise when the claims and interpretations of some actors preclude others from accessing heritage.

4   *Eszter Gantner and Heike Oevermann*

To sum up, in the last decade, the understanding of heritage has broadened to include uses of heritage and cultural processes as participation in defining what heritage is; furthermore, the understanding includes intangible aspects of heritage (Pendlebury, Townshend, & Gilroy, 2004; Smith, 2006). At the same time, we can also recognize shifts in the understanding of cities towards claiming rights to the city, manifold urban interventions, powerful subcultures, and the discovery of neglected sites (Lefebvre, 1996; Carmona, 2010, Patti & Polyák, 2017). The shift in the heritage field—towards processes and people—fuels discussion of urban heritage sites as symbolic places of history, *and* of contemporary uses within complex and dense environments. Therefore, the point of departure for our book is: Access and use of heritage, and agents, are strongly interlinked. We understand access to heritage sites as a precondition for present and future uses. Access can be physical, virtual, sensitive, intellectual, and more. Access to heritage is not only part of local practices, identities, and cultures, but—as the European Year of Cultural Heritage and the UNESCO World Heritage Programme demand—also something to be shared.

Securitization and access

The classical explanation of securitization, coined by the Copenhagen School, has been applied to analyses of state foreign policy behaviour (Abrahamsen, 2005), the construction of transnational crime (Emmers, 2003) and HIV/AIDS (Elbe, 2006) as security threats, various dimensions of the 'war on terror' (Buzan, 2006), and to minority rights (Claessens, Van Eerde, Rutte, & Roe, 2004). Furthermore, securitization is often viewed as *"shorthand for the construction of security"* (McDonald, 2008, p. 3), in which the assumption of security politics as negative and exclusionary is rarely interrogated beyond the contexts of particular case studies. The understanding of security and securitization as a 'regime' that is oppressing and limiting the diversity of the city (Davis, 1992; DeVerteuil, Marr, & Snow, 2009; Minton, 2009; MacLeod & Johnstone, 2011) is already a well-researched assumption, especially in the broad context of urban studies.

In the last decade, public urban space has acquired a renewed urgency for the practice and performance of contemporary (and often confrontational) politics, from Kiev to Cairo, Hong Kong to Istanbul. This includes securitization of urban public space—ranging from smart closed-circuit television sensors to restricted access to streets, plazas, and buildings. Yet, simultaneously—and seemingly in denial of this increasingly securitized reality—our cities place ever-greater importance on various notions of heritage in shaping their images and 'city brands' as they compete for tourism and talent in future economies. This raises difficult questions, especially concerning access: In Paris, the Eiffel Tower as symbol of the city is now heavily blockaded by bulletproof glass walls (Landauer, 2017). Exactly these contemporary practices were described by the German design theorist

Friedrich von Borries (2016) as *Sicherheitsdesign* (security design). However, going a step further, von Borries argues that Haussmann's vision of Paris could always be interpreted as security design, originally serving the aims of surveillance and military control over certain social groups in the city; and Von Borries further identifies security design in general with subjugation, which has to be undermined (2016, p. 72).

A similar position is presented by Rem Koolhaas, a leading contemporary critical architect and urban planner who discusses the ongoing transformation of cities towards smart cities and notices a shift in values: "A new trinity is at work: Traditional European values of liberty, equality, and fraternity have been replaced in the 21st century by comfort, security, and sustainability" (Koolhaas, 2014, p. 1). Koolhaas argues that, by implementing these values through the smart city concept, we face greater surveillance, more exclusive public spheres, and the treatment of urban inhabitants as infants.

We presume that the ongoing securitization of urban public spaces worldwide brings new agents and regulated access to sites, we are formulating two questions: Does securitization limit the access to heritage sites? Or does it potentially broaden possibilities of access to heritage sites? Within these frameworks, access is understood as a premise and prerequisite of urban heritage, whereas securitization corresponds to the assemblage of urban practices of *threat design* and *threat management*. Hence, we intend to elaborate on the ways in which securitization—as both concept and practices—is transformed in relation to urban heritage and its management of threats. By doing so, we seek to understand how securitization hinders and/or facilitates access to heritage sites.

Structure of the book

We use the understanding of securitization based on the discourse in urban studies and social sciences, and follow the path of Macdonald (2008) in transferring this to the heritage field. The various case studies present our interdisciplinary approach, including methods from the fields of history, art history, sociology, and anthropology. These case studies are linked by the introduced framework and by a conclusion that opens new perspectives developed from the results of the case studies. Thus, the book offers a strong theoretical and empirical contribution to further research on urban heritage. Furthermore, all of the chapters address the ways in which security concerns are enacted and transformed in relation to urban heritage and its management. We establish a kind of matrix between securitization, access, agency, and heritage sites, to analyse the versatile and changing relations between these coordinates. All of the case studies address these coordinates, but each employs a different approach and focus and consequently highlights different aspects of the transformation of securitization.

6 Eszter Gantner and Heike Oevermann

Part I: Agents and forms of agency

In the first part of the book, titled "Agents and forms of agency", case studies by Christophe Foultier and Katarzyna Puzon focus and elaborate on the question of *agency* and the various ways in which urban citizens are involved in shaping access to heritage sites. The connected security measures are in many cases based on automatisms against minorities or groups that are perceived as different, such as immigrants. As Foultier formulates it:

> Expecting that residents play the roles of users, experts, and citizens in security issues, the heritage management results in a categorization of individuals and groups through a sort of *'identification'* with, *'rejection'* of, and *'allegiance'* to the community standards: it becomes both an inclusive and exclusive process.

Both Foultier and Puzon emphasize more the exclusionary aspect of this process, understanding security and securitization as an assemblage of threat management, whereas Olimpia Niglio offers a different approach. Introducing her case studies of Kyoto City and Osaka in the form of an ethnographic "thick description", she highlights the inclusionary aspect, arguing that the Japanese approach and practice of including different groups and generations are seen as guaranteeing the long-term security and protection of cultural heritage. In this Japanese context, securitization as Foultier and Puzon reflect on it—urban practices of threat design and threat management—is totally unknown. In Niglio's explanation, the Japanese approach is exemplified by its intimate relationships between community and the use of cultural heritage. Therefore, questions of access to heritage sites in urban public space do not arise; such access is a given since, in this 'philosophy', cultural heritage and community are in unity. Additionally, the heritage sites in question are 'movable' and 'intangible', such as Kyoto's Gion Matsuri festival, thereby both contributing to and confirming the close relationships described between heritage and community.

Dennis Rodwell's approach also argues for inclusion, in analysing the practices and understanding of the authorized heritage discourse, pointing out how this "disassembles the complexity of established cities, focusing on exemplar historic areas". Moreover, he emphasizes that the authorized heritage discourse did not realize that a shift was necessary or already underway—already moving from the selective survival of heritage sites as monuments towards 'open avenues' that integrate communities, their resources, and values in the process of securing the heritage for the future. Regarding this shift, Rodwell discusses the central issue of sustainability in terms of a site's reuse, both environmentally and concerning the temporal dimension of securing heritage sites.

Introduction 7

Part II: Technology, heritage, and access

While the first part of the book elaborates on the different relationships between agents and securitization, the second part—"Technology, heritage, and access"—brings into play the opportunities and challenges of both obsolete and emerging technologies. These chapters look at new means of protecting heritage sites, focussing on the positive relationships between providing site access and ensuring their long-term security. Piotr Kuroczyński and also Torben Kiepke and Hans-Rudolf Meier examine forms of securitization through digitization, whereas Anna Storm, Fredrik Krohn Andersson, and Eglė Rindzevičiūtė elaborate on a form of security 'theatre', introducing aspects of the discourse on environmental studies and showing in this context the transformation in the meaning and concept of securitization.

Kuroczyński and also Kiepke and Meier analyse the opportunities and potentials that forms of digitization offer for long-term securing of heritage: While Kuroczyński introduces the potentials of reconstructing vanished and demolished heritage, Kiepke and Meier examine community initiatives for creating informal inventories of heritage sites. Their contribution also demonstrates the multiplication of actors, knowledge, and temporal layers involved in this process of documenting and securing architectural post-war modernity.

Additionally, the contribution of Storm and colleagues examines how introducing issues of risk and risk perception enriches this multiplication process regarding security and heritage, which again emerges through an innovative technology but, in this case, one from decades past. They discuss the paradoxical nature of nuclear reactors as industrial heritage sites—so-called atomic heritage. On the one hand these sites represent a particular historical period along with its highly specific knowledge, technology, expertise, and politics; on the other hand, such sites are based on their materiality—for that they are protected; and they correspond to risk and threat through their former radioactivity on a long-term perspective. This complexity of temporality, risk, threat, and security is analysed by the authors through the concept of security 'theatre', demonstrating that: "The sense of remaining risks is well substantiated by a broader public imaginary of nuclear and radioactive dangers and disasters, and urban reactors are thereby brought into a category of difficult heritage and dark tourism practices".

Part III: Securing urban heritage in time and space

The various approaches of *securitization* and *securing* overlap each other in the Part III chapters by Juli Székely; Eszter Gantner and Ayse Erek; Ricardo Duarte Bajaña; and Nadine Siegert. Each chapter in "Securing urban heritage in time and space" analyses those processes, which result in close but ambivalent relationships between securitization and securing in the sense of

8 *Eszter Gantner and Heike Oevermann*

protecting heritage. Székely's case study examines Budapest's 200-year-old City Park, which is both a heritage site and a place of strong identification for the city's residents. On the one hand, the park is used to control those citizens through securitization measures; on the other hand, the citizens themselves are attempting to secure City Park for the future by demonstrating against a collection of megalomaniacal construction projects imposed on the area.

A similar case from Saint Petersburg is introduced by Eszter Gantner, where there are plans to turn Degtyarnyy Lane, a central industrial heritage site, into a political and economic hub with high-security measurements such as closed-circuit television—doing so against the will and interests of the neighbourhood residents. In contrast, local civic activities have developed more-inclusive proposals that would instead protect and secure this industrial heritage site for future generations. However, as in the Istanbul cases of the Emek Theatre and Roma Garden sites introduced by Ayse Erek, the securitization measurements introduced to urban public spaces clash with the concept of securing these places in the long run, as evidenced by the opposition expressed by civic activists and local groups. Moreover, this clash includes the conflict between local associations, urban citizens, and political authorities concerning understanding of the past and interpretation of the heritage.

All these elements and conflicts also appear in Ricardo Duarte Bajaña's case study, which deals with intangible heritage—the rituals, symbols, and representations of soccer fan clubs in Mexico. Their activities are perceived by official actors as acts of violence and as a threat to public order. In response, the soccer club, police, and city authorities have implemented various security measures in public spaces in an attempt to control the heritage-making activities of this fan group.

While Duarte Bajaña's case study discusses the securitization of social practices, Nadine Siegert's chapter introduces the practices of contemporary memory culture around a contested heritage site in Luanda, Angola. The mausoleum of Angola's first president, Agostinho Neto, initiated during the country's socialist period, and a social realist mural at the Military Hospital have been renovated and seemingly considered as heritage in Luanda. However, the Angolan state has abandoned its former political ideology and so, despite renovating these sites, the state's relationship with its socialist past and the era's remaining heritage is ambivalent. These sites are included in debates on reconciliation following the trauma of Angola's civil war; however, rather than having a critical discourse on its history with all its complexities, socialist history has instead been incorporated into the nation's post-war narrative. Consequently, these sites are secured by practices of contemporary culture and newly developed historic narratives, embedded in processes of memorization. In that way, socialism—and with it the mural and mausoleum—becomes 'an unquestioned part of that history and serves to communicate a story of heroism and pacification'.

Introduction 9

As mentioned previously, the book thematizes the complex and changing relationships between securitization, access, agency, and heritage sites. The first section introduces the theoretical framework, and in the second section the case studies elaborate the transformation of securitization in various geographical, and social, settings. Finally, the third part focusses on the strong interrelations between spatial and temporal dimensions of urban heritage. However, the book closes with a conclusion, as the transformation of securitization is an ongoing process that raises new questions and thereby challenges the established understandings of heritage, access, and agency in cities worldwide. We argue that analysing and understanding these relationships is important, since access for all agents is a premise and prerequisite for defining and securing urban heritage.

References

Abrahamsen, R. (2005). Blair's Africa: The politics of securitization and fear. *Alternatives, 30*, 55–80.
Balzacq, T. (2015). *Contesting security. Strategies and logics.* London: Routledge.
Bandarin, F., & van Oers, R. (2012). *The historic urban landscape: Managing heritage in an urban century.* Oxford: Wiley-Blackwell.
Buzan, B. (2006). Will the "global war on terrorism" be the new Cold War? *International Affairs, 82*, 1101–1118.
Carmona, M. (2010). *Public places, urban spaces: The dimensions of urban design.* New York: Routledge.
Choay, F. (2001). *The invention of the historic monument.* Cambridge, MA: Cambridge University Press.
Claessens, B. J. C., Van Eerde, W., Rutte, C. G., & Roe, R. A. (2004). Planning behavior and perceived control of time at work. *Journal of Organizational Behavior, 25*, 937–950.
Davis, M. (1992). Fortress Los Angeles: The militarization of urban space. In M. Sorkin (Ed.), *Variations on a theme park* (pp. 154–180). New York: Hill and Wang.
DeVerteuil, G., Marr, M., & Snow, D. (2009). Any space left? Homeless resistance by place-type in Los Angeles County. *Urban Geography, 30*(6), 633–651.
Elbe, S. (2006). Should HIV/AIDS be securitized? The ethical dilemmas of linking HIV/AIDS and security. *International Studies Quarterly, 50*, 119–144.
Emmers, R. (2003). *The securitization of transnational crime in ASEAN.* Retrieved from: http://hdl.handle.net/10220/4440
Kaschuba, W. (2016). Vom Tahrir-Platz in Kairo zum Hermannplatz in Berlin. Urbane Räume als claims and commons? Raumanthropologische Betrachtungen. In E. Bertuzzo, E. Gantner, J. Niewöhner, & H. Oevermann (Eds.), *Kontrolle öffentlicher Räme* (pp. 20–57). Berlin: LIT-Verlag.
Koolhaas, R. (2014). *Are smart cities condemned to be stupid?* Retrieved from: www.archdaily.com/576480/rem-koolhaas-asks-are-smart-cities-condemned-to-be-stupid
Labadi, S., & Logan, W. (2016). *Urban heritage, development and sustainability: International frameworks, national and local governance.* New York: Routledge.
Landauer, P. (2017). Paris, das Gespenst der offensiven Stadt. *StadtBauwelt, 6*, 32–28.

10 Eszter Gantner and Heike Oevermann

Lefebvre, H. (1996). The right to the city. In E. Kofman & E. Lebas (Eds.), *Writings on cities* (pp. 3–60). Cambridge, MA: Wiley-Blackwell.

Macleod, G., & Johnstone, C. (2011). Stretching urban renaissance: Privatizing space, civilizing place, summoning "community". *International Journal of Urban and Regional Research*, 36, 1–28.

Mavelli, L. (2017). Governing populations through the humanitarian government of refugees: Biopolitical care and racism in the European refugee crisis. *Review of International Studies*, 43(5), 809–832.

McDonald, M. (2008). Securitization and the construction of security. *European Journal for International Relations*, 14(4), 1–36.

Minton, A. (2009). *Ground control: Fear and happiness in the twenty-first century city*. London: Penguin.

Morris, W. (1878, April 17). Destruction of city churches. *The Times* (London), p. 6. Letter written on behalf of the SPAB.

Patti, D., & Polyák, L. (2017). Funding the cooperative city. Vienna: Cooperative City Books.

Pendlebury, J., Townshend, T., & Gilroy, R. (2004). The conservation of English cultural built heritage: A force for social inclusion? *International Journal of Heritage Studies*, 10(1), 11–31.

Protect. (n.d.). In *Cambridge English Dictionary online*. Retrieved from https://dictionary.cambridge.org/dictionary/english/protect

Secure. (n.d.). In *Cambridge English Dictionary online*. Retrieved from https://dictionary.cambridge.org/dictionary/english/secure

Simpson, J. A., & Weiner, E. S. C. (Eds.) (1989). *The Oxford Language Dictionary*. Vol. XII, 2nd ed. Oxford, Oxford.

Smith, L. (2006). *Uses of heritage*. New York: Routledge.

Society for the Protection of Ancient Buildings (SPAB) (1877) *Manifesto of the society for the protection of ancient buildings*. The William Morris Internet Archive. Retrieved from: www.marxists.org/archive/morris/works/1877/spabman.htm

Tunbridge, E. J., & Ashworth, G. (1996). *Dissonant heritage: The management of the past as a resource in conflict*. Chichester: Wiley.

UNESCO (1972). *Convention concerning the protection of the world cultural and natural heritage*. Retrieved from: https://whc.unesco.org/archive/convention-en.pdf

UNESCO (2017). *Operational guidelines for the implementation of the World Heritage Convention 2017*. Retrieved from: https://whc.unesco.org/en/guidelines/

Von Borries, F. (2016). Weltentwerfen. Eine politische Designtheorie. Frankfurt am Main: Suhrkamp.

Part I
Agents and forms of agency

1 Community involvement in times of social insecurity

Christophe Foultier

Social tensions within local communities often emerge from a paradoxical injunction in the public arena, which consists of controlling residents that it seeks to involve. In the name of an emancipatory experience, community strategies can even contribute to activating inhabitants through preventive devices. Using a notion from Tunbridge and Ashworth (1996), I argue in this chapter that the contradictions involved in the management of heritage in cities can be conceptualized in terms of a 'dissonant heritage' (Tunbridge & Ashworth, 1996). Understood as a 'selective use of the past' (Ibid., p. 6), the notion of *heritage* is deliberately open to interpretation and controversy. To what extent does the heritage dimension in community development bring to light new forms of co-operation and controversies in matters of civil rights?

In this chapter, the notion of heritage is understood as a political resource— that is to say an instrument in public policy by which local governments implement forms of civic involvement and techniques of securitization in public urban spaces. In particular, the question of heritage becomes highly controversial in local development strategies, when local stakeholders contribute to designing a community-based development through the construction of an imagined past (Tunbridge & Ashworth, 1996, p. 4). Searching for recognition in an imagined community, the involved citizens and local stakeholders become exposed by a sort of 'allegiance' and 'rejection' in terms of class, ethnicity, or gender (Rose, 1999, pp. 177–178). Four issues will be addressed in this chapter.

First, I argue that participation and securitization are techniques and methods devoted to the design and management of heritage sites. From a theoretical viewpoint, the junction of participatory devices and security measures models a political resource that generates various practices of co-operation. These techniques lead local agents to produce political narratives on rights, duties, and values in cities, and are deeply embedded in controversies and conflicts that occur locally in times of insecurity.

Second, the analysis of a heritage dimension in cities exposes how politicians use historical references as a political resource in matters of civic

14   *Christophe Foultier*

participation and securitization. A case in point is the heritage of Saint-Denis, an old industrial city north of Paris, against the backdrop of social insecurity. I examine the rise of a *right to city* throughout the deindustrialization process and the urban renaissance of Saint-Denis in order to understand the significance of notions such as participation and security in a policy process.

Third, the management of such heritage in the city illustrates how participative devices and security procedures are articulated in a community development strategy. At the district level, the municipal strategy consists of reducing social and civil insecurity by increasing citizen participation in local democratic devices. In practical terms, the development of co-operation contributes to promoting various types of heritage, which are mostly dissonant in a securitization process.

In the concluding section, I emphasize the major effects that the management of a 'dissonant heritage' implies in times of social insecurity. The dissonant heritage implies a series of temporal shifts—in the development of political community standards—that raise normative questions, notably if they are examined through the prism of identity and belonging.

This chapter is based on research concerning the neighbourhood of Le Franc-Moisin–Bel-Air in the municipality of Saint-Denis. The empirical work includes public-document analysis, interviews, and observations. In particular, I have undertaken series of interviews to clarify the notions of participation and security in the urban strategy of the municipality. Seven preliminary interviews with researchers, experts, and institutional representatives gave me comprehension of the discourse, the orientations, and the organizational logics. I conducted 17 interviews with local players according to a chain of accountability: politicians, managers, technicians, consultants and architects, developers, and social workers. Finally, I planned sequences of observation with civic representatives and interviews with engaged residents recognized by the institutions as *referents*.

Participation versus securitization: revisiting the paradox

During the past decade, notions such as *urban citizenship* and *right to city* have been broadly commented upon through the lens of securitization and/ or civic participation (Donzelot et al., 2003; Oblet, 2008; Harvey, 2008; Mayer, 2012; Eick & Briken, 2014). In this theoretical part, I argue that the rise of participatory devices and security measures in urban policy signal the development of a new political resource by which local governments manage the tensions inherent to the heritage dimension of the city. The notion of heritage is understood as an instrument in a policy process devoted to the management of urban renaissance programmes. In particular, the reference to heritage aims to adjust urban changes that arise in the regeneration of city districts. My argument emphasizes the confluence of participatory devices and security measures in urban regeneration strategies and the way this

Community involvement and social insecurity 15

process models a political resource that lies in various forms of co-operation and co-ordination.

Influenced by Michel Foucault's concept of governmentality, I argue that the notions of participation and security can be described as techniques that support instruments of government. They constitute a political resource that incorporates the "multi-facets of the urban heritage" as Heike Oevermann and Eszter Gantner put it in the introduction section of this book. Rethinking the notion of power in this more decentralized context, certain French scholars such as Jacques Donzelot have been reluctant to reduce local development policies to a spatial treatment of poverty. In replacing a planning strategy by the co-ordination of territorial policies, the state gave itself the means to negotiate "the relationships between individual autonomy and the responsibility of all" (Donzelot, 1994, p. 260). From that perspective, territorial authorities open up possibilities through partnership, negotiation, and political participation in local contexts.

In the line of Foucault, the idea of participation is understood in this chapter as a "technology of the self" in which individuals, volunteers, and activists can "affect by their own means, a certain number of operations on [...] their own conduct, and this in a manner so as to transform themselves" (Foucault, 2004, p. 654). In engaging in a dialogue with the local actors and residents of targeted districts, the individual subject's rational choice, her action, her responsibility, her vigilance in a community development all became issues of study. As Mitchell Dean puts it, the 'cosmopolitan individual' and the 'individual as a life-planner' become the dominant narratives by which political reforms allow governing the individual conduct (Dean, 2007, p. 78). Thus, individuals are devoted to a new role: to promote themselves and their own values and rights (Rose, 1999, p. 265).

I argue in this respect that the political subject becomes a producer of her environment in the renaissance of cities: The exercise of 'self-training' or 'practice of the self' is potentially translated into a 'process of identification' in the development of public urban spaces. For instance, the examination of some figures of activism in the Le Franc-Moisin district of Saint-Denis sheds light on various motivations and perceptions in matters of civic affairs: partisans of civility and civic responsibility based on a local reading of national citizenship; partisans of associative mediation or of negotiations between institutions and society; and partisans of social transformation through grassroots movements. Under such circumstances, several local agents contribute to developing new practices of co-operation in the discussions of community standards.

The notion of securitization can also be useful to depict urban strategies if it is understood as a set of new techniques or methods that support instruments of government in liberal democracies (Huysmans, 2006, pp. 30–44; Bigo, 2008, p. 113). As Oblet observed about American urban theory, insecurity is a constituent dimension of urban life, being itself "the

16 *Christophe Foultier*

counterpart to the freedoms that the city affords" (Oblet, 2008, p. 3). Thus, a security process can be seen as a preventive means that allows administrating individuals and collectives in targeted areas (Foucault, 2004, p. 61–62).[1] As we shall see in Saint-Denis, the notion of security is historically constructed as a social-prevention method that consists of stimulating associations in targeted districts and promoting a deliberative process in which volunteers take part in public decisions. In particular, this policy process constitutes a political support in times of insecurity: Against the backdrop of deindustrialization in northern Paris, the values of volunteering and activism serve to affiliate residents with their residential environments.

According to my argument, the instrumentalization of participation and security in urban strategies cannot be understood without re-examining the local history of the city. Techniques of involvement and safety measures establish their legitimacy with a discourse on the heritage of the city, without which one cannot understand how local stakeholders design civic requirements and community ideals. Let us illustrate in detail how the heritage dimension is used in the city of Saint-Denis.

Heritage as 'instrument': revisiting the notions of participation and security in the city of Saint-Denis

This section puts in perspective the way in which the notion of heritage can be understood as a political resource. Through the deindustrialization of Saint-Denis, the municipality defined a vast urban renaissance programme that aimed to promote a new identity for the 'banlieue rouge' (Bacqué & Fol, 1997) (see Figure 1.1). The renaissance of the city was an opportunity for local politicians to promote new political standards, democratic values, and rights. In this part, I illustrate the extent to which this political resource is based on a "reconstruction of an imagined past" (Tunbridge & Ashworth, 1996, p. 4). The renaissance of the city, which draws its strength from the heritage of the industrial city, implies "a series of accepted judgements" for the present and future (Barraclough, 1955).

First, the municipal strategy in Saint-Denis consists of moving from a right to housing throughout the course of industrialization, to the right to city during the deindustrialization process. Local politicians supposed, in particular, that the traditional affiliations of the industrial city were on the decline, and that city renewal projects would generate a new, inclusive function, enabling the mobilization of local stakeholders, citizens, and residents in their close environment. Second, the municipal strategy aims to reduce social and civil insecurity by increasing citizen participation in local development strategies. The municipality implicitly supposes that the feeling of insecurity—which explains the rise of incivility and delinquency—results from social disaffiliation in the city. Let us look closer at these two core arguments against the backdrop of deindustrialization processes in Saint-Denis.

Figure 1.1 Public places and high-rise housing estate in the district of Franc-Moisin-Bel-Air. © 2013 Christophe Foultier.

From urban renaissance to the rise of a right to city

The first important argument used by the municipality to define a heritage dimension in the city is grasped during the transition from an extensive urban strategy—industrialization and the right to housing—to intensive urban development: deindustrialization, urban renaissance, and access to public space. The urban renaissance programme in particular is intended to generate a new territorial identity and a new system for affiliating the residents in the city development.

During the deindustrialization process, the city of Saint-Denis faced growing socio-spatial fragmentation that contributed to the increasing relegation of immigrant populations to social housing districts. Already at the end of the 1970s, the deputy mayor of Saint-Denis could not tolerate that the city of Saint-Denis be turned from the industrial cradle of France into an impoverished city (Bacqué & Fol, 1997). This process of the population's disaffiliation became a political issue for which local politicians had to forge a new political instrument (*Saint-Denis notre ville*, 1981).[2]

In Saint-Denis, the development of social housing areas was consubstantial with the industrial expansion that occurred in the northern suburbs of Paris. From the early 1900s until the end of the 1970s, the industrial area of La Plaine Saint-Denis became one of the French industrial jewels. At the end of the Second World War in particular, housing became a key theme of the political discourse of Auguste Gillot (mayor from 1945 to 1971) and then of Marcelin Berthelot (deputy of Seine Saint-Denis from

18   Christophe Foultier

1968 to 1978 and mayor of Saint-Denis from 1971 to 1991). Successive mayors denounced social injustice and the exploitation of the working class and demanded state funding to develop social housing and eliminate units that were unfit for habitation. Several outbreaks of fire in the slum districts of Saint-Denis exposed the inadequate housing conditions, leading in turn to an initial series of legislative measures. In the wake of a visit by government representatives to the slum district of Le Franc-Moisin, the Vivien Decree was promulgated on 10 July 1970 to speed up the first operations aimed at reducing the proportion of housing that was unfit for habitation. In such a context, for instance, the municipality obtained financing in 1970 to construct 900 housing units in the district of Le Franc-Moisin. Thus, local politicians who claimed a 'right to housing' developed a political stance that became the starting point of a massive social housing development in Saint-Denis: home-buying programmes that enabled social tenants to buy the right to housing; large high-rise estates of the 1970s that promoted a social-mix policy; and urban renewal projects at the turning point of the 1990s (Bacqué & Fol, 1997; Magri, 2008, pp. 173–183).

During the early 1970s, the deindustrialization of the city signalled a drastic shift from extensive development to intensive urban growth. The industrial development outside Paris, far from Saint-Denis and the 'red suburbs' (*la ceinture rouge*) encircling the capital, was the result of a strategy adopted by the large industrial groups, banking on 'industrial deconcentration' to modernize their production systems, and on highly skilled workers and advanced technology for increasing productivity. This intensive development had major consequences for the urban development of the city and its close industrial fabric (Adda & Ducreux, 1979, pp. 39–46). The metropolitan area of Saint-Denis was retrospectively presented as an aggregate of 'working-class municipalities' that underwent 'destructive economic transformations' in a region with 'much polluted terrain' and 'severance of the urban fabric' associated with physical severance by the railway and highway networks. These arguments clearly illustrate the motives of the vast renaissance programme that will be defined in Saint-Denis. At the turning point of the 1990s, the city's urban renaissance programme notably incorporated:

- The development of a regional business centre, including the construction of the national sports stadium, *Le Stade de France*;
- Better access to the city, with construction of several regional railway stations in La Plaine Saint-Denis, and extension of the underground railway to the University of Paris 8, in the north part of the city;
- Renovation of the historical centre, including a social-mix policy for housing;
- The launch of urban renewal projects and community development strategies in most of the marginalized districts of the city.

Community involvement and social insecurity   19

In the course of this intensive urban growth, the city of Saint-Denis presents contrasting socio-economic characteristics. On the one hand, the city gained significant economic development with the promotion of new strategic sectors such as the communications and entertainment sectors in connection with the presence of 4,600 firms. On the other hand, the municipality of Saint-Denis was confronted with the "development of significant exclusions, correlated with the rise in structural unemployment and the emergence of spatial segregations, added to the isolation of entire neighbourhoods" (Projet de Rénovation Urbaine de Saint-Denis, 2005).

In summary, the inhabitants of the city did not take part in the economic revival of Saint-Denis, and social differentiation in the workplace led retrospectively to a deep divide between politicians and the residents of Saint-Denis (Sintomer, 2000, p. 3; Vidal, 2004, p. 57).[3] This former Communist Party stronghold had an efficient mode of affiliation until the early 1970s due to the fact that the locally elected officials represented a countervailing force to national politicians in the structured framework of the party. This was no longer the case after the Socialist and Communist parties agreed on a common programme at the end of the 1970s. "The 'party' form is dead as a political organization", (Faraldi, 2005, p. 54) declared Patrick Braouezec, Communist Party deputy mayor of Saint-Denis from 1991 to 2012 and now president of the Plaine Commune agglomeration community.

Thus, the urban renaissance could not possibly be developed without a new system of territorial affiliation. The political vision was to include the inhabitants in the definition of a new identity for the *banlieues rouges*. In particular, civic participation appeared as a core political resource in the contemporary history of Saint-Denis, allowing the municipality to develop an attractive business centre at the regional level and to promote a 'right-to-city' at the local level. Against the backdrop of the deindustrialization process, the notion of urban renaissance embodies a mythical function that is essentially aimed at mobilizing local actors.

Coupling social insecurity with civil insecurity

The second argument of the municipality of Saint-Denis is that the shift from the factory to the neighbourhood of 'social conflictuality' is a permanent feature of the problem of insecurity. In the city of Saint-Denis, it is assumed that "social and civil insecurity intersect and feed one another" as Robert Castel puts it (2003, p. 5). Through the urban renaissance of the city, associative representatives and residents were directly perceived by the municipal team as a *living* political resource that could act on the feeling of insecurity in districts. The urban renewal of districts was also seen as an opportunity to revive social bonds and stimulate a network of associations through sports and socio-cultural activities. The development of associative activity around channels of financing is not really synonymous with resident engagement in

20   *Christophe Foultier*

decision-making. The participative strategy was intended here to create collective action and social control. It implicitly acknowledged that solidarity was not an active principle in society, but rather a project to be constructed on a political basis.

The first municipal newspaper to mention social insecurity as a dimension of the security topic was printed in May 1978 (*Saint-Denis notre ville*, 1978). Mayor Berthelot considered security as a 'complex' notion in which working conditions forged 'worries about tomorrow' (Ibid., pp. 8–11).[4] "Austerity generates insecurity", Berthelot insisted, and called for the elaboration of new "forms of prevention" (Ibid., pp. 12–14). With the coming of the Left to power nationally in the early 1980s, municipal discourse focused in particular on the social dimension of the notion of insecurity, in identifying "its roots in the deterioration of living conditions, the unpreparedness of youth for careers and jobs, academic failures, unemployment, and the poverty of working-class populations" (*Saint-Denis notre ville*, February 1982). For municipal representatives, the emergence of 'petty delinquency' in the 1980s was the flashpoint on the surface of events that essentially emerged from the spread of social insecurity. These social risks were explicitly regarded as the result of the economic crisis undermining the local social fabric.

> The situation [...] finds its source in the global crisis that emerged in the early 1970s. [...] We are basically dealing with petty delinquency in Saint-Denis. Repression is not the only answer to this. There is a social dimension. This delinquency is the product of the socio-economic situation, unemployment, social and racial segregation, the sense of being uprooted, the lack of professional training, and academic failure.
>
> (*Saint-Denis notre ville*, June 1984)

In this old industrial city, juvenile delinquency gradually replaced traditional forms of conflict in the labour society and, by the 1980s, raised particularly strong issues in terms of socialization, citizenship, and integration. The municipality responded to these new forms of conflict in the mid-1980s by laying the foundations for a participative development project throughout all districts of the city.

Civic involvement and security in the management of heritage sites

Let us look at the manner in which this heritage was integrated into participative devices and security procedures. In general terms, the assessment of the past is intended to define community standards around non-governmental actors. During the renaissance of Saint-Denis, the municipal approach stipulated that civic participation and security measures were not to be considered as an adversarial procedure. At the district level, the municipal

Community involvement and social insecurity   21

strategy consisted of reducing social and civil insecurity by increasing citizen participation in community development.

However, through the development of practices of co-operation in this matter, contrasting visions of the heritage of the city were promoted. In Saint-Denis, security and participation became adjusting techniques that allowed the "management of the past as a resource in conflict", as Tunbridge and Ashworth (1996) put it. In the district of Le Franc-Moisin–Bel-Air in particular, community development demonstrated how the municipality of Saint-Denis internalized several channels of participation. Some of the channels endeavoured to affiliate the residents to a social-prevention strategy while others sought to extend institutional co-operation in surveillance and security matters in order to reduce delinquency.

Reducing social and civil insecurity by increasing affiliation in the district

Designed by Patrick Braouezec, who became mayor of Saint-Denis in 1991, the local democracy project sought to recreate an affiliation based on the social development of the Le Franc-Moisin–Bel-Air district. For the municipal team, this affiliation model constituted a lever for social pre- vention and civil support in the city districts. The values of volunteering and activism served to 'affiliate' residents with their residential environ- ment. Class relations, in which generations of migrant workers were embedded, gave way to other forms of socio-political mobilization: The issue at stake was not so much the improvement of working conditions as that of establishing systems of collective negotiation around residents' living conditions and environment, by promoting access to civic and social rights. This approach to participatory democracy was supported by three pillars: (a) the structure of participative democracy, (b) the public services centre, and (c) local associations.

- First, a grassroots platform brought local and national services closer together and proposed a shared reception structure. Resident par- ticipation was historically built on a grassroots democracy structure developed in 1996 by the municipality of Saint-Denis, the so-called *la démarche quartier*. An institutional partner, Espace de Services Publics (ESP, Public Services Space), facilitated the implementation of trans- versal undertakings[5];
- Second, the foundation of the district project is based on resident par- ticipation. The municipality involves *volunteers* in urban design, district management, and the decision-making process: Inhabitants contribute to diffusing information in public meetings, to consultation on issues of land-use planning, and to discussing financial options for development of the district;

22   Christophe Foultier

- The third affiliation mode is developed via the rich but fragile associative fabric. Many associations, whose development was linked to the district's history, were in touch with the director of *la démarche quartier*.

Thus, resident participation takes on extremely diverse forms in this framework, since the different channels of participation allow for different types of involvement. For instance, the district's associative fabric today comprises 20-plus associations. These include a few large professionalized structures with salaried employees seeking to meet social needs at the grassroots level; associations representing group interests; emerging associations dedicated to the development of various forms of solidarity from diverse perspectives; and small associations of amateur athletes. The profusion of associations makes it possible to maintain many varied contacts, frequent or spontaneous, with residents outside the institutional framework. As privileged relays for local residents, these associations have often acted as intermediaries in formalizing actions of solidarity, organizing events, calming community friction or conflict with the police, or taking stands and organizing rallies and marches.

In broader terms, the grassroots organization aims to forge some form of affiliation around a neighbourhood collective. Of course, the democratic approach has a functional dimension: public services being structured so as to better incorporate social needs in the decision-making process; residents participating to improve institutional work; stimulating the fabric of association to develop bonds between residents. But also, in its civic dimension, the aim is to promote volunteer work among inhabitants and the activism of association representatives to fight against social disaffiliation and insecurity. In particular, the organization of solidarity ties within the district must rely on a community of collective beliefs, values, and ideas to constitute the society. A consensus on this point appeared during the interview process in the district: The president of a local association spoke of 'collective consciousness' in the neighbourhood, a representative of *Soninké association* of a 'sense of the collective', and a volunteer of the 'harmony' of the community in the neighbourhood. In this district, it is the capacity of collective representation that forms the linchpin of strategies of engagement, in terms of rights and social justice.

Accessing public urban spaces through increasing responsibility and surveillance

The principle of neighbourhood policing was defined during the mid-1980s in the framework of social development issues. In this context the local government put particular emphasis on preventive responses. However, at the beginning of the 2000s, new mechanisms, which were set up under the impetus of the state, signalled a drastic shift in security matters.[6] New cooperation on security issues emerged between the local authorities, residents,

Community involvement and social insecurity   23

associative fabric, and the police, and reinforced the project development. The values of individual responsibility and civic volunteering served to raise residents' awareness of security matters within their local environment according to a chain of accountability.

First, the increased presence of security procedures and bodies in the steering mechanisms of the district impacted on the definition of the urban strategy. The urban strategy developed by the local authorities notably includes recommendations from the police in matters of urban design. From a technical standpoint, security measures focus on the visibility of places and their accessibility, recreating concrete slab passages for security forces and maintenance crews. Parallel to the security-based development, volunteering for the district board allows taking a position on subjects like civility, security, and cleanliness. For instance, if some residents feel that responsibility is a chief concern in their life, it is because they watch the day-to-day deterioration of their environment. In this respect, one of the volunteers recommends placing "cameras to see who's illegally dumping" even though the "city is not ready" for this. Her observations equally concern simple acts of incivility, because some people "have no respect for anything" and "lack education". She expects more from the city itself, "since the police cannot resolve everything".

Second, the municipal government incorporated surveillance systems in the development of urban projects. Indeed, the refurbishment of a public place became the occasion for a 'trench war' between some youth gangs and the public institutions. The destruction of a number of sites 'disturbed' drug trafficking in the district. Surprised by the radicalization of the conflicts with the youth, the local stakeholders developed new, professional routines during meetings between the agglomeration community, the city, the housing providers, and the police: visualization of incivilities during a presentation of the district to the police; taking elements of urban design into account in repressive mechanisms; and co-ordinating interventions between the project head and the police representatives during a new construction phase. In particular, every phase in the construction work had to be accompanied by added surveillance in order to prevent its immediate destruction. A few district residents were employed as on-site mediators and were in charge of identifying problems related to use of the places and damaged urban installations.

Third, in response to issues of daily incivility and delinquency, various connections were developed between the district residents and institutional representatives. For instance, a police mediator position was created to promote resident comprehension regarding the work of patrols. Four years after taking up the position, the police delegate had developed contacts with the neighbourhood associations and residents. He refuses to think in terms of 'informers', since that runs counter to his deontology, but he knows details of everyday life, practices, times, places, and illegal activities: "You see this boulevard: there's lots of pickpocketing and thefts from cars. Many are

24 Christophe Foultier

middle school students who come here during classes", he explains during a visit to the neighbourhood. These new connections tended to individualize modes of dialogue and thereby upend power relations in the district by warding off the effects of massive mobilization. Through ordinary civility, the stakeholders establish a set of values that underpin the responsibility of the residents and its role in the prevention of 'deviant' behaviours.

Facing various dangers and risks, local partners develop co-operation with various institutions by implementing systems of social-risk prevention, the elaboration of new social norms, or the development of a 'new military urbanism' in metropolitan areas (Bigo, 2008, p. 100; Graham, 2011, p. xxvi). These new chains of accountability can also be considered as part of the heritage management, since the community standards have always emphasized the relationship between social insecurity and civil insecurity in public urban spaces. In particular, the adjunct mayor points out that access to public space must very concretely ensure that "the appropriation by some residents is not achieved to the detriment of others". This point fits perfectly with the volunteers who reject 'community insularities', 'drugs, dealers, carjacking, and more', and promote the values of citizen responsibility and civility between inhabitants.

Managing a dissonant heritage in times of insecurity: a potential extension of security norms in the city

This concluding section emphasizes the major effects of the management of a dissonant heritage in times of insecurity. The development of a vast urban renaissance programme, which appears as a comprehensive political solution to social, cultural, and spatial problems, inevitably comes up against the multiple facets of the city heritage. In this chapter it is argued that the heritage of the city is understood as a political resource and that the dissonance—which arises with new expressions of civic rights and sociocultural values such as voluntarism, activism, civility, or responsibility—lies in the extension of security issues to the system of affiliation.

In general terms, one can argue that security-related procedures are subject to a hierarchical and functional logic bound up with the sovereign function of the state. At the district level, however, I have shown that multiple connections exist between residents, associative representatives, and institutional actors—first and foremost the national police—in matters of security. My argument is that the notion of *insecurity* is politically constructed according to territorial development and thus can vary drastically from one city to another. In Saint-Denis, the prevention and security-based procedures lead to defining new chains of responsibilities and to developing locally hierarchical layers of decision-making. While the increasing involvement of local actors aims to establish community standards through social-prevention measures, the complex institutional co-operation generates bridges between social development, professional training and employment (social prevention), urbanism (urban safety), public order (repressive measures), and surveillance (dissuasive approaches). Consequently, the involvement of a multiplicity of agents in various co-operative projects gives rise to discussions about a large number of matters, from social exclusion to petty delinquency.

In fact, forms of co-operation on security concerns mask major issues of urban heritage in Saint-Denis. Indeed, within the renaissance of the city, many heritage dimensions have been forgotten in the construction of a new territorial identity. As a political resource, the heritage of Saint-Denis has mainly been used to tackle the insecure deindustrialization process in La Plaine Saint-Denis. However, through the promotion of a new territorial identity, the municipal strategy did not anticipate the *uncertainty factor* that the negotiations and controversies have generated in matters of community standards. As Franck Scherrer (2013, p. 23) puts it, "the reversibility [of spaces that arise with vast urban regeneration programmes in cities] qualifies the relation that one constructs with futures in the same way as the patrimony has become the filter of our relation with the past".

At the turning point of the 1990s, the grassroots organization was concentrating efforts on social development and social prevention. During the 2000s, local stakeholders reoriented the strategy towards defining new standards of civility and systems of control in public places. These facets of the heritage of Saint-Denis are still subject to interpretation and controversy in public meetings.

For instance, during a public meeting on violence in public places, organized by the municipality and the national police, a resident presents a contrasting vision of security development according to various periods, when he considers: "In the 1980s, there were beat officers and all went well. Then came the community policing, and one day a policeman said to me: 'Hey, you, dirty Arab, get off your bike!'" The commissioner, standing in the middle of the room, replies, "But things have changed a lot since the beat officer days".

A member of the district board of Le Franc-Moisin–Bel-Air, a volunteer of the district, also presented the 'security-related problem' in the area as a social issue that manifests as incidences of incivility and delinquency. Inherited from the deindustrialization of the city, petty delinquency, pickpocketing, and drug dealing are only manifestations of a much deeper malaise linked to the withdrawal of public welfare and the decline of supportive networks in the district: lack of parental support, situations of institutional precariousness and poverty, social inequality, unemployment, and the rejection of others. He declared that

> young people—even those with diplomas—and the unemployed are not benefitting from the local development plan. Young people complain about police profiling and rudeness, which they take very badly. Violent police interventions, in particular the use of teargas on Rue de Montfort

26 *Christophe Foultier*

last November in the presence of children and parents, represent dispro-
portionate measures.[...] Residents have seen regular aggression, pickpocketing on Rue du Flot or along the canal, drug dealing, with addicts
leaving needles in the street, noise pollution from mopeds, robberies,
illegal parking.

We can also consider the heritage as dissonant when a resident denies one
interpretation of the past that the members of the district board present in
matters of security processes: "We know all that. No point in repeating what
everyone knows!"

For this representative of the local society, the prevention policy, which
constitutes a key aspect of the heritage in Saint-Denis, emerges as an undesirable past. One resident sums up the point when he says to the commissioners
of Saint-Denis: "You're in a hard-hit district because of the insecurity, and
you talk to us of progress!" When residents call the idea of progress into
question, we see the extent to which insecurity is associated with uncertainty.

As Oevermann and Gantner previously noted in the introduction to
this volume, "the focus of the heritage movement's activities" can easily be
reoriented "from the past to the future" and thus ends up in an imagined
community. The heritage is 'dissonant' when the socially and politically
constructed notion of security is too ambivalent to be fruitful in local
social networks and community-based associations. In Le Franc-Moisin–
Bel-Air, for instance, an associative representative points to the risk that
residents who take charge of security in the neighbourhood may become
'vigilante groups'. For him, it is well known that, in looking for 'sociological
explanations', the associations and activists often become 'complicit' in
misdeeds. At the same time, a volunteer of *La démarche quartier* looks for
a means to change 'the way people behave' in the district. She points to
the development of 'socio-ethnic ties' as a civilian problem—amongst the
'Malians', among others—because she regards it as an expression of insu-
larity and of rejecting others: "People do not approach outsiders; they greet
only people from their own community". Another associative representative
argues that the problem of insecurity is connected to the absence of cultural
values: "The youth run away from talks" and "the parents are disarmed" to
deal with the "very troubling insecurity in the district" with young people
snatching handbags, burning cars, smoking, selling drugs, and so on. This
resident, who is convinced that young people have lost 'a sense of values',
works on projects related to reinforcing intergenerational and ethnic bonds.
Securitization develops through the tangle of emotions that arises in civic
affairs and social matters against the backdrop of city renaissance. Indeed,
local forms of engagement can generate misunderstanding, suspicion, and
conflicts in public urban spaces, and thus contribute to extending—if not
refining—techniques of prevention, dissuasion, and repression.

The participatory procedures influence the conduct of participants, who
express subjective thoughts on identity, belonging, and public urban spaces.

In the daily life of the neighbourhood, the dissonant visions of heritage tangibly impact public meetings, and assemblies often turn into altercations. In particular, the public discussions on social insecurity and incivility become occasions for heated disagreement on matters of ethnicity and gender—not only between inhabitants and public institutions, but also among inhabitants.

Let us return to the words of the district residents who express this dissonant heritage in a local environment: A resident comments: "I must say that the parents have a role to play. Don't forget it's the immigrants who are a problem". This barely concealed xenophobia and almost commonplace arrogance do not call for an answer in the assembly. Five minutes later, a man gets up and says that he has children and that he educates them well: "When you arrest a minor for a petty crime, you take them away, but do the parents get a reminder of the law? If they give their kids a beating, the kids call a hotline!" One young adult replies angrily: "Our minors are our children. The juvenile delinquents are our brothers and sisters. There are no walls. Fortunately, it's the minors who are getting into trouble, not the grown-ups!" thereby countering the attitude of most of the assembly. "Whoah!"—the collective interjection rises from the gathering. "But we haven't even spoken about the violence against women, and it's an important subject here", a young woman remarks.

Expecting that residents play the roles of users, experts, and citizens in security issues, the heritage management results in a categorization of individuals and groups through a sort of identification with, rejection of, and allegiance to the community standards: It becomes both an inclusive and exclusive process. Moreover, in seeking to foster civil involvement, the institutional procedures can expose residents and social groups to taking responsibility for criminality or incivility. This system of affiliation, which is supported by a strong institutional discourse on insecurity, fuels discriminatory representations (Uitermark, Rossi, & Houtum, 2005, p. 635).

Through the example of Saint-Denis, it becomes clear that the notion of insecurity contributes to qualifying the relationships that individuals, volunteers, and activists have to the past, while the notion of uncertainty calls into question their relationships to the future. The point is that the temporal shifts that occur through expressions of insecurity and uncertainty pave the way for a dissonant heritage. Through the use of the past, the understanding of the securitization process clearly depends on the periods and places to which the stakeholders are referring.

Notes

1 Foucault emphasizes three features that characterize a securitization process: (a) a way of individualizing a collective phenomenon or of collectivizing phenomena; (b) a knowledge based on the ability to spot individuals or groups through series of data such as place of residence, etc.; and (c) the emergence of "risk zones" (Foucault, 2004, pp. 61–62).

28 Christophe Foultier

2 In particular, the deputy mayor of Saint-Denis denounced the formation of ghettos in the city:

> The housing situation deteriorates and many French and immigrant families find themselves refused HLM [Habitation à loyer modéré] attributions [...]; difficulties at school are aggravated: the children of immigrants make up 80 per cent of some classes in our city; municipal costs for social assistance and health rise considerably [...]. What the state is looking for in Saint-Denis as in other working-class cities is the constitution of genuine ghettos of immigrant populations. We cannot tolerate this, [... we] reject the creation of these ghettos in Saint-Denis, [...] demand a fair distribution of immigrant workers in all the cities of the greater Paris area, [...] along with an end to official and clandestine immigration so as not to add to the number of French and immigrant jobless [...].

> (*Saint-Denis notre ville*, 1981)

3 Voter turnout dropped significantly between 1960 and 2000, from 60–65 per cent to 20–25 per cent (Sintomer, 2000, p. 3). Voter registration in Saint-Denis plummeted in particular between 1982 and 1990, factoring in demographic variations (Vidal, 2004, p. 57).

4 The mayor noted various infringements to basic rights. Protecting the exercise of trade union activities in industrial companies, maintaining the healthcare system, and sustaining higher living standards in the environment (housing construction, transport, and air and noise pollution) became 'local' issues.

5 The ESP was a grassroots structure created in 1995 by the municipality. It brought local and national services closer together and proposed a shared reception platform. The aim of the public service space was to support residents in their administrative procedures through specialists available to help households understand a particular procedure or answer a specific difficulty (e.g. legal problems caused by the loss or theft of documents).

6 The national government got involved in local debates by establishing a battery of more robust mechanisms in the district, while the local government endeavoured to draw a sharp distinction between prevention and repression. A series of mechanisms were set up: defining the Local Council for Security and Delinquency Prevention (CLSPD), implementing the Local Group for the Treatment of Delinquency (GLTD), and creating a Local Territorial Unit of the National Police (UTEQ).

References

Adda, S., & Ducreux, M. (1979). L'usine disparaît. L'industrialisation remise en question. Saint-Denis, Aubervilliers. *Les Annales de la Recherche Urbaine*, 5, 27–66.

Bacqué, M. H., & Fol, S. (1997). *Le devenir des banlieues rouges*. Paris: L'Harmattan (Habitat et Sociétés).

Barraclough, G. (1955). *History in a changing world*. Oxford: Blackwell.

Bigo, D. (2008). Security: A field left fallow. In M. Dillon & A. W. Neal (Eds.), *Foucault on politics, security and war* (pp. 93–114). London: Palgrave Macmillan.

Castel, R. (2003). *L'Insécurité sociale. Qu'est-ce qu'être protégé?* Paris: Seuil.

Dean, M. (2007). *Governing societies: Political perspectives on domestic and international rule*. New York: Open University Press.

Community involvement and social insecurity 29

Donzelot, J. (1994). *L'Invention du social. Essai sur le déclin des passions politiques.* Paris: Seuil.

Donzelot, J., Mével, C., & Wyvekens, A. (2003). *Faire société. La politique de la ville aux états-unis et en France.* Paris: Seuil.

Eick, V., & Briken, K. (2014). Urban (in)security—An introduction. In V. Eick & K. Briken (Eds.), *Urban (in)security: Policing the neoliberal crisis* (pp. 9–26). Ottawa: Red Quill Books.

Faraldi, L. (2005). *La participation et la démocratie locale. Section I, l'État central. La politique de la ville, Sections III & IV, Les élus locaux—les associations. Délégation Interministérielle à la Ville (DIV)/Observatoire National des Zones Urbaines Sensibles (ONZUS).* Retrieved from http://deey.free.fr/documents/Documents%20Citoyennete,%20Espace%20et%20Politique%20publique/Rapport%20démocratie%20participative%202006.pdf

Foucault, M. (2004). *Sécurité, territoire, population, cours au collège de France 1977–1978.* Paris: Gallimard–Seuil.

Graham, S. (2011). *Cities under siege: The new military urbanism.* London & New York: Verso.

Harvey, D. (2008). The right to the city. *New Left Review, 53*, 23–40.

Huysmans, J. (2006). *The politics of insecurity: Fear, migration and asylum in the EU.* London: Routledge.

"Le Projet de Rénovation Urbaine de Saint-Denis (PRU), demande de subvention auprès de l'Agence Nationale pour la Rénovation Urbaine Saint-Denis", Municipality of Saint-Denis, 5 July 2005.

Magri, S. (2008). Le pavillon stigmatisé. Grands ensembles et maisons individuelles dans la sociologie des années 1950 à 1970. *L'Année Sociologique, 58*, 171–202.

Mayer, M. (2012). The 'right to the city' in urban social movements. In N. Brenner, P. Marcuse & M. Mayer (Eds.), *Cities for people, not for profit: Critical urban theory and the right to the city* (pp. 11–23). London: Routledge.

Oblet, T. (2008). *Défendre la ville. La police, l'urbanisme et les habitants.* Paris: Presses universitaires de France.

Rose, N. (1999). *Powers of freedom: Reframing political thought.* Cambridge: Cambridge University Press.

Saint-Denis, notre ville (1978). *Dossier: la sécurité. 32. 5.* Retrieved from http://archives.ville-saint-denis.fr/archive/resultats/bulletinsmunicipaux/vignettes/FRAM93066_BM/n:36?RECH_TYP=and&RECH_mandats%5B0%5D=Marcelin+Berthelot++%281977–1983%29&type=bulletinsmunicipaux

Saint-Denis, notre ville (1981). *Immigration: Qui est raciste. 55. 3.* Retrieved from http://archives.ville-saint-denis.fr/ark:/15391/vta52d7619c64e7d/dao/0#id:2094599679?gallery=true&brightness=100.00& contrast=100.00&center=1021.000,-871.000& zoom=5&rotation=0.000

Saint-Denis, notre ville (1982). *Des ilotiers dans ma cité. 11. 10–11.* Retrieved from http://archives.ville-saint-denis.fr/archive/resultats/bulletinsmunicipaux/vignettes/FRAM93066_BM/n:36?RECH_TYP=and&RECH_mandats%5B0%5D=Marcelin+Berthelot++%281977–1983%29&type=bulletinsmunicipaux

Saint-Denis, notre ville (1984). *Un comité pour une meilleure sécurité, une interview de Jean-Pierre Jeffroy, maire-adjoint à la sécurité. 26. 10–11.* Retrieved from http://archives.ville-saint-denis.fr/archive/resultats/bulletinsmunicipaux/vignettes/FRAM93066_ BM/n:36?RECH_TYP=and&RECH_mandats%5B0%5D=Marcelin+Berthelot++%281977–1983%29&type=bulletinsmunicipaux

30 Christophe Foultier

Scherrer, F. (2013). Villes, territoires, réversibilité: Pas à pas. In F. Scherrer & M. Vanier (Eds.), *Villes, territoires, réversibilité*. Paris: Éditions Hermann.

Sintomer, Y. (2000). Désaffiliation politique et vote frontiste dans l'ancienne banlieue rouge. L'exemple du quartier Allende à Saint-Denis. In F. Haegel, H. Rey, & Y. Sintomer (Eds.), *La xénophobie en banlieue. Effets et expressions*. Paris: L'Harmattan.

Tunbridge, J. E., & Ashworth, G. J. (1996). *Dissonant heritage: The management of the past as a resource in conflict*. Chichester, UK: John Wiley.

Uitermark, J., Rossi, U., & Houtum, H. V. (2005). Reinventing multiculturalism: Urban citizenship and the negotiation of ethnic diversity in Amsterdam. *International Journal of Urban and Regional Research*, *29*, 622–640.

Vidal, J. C. (2004). Saint-Denis, évolution électorale sur un long terme, *Saint-Denis Au fur et à mesure*, *42*.

2 Participatory matters: access, migration, and heritage in Berlin museums

Katarzyna Puzon

Can one really speak of taking a part when one takes part?
(Hans-Georg Gadamer, 2007)

Introduction

Situated on the fourth floor of the Friedrichshain–Kreuzberg Museum, the *Ferngespräche* (Distant Conversations) exhibition started receiving visitors around 7 P.M., shortly before the time scheduled for its opening. One had to climb the stairs of the five-storey building, a former commercial space, to reach the event room. The museum is located in the backyard of the plot adjacent to Zentrum Kreuzberg, a complex comprising a 12-storey wall of apartments and shopping areas, and in the vicinity of the (in)famous Kottbusser Tor in Berlin's Kreuzberg neighbourhood. The opening took place on 6 April 2017 and featured a short speech by district councillor Clara Herrmann. Denoting the exhibition as an *Integrationsprojekt* (integration project), she praised the museum and the two project leaders for providing newcomers with space to talk about and share their perspectives and experiences of living in the capital city.

In 2015, Germany received a large number of refugees fleeing the war in Syria. Berlin's museums, among other institutions, responded to changes in the social landscape in various ways. This is exemplified by a number of participatory projects, such as the aforementioned Ferngespräche project, the exhibition *daHEIM: Einsichten in flüchtige Leben* (daHEIM: Glances into Fugitive Lives) hosted by the Museum of European Cultures, and the project *Multaka: Treffpunkt Museum—Geflüchtete als Guides in Berliner Museen* (*Multaqa: Museum as Meeting Point—Refugees as Guides in Berlin Museums*). These initiatives bring to the fore questions of access and belonging and the ways in which participation is thought of and regulated in (city) museums deemed 'agents' of heritage (Kirshenblatt-Gimblett, 2004).

This chapter takes as its subject the relationship between heritage, migration, and a city, with special emphasis on access and participation in the museum context. Approaching local museums as agents of urban heritage, I primarily examine the practices of the Friedrichshain–Kreuzberg

32   *Katarzyna Puzon*

Museum and their engagement with the recent developments, including the 'refugee crisis', which is also termed "a reception crisis, a solidarity crisis" (Christopoulos & Souvlis, 2016) or the "long summer of migration"—the phrase favoured, albeit not exclusively, by some scholars in the German setting (Hess et al., 2016; Römhild, Schwanhäußer, zur Nieden, & Yurdakul, 2018). I also look at the exhibition daHEIM: Glances into Fugitive Lives at the Museum of European Cultures in Berlin's Dahlem neighbourhood. Keeping in mind the idea of securing heritage for the deliberations falling within the scope of this volume, I explore the interplay between access, participation, and migration in museums. Against the backdrop of ongoing debates on displacement and mobility, I ask how migration informs museum practice in terms of access and participation. What do city and neighbourhood museums mean when they declare that they foster participation in their spaces? And how do they make it happen? These are pertinent questions worth investigating with regard to heritage-making in cities, and my contribution reflects upon some aspects of those processes.[1]

Heimat and district museums

At the turn of the 20th century, the concept of *Heimatmuseum* developed around Germany and gained momentum in the 1920s, giving rise to the movement dubbed *Heimatmuseumsbewegung* (Heimat museum movement).[2] Its popularity declined in the second half of the 20th century. Some Heimat museums turned into district museums (*Bezirksmuseen*) and city museums (*Stadtmuseen*) (Büchert, 2011, p. 20). In Berlin, for example, the Heimatmuseum Friedrichshain removed that descriptor after merging with the Kreuzberg Museum in 2004; as did another district museum in the same year—an institution formerly called the Heimatmuseum Neukölln and affiliated with the Neukölln Cultural Office. Linked with Germany's Nazi era and regarded as exclusionary, Heimat has a contentious history and has become a problematic construct over the past few decades.[3] Lately, however, we observe a revival of this term in Germany. For instance, the Federal Ministry of the Interior, Building, and Community has recently added *Heimat* to its official name (*Bundesministerium des Innern, für Bau und Heimat*).[4]

In lieu of Heimat, Beate Binder (2010) puts forward the concept of *Beheimatung*, which denotes a process, a 'feeling at home' encompassing belonging and being at home not defined by the place of origin. In a similar vein, there have actually been attempts to reclaim the idea of *Heimat*, and some propose its use in the plural form. For example, the Museum of European Cultures has recently launched the project *Gib Uns Dein Heimat* (Give us your Heimat) to collect *Heimaten*, the plural of *Heimat*, and visitors' thoughts and reflections on this somewhat controversial term.[5] Berlin's district museums, whose origins are inevitably rooted in the Heimat debate, offer a good space, somewhat destined to deal with the questions of place, belonging, and heritage, notably those centring on urban spaces marked by mobility and migration, such as the districts of Kreuzberg and Neukölln. This rescaling (see also Purcell, 2003; Çaglar & Glick Schiller, 2018) of the focus of heritage holds the promise of inducing a sense of belonging and community, as is often the case with heritage-making (e.g., Basu, 2006; Hoelscher, 2006), within the city. Those local agents and initiatives can thus potentially challenge the notion of heritage as a conceptual stronghold of the nation state, frequently entangled with a securitization perspective. The implications of such challenges vary across institutions, embedded in their respective histories, legacies, and power structures.

Securing heritage

Drawing on the Copenhagen School of International Relations, anthropologist John Gledhill analyses securitization as a social construct and argues that

> [wh]en an issue is securitized it is transformed from a question that is politicized in the normal sense into one that supposedly threatens the very survival of states and their citizens. This involves the deployment of a discourse that redefines particular issues as matters of security and thereby justifies the use of exceptional measures to deal with them.
>
> (2009, p. 2)

Gledhill's definition resonates with Matt McDonald's take on securitization as a political tool, and security as a "normative goal or expression of core values" (2008, p. 564). This possibly applies to migration and the way it is debated in the context of the current securitization of forced migration and the regulation of the 'refugee crisis', accompanied by certain understandings of values, space/territory, and identity, all of which can be mobilized and linked with 'heritage' as an insular phenomenon threatened by foreign elements and entities. Both migration and heritage emerge as securitized categories that are interwoven, as the former potentially poses a danger to the latter and is thus alleged to be a threat to national security. In this vein, a securitization perspective is problematic, and other approaches might be much more productive for our thinking about and dealing with (urban) heritage, especially given ongoing discussions on migration and the resurgence of nationalist sentiments. Here, I propose a participation model by drawing on my research at two Berlin-based museums, the Museum of European Cultures and the Friedrichshain–Kreuzberg Museum, both of which have been preoccupied with migration, although in quite distinct ways.

The interplay between participation and migration in museums brings to the fore the role of the museum as a steward of collections—one that attempts to foster community engagement or a participatory approach. This is demonstrated by *Multaka: Treffpunkt Museum—Geflüchtete als Guides*

34   *Katarzyna Puzon*

in Berliner Museen, a project that operates in four Berlin-based national museums (the Museum of Islamic Art, the Bode-Museum, the Museum of Ancient Near East, and the German History Museum). Through tours guided by migrants or refugees, mainly of Iraqi or Syrian background, and arranged for recently arrived refugees, the participating museums seek to act as "a connecting link between the refugees' countries of origin and their new host country" (Multaka. Treffpunkt Museum, n.d.; see also Gram, 2018). They are introduced to 'shared heritage' exhibited in German museums, somewhat in line with the 1972 World Heritage Convention that embodies a universalizing logic of the protection of 'world heritage'. The securitization attempts of such institutions as the United Nations Organization for Education, Science and Culture (UNESCO) or the International Council of Museums (ICOM) reinforce 'the greater good' thinking about heritage and the ways in which it needs to be preserved, often without giving much space to the voices of those directly involved, or leaving little room for local visions and strategies for heritage protection. My analysis does not, however, centre on the museum as an institution safeguarding or securing (urban) heritage, but rather examines the ways in which access is bound up with participation in the context of migration, moving beyond a securitization perspective as well as the 'on behalf of' approach that ventures to act 'for the greater good' (Graham, 2017).

Participation

Participation is nowadays a buzzword in Berlin's museum world. This trend is not a new phenomenon, as the term has been circulating for quite a while and keeps re-emerging at various moments and in different spaces. Participation and community involvement in museums and heritage are tightly associated with the advent of the new museology in the 1980s (Vergo, 1989), preoccupied with the practices of exclusion/inclusion and the democratization of museums, among other issues. The new museology, by and large, concentrates on the social relevance of museum theory and practice. Peter van Mensch and Leontine Meijer-van Mensch (2011) identify access, along with participation and representation, as one of the key forms of inclusion for museums.

Access in museums has already been explored in terms of participation (Bishop, 2006; Skartveit & Goodnow, 2010; Simon, 2010; Bluche, Gerbich, Kamel, Lanwerd, & Miera, 2013) and as a capability-based phenomenon (Labadi, 2018). In both cases, it has been conceptualized—and contextualized—variously and, for instance, examined as the permission to use a place or services and/or the means and opportunity to do so. Access and participation tend to be discussed as two distinct phenomena. The former might imply a less engaging and more passive modus operandi whilst the latter indicates an active involvement. In this respect, access entails visiting and using museum spaces and heritage sites as well as (at least in theory) the possibility of granting information concerning the locations and provenance of museum holdings. This, of course, differs across sites and institutions, and the participatory is defined diversely depending on context and the purpose of its use. Katherine Goodnow (2010) does not follow this distinction, but instead proposes four forms of participation in the museum setting: access, reflection, provision, and structural involvement. *Access* comes as the first level, pointing to physical design and admission fees to museums as typical examples and a somewhat literal meaning of accessibility—for instance the right to enter. The second form, *reflection*, is "one step beyond participation by way of access" (ibid.) and embraces consideration given to diverse audiences and their interests, which in turn entails collaboration with those outside the museum. The third form, *provision*, is envisaged as a natural consequence of *reflection*, and denotes reaching out to community members and asking them to supply stories and artefacts for exhibition purposes.

To include fully those whose lives and histories are represented, participation by *provision* requires yet another form of participation, that is, *structural involvement*. As Goodnow argues, this necessitates partaking in a decision-making process and moves beyond mere representation. That stage demands a reflective approach and presents a serious challenge. Bernadette Lynch (2018) recounts the repercussions of a paternalistic take on participation and the practice of assigning those outside the museum, primarily migrants, the role of consultants. "For many museum staff", she contends, "social inclusion functions as a kind of fantasy. Like any fantasy, it tells us more about its subject than its object. And, like any fantasy, it distorts the very object it believes it desires" (ibid., p. 235). Her observation accentuates the salience of negotiation over discovery and thus references James Clifford's contact zone not limited to consultation. In his conference talk, "*May you live in interesting times: The ethnographic museum today*", Clifford (2013) revisits the concept of "museums as contact zones", and expands upon the museum's main role in today's world, which he believes is essential to understand "how people get along with each other in the world".

One can identify three German terms that render the meaning of the English word participation: *Teilhabe* implies both having access (*Zugang haben*) and involvement, notably in a decision-making process (Knopp, 2014, p. 39), and on a structural level; *Teilnahme* indicates the possibility of taking part; and *Teilgabe*, much less widely used, embodies the idea of giving and envisaging reciprocal relationships. Marianne Gronemeyer (2002) puts forward the ensuing distinction between the last two terms: Teilgabe presupposes that each member of society contributes to shaping social interactions in all areas that affect their life; Teilnahme, on the other hand, is the claim to share in the distribution of 'the bigger cake' (*großer Kuchen*) (ibid., p. 79).

Migration, cities, heritage

The subjects of migration and mobility arise every now and then, and so the ongoing debates did not start with the events of 2015 and recent

36 *Katarzyna Puzon*

conjunctures. Migration is inevitably part of Berlin's urban heritage. Some scholars even suggest that the 'city is migration', such as sociologist Erol Yildiz (2011), who investigates urban developments propelled by immigration in the 19th century, which also concerned Berlin as it grew by 872 per cent at that time (p. 73). City museums, which appear as 'natural' agents and sites pertaining to urban heritage, have been addressing these questions for quite some time. In Berlin, they concentrate on a whole city, as in the Stadtmuseum Berlin, or on neighbourhoods, as in the Neukölln Museum and Friedrichshain–Kreuzberg Museum. Undeniably, discourses and practices of urban heritage play out variously in different cities and contexts (e.g., Herzfeld, 2009; Puzon, 2017; Beeksma & de Cesari, 2018; Panetta, 2018), and museums are not the only actors concerned with collecting and curating cities' past(s) and present. This is also of relevance to art galleries and archival centres. Berlin is a particularly interesting case due to the large number of neighbourhood-based museums functioning as spaces of and for local histories, memories, and stories, whose practices and visions nonetheless vary.

Denoted as a 'distinctive assemblage' (Macdonald, 2009), heritage is about processes and practices rather than final products, so to speak. As Sharon Macdonald astutely puts it, an assemblage perspective can "avoid imputing 'magical' notions such as, say, 'society' or 'ideology' as part of its explanations. Instead, it focuses on tracing the courses of action, associations, practical and definitional procedures and techniques that are involved in particular cases" (2009, p. 118; see also Stage & Ingerslev, 2015). In this vein, Teilhabe, Teilnahme, and Teilgabe, as well as their interconnections, are therefore best understood when observed in practice, and viewed not as being fixed but rather as playing out in an assemblage mode. To illustrate how this materializes on the ground, I discuss two projects that I see as going beyond the 'on behalf of' and 'forever, for everyone' thinking (Graham, 2017). These are daHEIM: Glances into Fugitive Lives exhibited at the Museum of European Cultures, and the Friedrichshain–Kreuzberg Museum's Ferngespräche. The Teilhabe approach was most commonly employed by those who initiated or partook in those projects and thus might best reflect the character of practices in which they were engaged.

daHEIM: glances into fugitive lives

In March 2016, the art group KUNSTASYL (Art Shelter) started work on an exhibition at the Museum of European Cultures (MEK), a neighbourhood, urban, and national institution based in Dahlem, which is part of Berlin's southwestern district of Steglitz-Zehlendorf.[6] Although the museum does not chiefly focus on urban heritage, its activities are inevitably involved in developments in the capital city, and recently more actively in the neighbourhood where it is situated. Through their collections and exhibitions, the institution had already brought to public prominence questions of migration and mobility.

The *daHEIM* project primarily revolved around asylum, migration, as well as the notions of home and belonging. Opening in late July 2016, the year-long exhibition was the fruit of collaborative efforts between the museum and KUNSTASYL. KUNSTASYL members are artists and creative people—as they describe themselves—including asylum seekers and those who hold refugee status in Germany. Some resided in a refugee shelter where the initiative started, in a building that formerly housed a health facility in Berlin-Spandau, one of the city's industrial areas. The exhibition incorporated objects, such as bed frames, as well as memories of that time and space. These were juxtaposed with material and immaterial legacies related to the KUNSTASYL members' travel—or 'adventure' as some would call it—to and within Europe, as well as their experiences after arriving in Berlin.

Regarding the project as participatory, the museum characterized it in terms of hosting, and KUNSTASYL identified their work at MEK as a friendly takeover of designated spaces. To Berlin-based artist Barbara Caveng, who founded the KUNSTASYL project, the institution proffered an alternative kind of access and participation. As she posits, "the museum renounced its claim to representation: instead of a paternalistic gesture of participation, it granted autonomy. What started in a home (*Heim*) became possible in the museum: *Heim* became daHEIM (at home)—a fragile construct into fugitive lives" (2017, p. 11). In this statement, she alludes to KUNSTASYL's strong presence in the museum throughout the entire process of exhibition-making and, implicitly, critically appraises the questions of belonging and migration against the backdrop of current and past events in Berlin, Germany, and Europe at large. Rather than exhibiting 'on behalf of' the museum allowed 'those directly concerned'—to reference Helen Graham's (2017) definition of participation—to speak for themselves. This involved a degree of tension, in particular in the early stages of the collaboration. In addition, Teilhabe manifested through direct processes of decision-making, in terms of the format and content of the exhibition. In some cases, these were negotiated with the museum, also with respect to objects the staff were planning to display and thus their contribution to the exhibition 'collection-wise'. The project fostered interpersonal relationships, both within KUNSTASYL and between the museum and the group, even if only temporarily in some cases. To a certain extent this references Clifford's call for "understanding how people get along with each other in the world"—and perhaps, in the present case, for creating other ways of engaging in/with the museum world. The daHEIM project is a good example of how participation and heritage might work in practice in an institutional setting, and how this is imagined and enacted through collaborative exhibition-making. The next case study further probes this interrelationship by investigating the ways of (self-)

38 Katarzyna Puzon

positioning of those who hold refugee status, with special emphasis on its urban and translocal character.

The Friedrichshain–Kreuzberg Museum and Distant Conversations

In 1978, the Kreuzberg Museum opened under the auspices of the Kreuzberg Office for the Arts. Moving to its current site in Adalberstrasse in 1990, at the turn of the new millennium it merged with the Heimatmuseum Friedrichshain. In 2004, both institutions combined their efforts and have since operated as a single institution, the Friedrichshain–Kreuzberg Museum, also known as the FHXB Museum. The museum serves two general purposes: it researches, collects, and displays local history and developments within the Friedrichshain–Kreuzberg district and strives to function as a space for the local community to foster resident participation in conceptualizing its main exhibitions. Natalie Bayer, the newly appointed museum director, highlighted that the institution's goal was to include multi-perspectivity and specific or individual narratives, rather than engaging in 'history telling'.[7]

Since its inception, the institution has tackled the question of migration in Kreuzberg, part of the Friedrichshain–Kreuzberg borough since 2001. Viewed as an 'arrival neighbourhood', Kreuzberg, along with Wedding and Neukölln, has Berlin's largest population of migrants and those with a *Migrationshintergrund* (migrant background).[8] This immigration started in the 17th century with the settlement of Huguenot refugees forced to flee France (see also Kil & Silver, 2006). Over the years, the museum has held events and exhibitions devoted to histories of the district, mobilities, and residents' everyday practices. This was exemplified by the theme of their 2005–2010 exhibition "*ein jeder nach seiner Façon? 300 Jahre Zuwanderung nach Friedrichshain–Kreuzberg*" (Everyone Their Own Way? 300 Years of Migration to Friedrichshain–Kreuzberg). The museum's involvement in the ongoing refugee debates came as an expected response.

In 2015, the institution hosted a temporary exhibition in the museum stairway, entitled We will Rise'. Refugee Movement—Exhibition and Archive in Progress. Mounted by the Refugee Movement, it addressed the events of 2012–2014 and memories of a protest camp at Kreuzberg's Oranienplatz, popularly known as the O-Platz. The O-Platz was the final stop of a protest march from the city of Würzburg, in northern Bavaria, situated 600 kilometres from Berlin. The decision to walk to the capital city was a response to harsh living conditions in Germany's refugee camps and was prompted by the suicide of Mohammad Rahsepar, an Iranian citizen seeking asylum in Germany who resided in Würzburg's detention centre at the time of his tragic death.[9] The occupation of the O-Platz lasted 17 months and ended in 2014 (see Figure 2.1).

Figure 2.1 The refugee protest camp at the O-Platz. © 2014 Katarzyna Puzon.

Distant Conversations

The Ferngespräche (Distant Conversations) project started in summer 2016 and was dedicated to showcasing New Berliners' perspectives on, and experiences in, the city.[10] The exhibition rendered the results of a six-month project in posters, visuals, and video recordings. It was initiated by two affiliated members of the museum, Stefanie Kuhn and Sophie Perl, who collaborated with refugees, asylum seekers, and local artists. Ferngespräche was a companion to an exhibition titled *Ortsgespräche* (Local Chats), which was designed as part of a participatory project with local residents and opened in 2012, and into which Ferngespräche was subsequently incorporated. Ortsgespräche displays the history of the district as one of migration and uses Kreuzberg's public places as anchors for overlapping stories. A giant floor map of the district shows numbered locations and consists of approximately a hundred recordings of residents' stories; the exhibition also employs new media.

Ortsgespräche was a starting point for the Ferngespräche project, which was conceptualized as a space in which those holding refugee status or seeking asylum in Germany could develop multi-modal contributions to

40 Katarzyna Puzon

communicate with the public. Ferngespräche was divided into three thematic groups: Reclaim your Space addressed public space in a more theatrical way; Euphrat und Spree (Euphrates and Spree) involved historical canoe tours; and Dialog am Ort (Local Dialogue) constituted an intense biographical work. Three teams of seven to eleven individuals were assigned to respective topics and engaged in a workshop-like process. The exhibition was composed of, among other works, twelve video collages created over the course of eight workshop series and made in co-operation with filmmakers and performance artists. Each group centred on one general subject and addressed access, memory, the process of arrival in Berlin, in particular concentrating on the Kreuzberg neighbourhood, as well as the participants' movements around the city (Figure 2.2). Several works covered sites and spaces outside Germany, chiefly those inscribed in their life trajectories. For example, Omar, a Muslim man from Chad, came up with the idea of sharing his religious day-to-day life with the project participants and museums visitors. He resides in Teltow, a town within the Berlin-Brandenburg region, but spends most of his time in Kreuzberg. The video featured his story of praying in a village in the Sahara, and also at the Bosnian Cultural Centre close to the museum. A few other exhibits included recordings with asylum seekers and those who hold refugee status. Some of them came to Germany during the "long summer of migration," and others prior to that period. Despite being contextualized within the recent developments of the "refugee crisis," the project referenced the 2012–2014 events, partly by virtue of the involvement of those who were part of the O-Platz movement (see Figure 2.2).

The events of 2012–2014 were a source of inspiration for the project convenors. They argued that Kreuzberg became a central place for refugees, once again, so to speak, because of the legacy of the O-Platz around which the entire infrastructure and networks emerged at the time of its occupation. Many refugee initiatives and resources were already in place when nearly one million asylum seekers arrived in Germany in 2015. Among other things, this attracted the project participants to the neighbourhood. Finding accommodation in Kreuzberg was not within their grasp, mostly due to the shortage of affordable housing; also for this reason, the district has relatively few refugee shelters. Accustomed to crossing the entire city every day, the participants would travel to the museum, often as part of other visits to the neighbourhood, from different locations in the metropolis and the surrounding region of Brandenburg.

In addition, the Ferngespräche project was guided by the theme of remoteness. The prefix *fern* has temporal and spatial connotations in German, referring to distance in terms of space and in relation to the past and the future. Here, *Ferngespräch* means a long-distance call, partly in contrast to *Ortsgespräch* which signifies a local call. Multi-perspectivity, as advocated in the Ortsgespräche project, proved to be slightly redundant, hence the idea of expanding the focus from one place (*Ort*) to the interconnection and interrelation between sites, including very distant (fern) ones. Placing these

Participation, access, migration in Berlin museums 41

Figure 2.2 Participants of the Reclaim Your Space team holding their posters. © Wie-yi Lauw. Reproduced courtesy of Stefanie Kuhn, Sophie Perl, the Friedrichshain–Kreuzberg Museum, and the Society for Interregional Cultural Exchange.

two exhibitions within one space resulted in multi-sited and multi-scalar conversations, both local and global, thereby becoming in a way translocal (Puzon, 2018), both temporally and spatially. This translocal perspective can be detected not just in the themes that simultaneously tackle various locations and places. Moving beyond the emphasis on one specific place, it traces the interrelations between sites and spaces, as well as "situatedness across different locales" (Brickell and Datta 2011, p. 4). One of the project leaders explained the rationale for this juxtaposition:

> If you come from one place and live in another place, you kind of always have these two places in your mind, whatever that ends up meaning. A lot of stories somehow address this fact of being here and dealing with concrete places in Berlin, but also still having some part of your mind and your heart in another place.

Hence the exhibition was to amplify the interrelationship between "more places that simply come together" (*mehrere Orte, die einfach zusammen kommen*), to address a sense of simultaneous attachment to two or more

42   *Katarzyna Puzon*

places, and to reveal migration as part and parcel of Kreuzberg's heritage and city-making at large (cf. Çaglar & Glick Schiller, 2018). These issues naturally emerged during the workshop discussions and in the course of making the exhibition.

The initiative took the shape of a co-creative project in terms of participants' crucial role in the decision-making process, especially at later stages of the project, and thus their significant contribution to its form and content. Unlike the local politician who depicted the initiative as an *Integrationsprojekt* for newcomers, the project leaders were hesitant about denoting it as such, and one of them remarked, "I don't like the word [integration]. It seems very normative and externally imposed. Integration as a goal—it does not need to be a goal; it's not everyone's goal". She admitted that the project actually made her more integrated into what was happening in the city. Addressing questions of mobility, the scope of their activities proved not to be restricted to a neighbourhood or city—if that is ever the case. The translocal perspective, in particular, exposes the salience of flows, relationships, and interconnections in the activities of museums operating in contexts where 'migrant heritages' intersect with urban ones. The project adopted the 'anyone approach' (cf. Graham, 2017), opening up to those who recently arrived seeking asylum in Berlin/Germany, rather than aspiring to act for everyone. Entering into collaboration with refugees—who are historically, spatially, and politically entangled in the history and memory of the district—offered the Friedrichshain–Kreuzberg Museum the possibility of expanding a network of people, objects, and places. Also, Teilhabe unfolded through translocal and assembled spaces and times that manifested in the form and content of the project, along with participants' involvement in the decision-making process.

Concluding remarks

This chapter situated questions of access and participation in the museum context and against the backdrop of recent migration and the 'refugee crisis'. My purpose was that of examining the practices of two initiatives that see the inclusion of—or a commitment to—participation, broadly and variously understood, as the cornerstone of their respective activities. The developments discussed here were intertwined with particular spatial and temporal moments in the city and the ways in which museums grappled with these by involving some of those directly concerned. The forms they took illuminate the heterogeneity of participatory processes and expose the ways in which people experience and conceive of certain places and spaces. By reflecting on participatory projects, my analysis shows the practices of regulating access in museums, thereby drawing attention to the ways in which migrants get to participate. In that regard, this can be important in terms of the dynamics of securitization and therefore deemed "a special form of regulation", as depicted in the Introduction to this edited volume.

The question is, however, not necessarily whether the participatory matters, but more how and when it does so. It seems that "[w]hile 'everyone' cannot really exist", as Helen Graham propounds, "individuals, groups, friendship networks and local networks do". She notes that

> investment in the type of small group work that has defined participation in museum and heritage contexts becomes a lot less problematic if, rather than successively (one group after another), it is seen as adding new nodes into a wider network.
>
> (2017, p. 84)

This is especially relevant to migration and the ways in which museums 'do belonging' in their participatory projects in this respect, as I have elucidated. Both the daHEIM exhibition and the Ferngespräche project positioned MEK and the Friedrichshain–Kreuzberg Museum as 'generators of participation', and not simply as collection-oriented institutions. While the Friedrichshain–Kreuzberg Museum has long-term experience of initiating participatory projects, this was the first such collaboration for MEK and some of its traces have already been included in the museum's permanent collection. Nonetheless, the sustainability of those approaches remains a challenge, along with the question of power relations that inevitably unfold in participatory processes. Last but not least, both institutions could have complemented their participatory endeavours by taking into account an audience perspective and the ways in which visitors partake. This may have afforded a more dynamic and diverse interaction between the museum and the audience, neither of which can really exist without the other.

Notes

1 The bulk of the research I discuss here was principally conducted as part of my ethnographic research within the project *Making Differences in Berlin: Transforming Museums and Heritage in the 21st Century*, and funded by the Alexander von Humboldt Foundation as part of the research award for Sharon Macdonald's Alexander von Humboldt Professorship.
2 The term Heimat has no equivalent in English and could be roughly translated as home, homeland, or a sense of belonging.
3 This question merits more in-depth exploration, which I am unable to offer within the space constraints of the current chapter.
4 Horst Seehofer, head of the ministry and a stark opponent of Chancellor Angela Merkel's open-door refugee policy, sparked controversy by stating that "Islam does not belong to Germany".
5 See http://blog.smb.museum/gib-uns-deine-heimat-wie-das-museum-europaeischer-kulturen-heimaten-sammelt/
6 See also http://kunstasyl.net/
7 Talk at a departmental seminar of the Institute of European Ethnology at Humboldt University, 24 April 2018.

44 Katarzyna Puzon

8 This applies to individuals who were not born as German citizens or who have at least one parent who was not born a German citizen. For more information, see www.bamf.de/DE/Service/Left/Glossary/_function/glossar.html?lv3=3198544

9 The protesters also opposed the policy of mandatory residence (*Residenzpflicht*), which requires asylum seekers to reside in the same area as their immigration authority office. Amendments to this law came into force on 1 January 2015, reducing this obligation to the first three months after registration.

10 See the project website: http://projekt-ferngespraeche.de/

References

Basu, P. (2006). *Highland homecomings: Genealogy and heritage tourism in the Scottish diaspora*. London: Routledge.

Beeksma, A., & de Cesari, C. (2018). Participatory heritage in a gentrifying neighbourhood: Amsterdam's Van Eesteren Museum as affective space of negotiations. *International Journal of Heritage Studies*. Pre-print online, doi: 10.1080/13527258.2018.1509230

Binder, B. (2010). Beheimatung statt Heimat: Translokale Perspektiven auf Räume der Zugehörigkeit. In: M. Seifert (Ed.), *Zwischen Emotion und Kalkül. "Heimat" als Argument im Prozess der Moderne* (pp. 189–204). Dresden: Leipziger Uni-Vlg.

Bishop, C. (Ed.) (2006). *Participation*. London: Whitechapel/MIT Press.

Bluche, L., Gerbich, C., Kamel, S., Lanwerd, S., & Miera, F. (Eds.) (2013). *NeuZugänge: Museen, Sammlungen und Migration. Eine Laborausstellung*. Bielefeld: Transcript.

Brickell, K., & Datta, A. (2011). Introduction: Translocal geographies. In K. Brickell & A. Datta (Eds.), *Translocal geographies. Spaces, places, connections* (pp. 3–20). London: Routledge.

Büchert, G. (2011). *Schauräume der Stadtgeschichte. Städtische Heimatmuseen in Franken von ihren Anfängen bis zum Ende des Zweiten Weltkriegs*. Berlin: Deutscher Kunstverlag.

Çaglar, A., & Glick Schiller, N. (2018). *Migrants and city-making: Dispossession, displacement, and urban regeneration*. Durham, NC: Duke University Press.

Caveng, B. (2017). I am a human. From READY NOW to KUNSTASYL—A chronicle. In: E. Tietmeyer (Ed.), *Glances into fugitive lives* (pp. 8–11). Heidelberg: arthistoricum.

Christopoulos, D., & Souvlis, G. (2016, 8 June). *Europe's solidarity crisis: A perspective from Greece. Roar Magazine*. Retrieved from https://roarmag.org/essays/europe-refugee-solidarity-crisis-greece/

Clifford, J. (2013, 19 July). *"May you live in interesting times": The ethnographic museum today*. Keynote talk presented at The Future of Ethnographic Museum Conference. Pitt-Rivers Museum: Oxford. Retrieved from www.prm.ox.ac.uk/PRMconference_lectures.html

Gadamer, H. (2007). *The Gadamer reader: A bouquet of the later writings* (R. E. Palmer (Ed. and Trans.). Evanston, IL: Northwestern University Press.

Gledhill, J (2009). *Securitization and the security of citizens in the crisis of neoliberal capitalism*. University of Manchester website. Retrieved from http://jg.socialsciences.manchester.ac.uk/Conferences/Securitization and the security of citizens in the crisis of neoliberal capitalism.pdf

Goodnow, K. (2010). Introduction: Expanding the concept of participation. In: H. L. Skartveit & K. Goodnow (Eds.), *Changes in museum practice: New media, refugees and participation* (pp. xxv–xxxvi). New York, NY: Berghahn Books.

Graham, H. (2017). Horizontality: Tactical politics for participation in museums. In: B. Onciul, M. L. Stefano & S. Hawke (Eds.), *Engaging heritage, engaging communities*. Woodbridge: The Boydell Press.

Gram, R. (2018). *Multaka. Treffpunkt Museum. An ethnography on museums and migration in Berlin* (Unpublished MA dissertation). Institut für Europäische Ethnologie, Humboldt-Universität zu Berlin, Berlin.

Gronemeyer, M. (2002). *Die Macht der Bedürfnisse. Überfluss und Knappheit.* Darmstadt: Wissenschaftliche Buchgesellschaft.

Herzfeld, M. (2009). *Evicted from eternity: The restructuring of modern Rome.* Chicago, IL: University of Chicago Press.

Hess, S., Kasparek, B., Kron, S., Rodatz, M., Schwertl, M., & Sontowski, S. (2016). *Grenzregime III. Der lange Sommer der Migration.* Berlin: Assoziation A.

Hoelscher, S. (2006). Heritage. In: S. Macdonald (Ed.), *A companion to museum studies* (pp. 198–218). Oxford: Blackwell.

Kil, W., & Silver, H. (2006). From Kreuzberg to Marzahn: New migrant communities in Berlin. *German Politics and Society, 24*(4), 95–121.

Kirshenblatt-Gimblett, B. (2004). From ethnology to heritage: The role of the museum. In: Among others: Encounters and conflicts in European and Mediterranean societies, 8th SIEF congress proceedings (pp. 73–80). International Society for Ethnology and Folklore, Marseille, 2004.

Knopp, R. (2014). Mehr Partizipation wagen. Die besondere Bedeutung von Partizipation im Keywork-Konzept. In: R. Knopp & K. Nell (Eds.), *Keywork4: Ein Konzept zur Förderung von Partizipation und Selbstorganisation in der Kultur-, Sozial- und Bildungsarbeit* (pp. 39–48). Bielefeld: Transcript.

Labadi, S. (2018). *Museums, immigrants, and social justice.* London: Routledge.

Lynch, B. (2018). Migrants, museums, and tackling the legacies of prejudice. In: C. Johansson & P. Bevelander (Eds.), *Museums in a time of migration: Rethinking museum's roles, representations, collections, and collaborations* (pp. 225–242). Lund: Nordic Academic Press.

Macdonald, S. (2009). Reassembling Nuremberg, reassembling heritage. *Journal of Cultural Economy, 2*(1–2), 117–134. doi: 10.1080/17530350903064121

McDonald, M. (2008). Securitization and the construction of security. *European Journal of International Relations, 14*(4), 563–587. doi: 10.1177/1354066108097553

Multaka: Treffpunkt Museum (n.d.). *Concept: The grand narrative – Connected through human cultural history.* Retrieved from https://multaka.de/en/concept/

Panetta, C. (2018). An 'alternative framework for development': state–citizen relations, urban revitalization, and downtown Cairo's passageways. *International Journal of Heritage Studies.* Pre-print online, doi: 10.1080/13527258.2018.1493703

Purcell, M. (2003). Citizenship and the right to the global city: Reimagining the capitalist world order. *International Journal of Urban and Regional Research, 27*(3), 564–90.

Puzon, K. (2017). Saving Beirut: Heritage and the city. *International Journal of Heritage Studies.* Pre-print online, doi: 10.1080/13527258.2017.1413672

Puzon, K. (2018). *Translocality.* CARMAH Paper 1 (pp. 27–39). Retrieved from www.carmah.berlin

46 Katarzyna Puzon

Römhild, R., Schwanhäußer, A., zur Nieden, B., & Yurdakul, G. (Eds.) (2018). *Witnessing the transition: Moments in the long summer of migration.* Berlin: Berliner Institut für empirische Integrations- und Migrationsforschung.

Simon, N. (2010). *The participatory museum.* Santa Cruz: Museum 2.0.

Skartveit, H. L., & Goodnow, K. (Eds) (2010). *Changes in museum practice: New media, refugees and participation.* New York: Berghahn Books.

Stage, C., & Ingerslev, K. (2015). Participation as assemblage. Introducing assemblage as a framework for analysing participatory processes and outcomes. *Conjunctions*, 2(2). doi: 0.7146/tjcp.v2i2.22850

van Mensch, P., & Meijer-van Mensch, L. (2011). *New trends in museology.* Celje: Muzej novejše zgodovine.

Vergo, P. (Ed.) (1989). *The new museology.* London: Reaktion.

Yildiz, E. (2011). Stadt ist migration. In: M. Bergmann & B. Lange (Eds.), *Eigensinnige Geographien: Städtische Raumaneignungen als Ausdruck gesellschaftlicher Teilhabe* (pp. 71–80). Wiesbaden: Verlag für Sozialwissenschaften.

3 Agents, access, and cultural policies of sharing in Kyoto City and Osaka

Olimpia Niglio

First dialogues with Western culture

The writing of John Ruskin was introduced to Japan only in 1888, in the popular magazine *Kokumin no Tomo* (Friends of the Nation) by Tokutomi Sohō, an important journalist and writer. In 1896 Shimazaki Tōson translated part of Ruskin's *Modern Painters*. In 1899 for the first time Murai Tomoyoshi introduced the socialist theories of John Ruskin and William Morris, in the magazine *Shakai Shigi* (Socialism). In Japan, this interest in the theories of Morris and Ruskin, both in the social and conservative field, had found important feedback for the protection of artisan heritage. In fact, the introduction of English theories fostered the development of cultural movements that promoted social respect and the preservation of human creativity.

William Morris was first introduced in Japan in 1891 by Shibue Tamotsu, in *Eikoku Bungakushi* (History of English Literature). In 1900 Iwamura Tōru published the first biography in Japanese of John Ruskin, in *Bijitsu Hyōron* (Art Criticism). In 1905, under the influence of Ruskin's aesthetics of nature, Kojima Usui founded the Japanese Alpine Club.

Ruskin's theories gained interesting adherents, especially after 1920 with the first important publications on socialism and on the decline of civilization and the degradation of society. In 1920 the philosopher Yanagi Sōetsu (1889–1961) founded the *Mingei Movement* (folk arts or arts of the people) in Japan. The movement adopted the ideas of Ruskin and Morris during a very crucial period for Japanese culture. The country was strongly influenced by Westernization, and industrialization dominated local arts and crafts (Kikuchi, 2004; Niglio, 2013).

Ruskin and Morris's ideas concerning the art of the people, and their proposals on social reformation and moral questions, interested the Japanese intellectual class, but there are important differences from the Japanese context of Yanagi Sōetsu, who had written about cultural values and morality reflecting on art. However, while Ruskin idealized medieval society and Gothic architecture and also art by craftsmen, in contrast, for Yanagi Sōetsu these values were very important, but it was the creativity of

48 Olimpia Niglio

unknown craftsmen that deserved to be valued and not only that which history has handed down.

Another important difference is that Ruskin's theories analysed the issue of *conservation* and of tangible heritage, while the Mingei Movement (Kikuchi, 2005) focused specifically on the theme of creativity and the protection of the creative process of art and therefore of its intangible part. Meanwhile, none of the opinions of Ruskin and Morris had repercussions in more recent theories regarding the theme of heritage conservation in Japan.

However, in Japan—whether it be the maintenance of artistic, architectural, or environmental assets developed in the past, or more generally any form of knowledge—the conservation of cultural heritage pursues constructive objectives to the extent that it enables each society to freely manage its own cultural interests and to exercise its own capabilities for the development of its own knowledge, in respect of the ethical values that distinguish each particular epoch and, consequently, the particular design paradigms of that epoch. For this reason, in Japan the criteria adopted for conserving historically important architectural assets are bound to be affected by the nature of social problems and their related aspects in the human ecosystem in which those assets are found (Niglio, 2011, pp. 7–8). The experiences in Kyoto and Osaka, analysed in this chapter help the reader to understand a different cultural approach to the conservation of cultural heritage.

The present observations relate to the conservation of architectural assets as experienced by the author during teaching and researching in Japan since 2012. All of the observations were elaborated through discussion with professors, students, state officials, citizens, and friends, and during academic conventions, international congresses, and informal meetings (Inoue, 2018).

The non-generalization of cultural postulates

The politics of conservation is a topic that affects many countries, especially in the West and the Middle East. Cultural policy in Japan is strongly focused on bringing the community closer to its heritage, and on how the community itself can collaborate in the protection of heritage. That heritage is: the population; the creativity of the people who in different centuries have built a country; and the cultural value of each citizen. The Japanese do not defend themselves against their fellow man; the Japanese people share and engage in dialogue. Approaching this cultural context means understanding its *cultural postulates*. In Japan the main cultural postulates are the concepts of *shūrisuru* (to repair), *hozonsurū* (to preserve) and *shūfukusuru* (to restore), therefore much more technical concepts. These postulates are applied to tangible heritage and mostly to temples, shrines, and public buildings (Ender & Gutschow, 1998).

However, after many studies and international comparisons, the international academic community has come to understand that the conservation of movable, fixed, or intangible assets pursues positive goals to the extent that it enables different human societies to live in relation to their own environments, and to exercise their own vital actions, as a function of the cultural values that characterize their own existence. This is because the methods that are used to critically establish how to recognize a *value* are strongly influenced by the specific social, economic, political, and above all the historical context in which any particular society acquired its configuration. Testimony of the different methods applied to heritage conservation are precisely the results that the individual communities have pursued in different countries worldwide.

In recent years we have witnessed the loss of many examples of human, material, and immaterial heritage, often due to lack of awareness of cultural differences and lack of appropriate tolerance and respect. Therefore, we are all invited to ask ourselves: What are the *values* of cultural heritage?

Civil sustainability and human heritage

Japanese culture promotes respect for others, for the community, and for what is not known. Japanese citizens do not work for themselves but for the community to which they belong, and everything is realized for others. The relationship between the *values* and *needs* of different cultures has to come into being, along with another related fundamental factor: Knowledge of the different ways in which the changes in the life conditions of different societies, as they are now, came about in the past and are still occurring— different ways of living together that can give rise to different requirements when it comes to defining the relationship between the *conservation* and the *use* of cultural heritage (Niglio, 2012). When we value the different concepts on the basis of which different cultures—for example between Far East and Western countries—have developed different interpretations of the past and the present, the resulting interpretations can be taken as the basis for constructing theories as to what kinds of action would be appropriate. These interpretations will also determine the different approaches to be adopted for safeguarding and conserving heritage, specifically *human heritage* and creativity (Niglio, 2016b).

In Japan, where the culture of conservation is constituted by practical community action, usable value is essential for ensuring the future continuity of cultural heritage. If a good cannot be used for community needs, then it is not a common good; this is a very important principle and applies to both public and religious goods. This relationship between use, community, and the cultural value of a good is not based on fixed or unquestionable criteria; it is caught up in a continuous process of reinterpretation that closely connects to its cultural environment of reference, and thus to a cultural postulate. Every cultural postulate must be understood as an *ethical act* that is the driving force for human activities and at the same time the justification for them. As such it can be analysed on the basis of the historical

50 *Olimpia Niglio*

considerations that produced it, although of itself it does not require justifying references. In Japan this ethical act commits the community to activate projects so that older people can teach young people the local cultural traditions. The transmission process is the main ethical act, and this process is implemented through programmes activated by municipalities and citizens' associations.

We will analyse some cases in Kyoto and Osaka (Kansai Prefecture). The requirements for conservation of cultural heritage come from addressing and satisfying those cultural postulates that define specific ethical acts. In order to do so in specific terms, a conservation project must first and foremost acquire knowledge about the asset, including historical knowledge, so that this factual information can then be used to determine what the requirements should be for conserving the asset, and what methods should be used for implementing them. The reference to a generalizable norm is not always credible but, differently, a local approach is credible if defined by direct knowledge. In Japan, for example, to know and to respect the opinion of a person and of the community is fundamental in order to better organize programmes for conserving and enhancing heritage.

This concatenation of factors makes it possible to identify suitable criteria that can guide the procedures to be followed; thus the work can be carried out in respect of the principles laid down by the cultural postulates— the motivating force that drives the activities of all human societies. Thus, knowing the criteria and methods of heritage protection in Japan requires widening our cultural perspective and not judging according to a general rule that has no reason to exist. Fortunately, cultural policies are increasingly oriented towards respect for local needs.

Training programmes in Japan are activated directly by citizens' associations together with municipalities, and participation is deeply felt and highly active.

The two cities, Kyoto and Osaka, and culturally differentiated situations that I have taken as my reference, make it possible to investigate the close interrelationship between knowledge of an asset and its conservation.

Although my choice of these two examples is coincidental in that it was the outcome of reflections suggested by personal experience, it does not seem merely casual. In fact, in both settings the cultural development that conditions the practice of architectural conservation has taken directions that were dictated by specific ethical principles and cultural postulates. For that reason, they cannot be generalized because they find their own motivations in the histories and environments to which they refer.

Cultural policy and ancient traditions in Kyoto

This analysis of cultural postulates is very important for understanding the reasons that determined choices and design solutions in Japan, especially in Kyoto and Osaka.

Cultural policies of sharing in Kyoto and Osaka   51

From what can be observed when investigating projects that follow one of the approaches currently employed in Japan's complex culture and practice of conserving cultural heritage, a first series of considerations emerges. It becomes evident that, in Japan, the approach differs in significant ways from the regulatory principles that are taken as the basis for practice in a European setting.

All this is very interesting and contributes to the construction of a path that we will now try to follow together in order to understand which cultural postulates encourage the conservation of heritage in Kyoto.

A very important topic in Kyoto is the respect for *human heritage* nurtured during more than 1200 years of history. Kyoto's multicoloured culture has shaped many public relations campaigns on the city's image and has always involved its citizens, even in the most complex historical periods. This multi-variegated character is still today translated into a balanced dialogue between tradition and modernity.

In both past and present, Kyoto has always promoted harmonious dialogue between various cultures and different contexts, such as those of aristocrats and commoners, city and countryside, Chinese and Japanese styles, and between Western and classic Suki styles. Kyoto's main characteristic (and increasingly so) is its acceptance of various cultures and new traditions, together with respecting and maintaining a balance between diverse groups.

The city of Kyoto has always been a mixture of aristocrats and warriors, temples and shrines, governmental structures and city associations: A culture in which the sharing of diversity has played a very important role during every age. Kyoto hosts important festivals that formed the basis of peoples' faith in history and religion. The *Gion Matsuri* (World Intangible Cultural Heritage, Figure 3.1 and Figure 3.2) is a ritual of the Yasaka Shrine, which has been closely connected to the local community since the Edo period (1603–1867). These historical facts clearly show that daily lives, lifestyles, and communities are inseparable. The Gion Matsuri is celebrated by the citizens of Kyoto as well as by visitors who come to the city in July especially for this occasion. The festival has its origins in 869, when Kyoto City was hit by an epidemic that led the imperial court to hold a purifying ritual at the Shinsen-en Temple in order to calm the wrath of the spirits of the dead. Today the tradition continues and, so, every summer (a traditional period for the spread of epidemics) the entire city is involved in organizing this historic cultural event (Tagaki, 1906; Tanibe, 2010).

Every year in June work starts on constructing large, traditional wooden wagons that in July parade through the city's main streets to welcome the god, calm the spirits of the dead, and invoke the god to protect the city from diseases and natural disasters.

This ritual is interesting in that the urban scene takes on a decisive and fundamental role for citizen involvement and inclusion, a theme that also

Figure 3.1 Picture of historical Gion Matsuri, Kyoto. © Olimpia Niglio.

involves the training and oral transmission of these traditions to the younger generations.

However, in order to organize this festival, which is a very important part of Kyoto's cultural heritage, the citizens work throughout the year. Thanks to the citizens' associations and municipal support during the year, every group—within their district of residence—promotes meetings, courses, and programmes where seniors meet young people and share knowledge of these ancient traditions. These comprise training projects supported by the municipality, where young people receive important lessons for transmission to the future of their ancient heritage, both tangible and intangible. In the Gion Matsuri, heritage is characterized by the techniques used to construct ancient floats of wood and jute rope, and by works of art, music, and rituals. The local associations bring together young people, adults, and the elderly, all committed to knowing and transmitting these highly complex cultural traditions (Shimada and Nishiyama, 2006). There are no books or writings from which to study this cultural heritage, but only oral transmission that opens important spaces for sharing and learning. Direct experiences in Kyoto have allowed us to analyse and attend these collective educational meetings and to verify and know these important local cultural policies that encourage the approach of young people, including foreigners, to the historical heritage of Kyoto.

Figure 3.2 Picture of present-day Gion Matsuri, Kyoto. © Olimpia Niglio.

Old pictures portray the Gion Festival and the formative meetings exactly as they happen today, where children learn ancient language, read original music, play traditional instruments, and learn the local traditions (Takagi, 1906).

Collaborations among people, and the transmission of local culture among different generations, are very important in Japan because history and traditions help the young generations and immigrants to know the cultural urban heritage, to respect it, and to protect it. Thanks to this specific educational approach of sharing heritage, access is secured for all, whether immigrants or not.

Another important aspect of conservation culture in Japan, which is very evident in this experience of Gion Matsuri, is the awareness that the characterizing feature of existence is change, a concept of *impermanence* that permeates all the philosophies and religions of the East; there is nothing in any of the fields to which we can refer (animate or inanimate, organic or inorganic) that could be defined as permanent. Inevitably, like all the rest of life, our material surroundings are destined to change and are in continuous metamorphosis. Therefore, in the field of architectural conservation as in everyday life, the impermanence of reality is a cultural postulate rooted in the principles of Zen Buddhism (Yamada, 2013).

54   Olimpia Niglio

From this we can infer that in Japan the existence of things does not correspond to any permanent physical reality; what prevails instead is experience of place, the poetic evocation of space in its beauty, which is linked to the nature contained in that space at the single moment in which it is perceived. Consequently, more than a desire to conserve physical material, the prevalent intention is to transmit knowledge of construction techniques and of the skills needed to carry them out (Shirō Inouye, 2008). In general, education in Japan proposes dialogue and participation, two fundamental principles through which to include everyone in the process of safeguarding cultural heritage.

Social inclusion and urban landscape in Kyoto City

In Kyoto the International Cultural Policy Research and Education Society with the Center for the Promotion of Excellence in Higher Education encourage programmes and comparative research (also with the support of foreign researchers) on the cultural heritage of Kyoto. These projects also have the great merit of fostering sustainable policies for social inclusion. Today Kyoto has a population close to 1.5 million that includes many immigrants from Korea and the Philippines. But only at the beginning of the new millennium in Japan were cultural policies adopted to promote social participation in government decisions. These policies encouraged the formation of local associations. Recently, Prime Minister Shinzo Abe has begun to open Japan up to immigration, mainly due to the lack of workforce. Immigrants are brought in and trained by the Japanese authorities depending on the job for which they are required. Most of the (still comparatively few) immigrants in Japan are Korean and Filipino, but in Japan it is not possible to create metropolitan communities of immigrants because integration and social inclusion are favoured.

These programmes have also promoted projects for the valorization of the urban landscape.

In Kyoto all citizens take care of the streets and public gardens; these are activities that encourage respect for the common good. Thanks to these programmes of inclusion the municipality, with the collaboration of academic institutions, has realized important projects to preserve ancient districts of Kyoto. This city is very important for temples and shrines, many of which have an important history and very ancient roots.

The Philosopher's Path in the north-eastern part of Kyoto represents an important route that unites many temples, from Gingaku-ji Temple to Nanze-ji Temple (Tanaka, 2017. Continuing southward there is Ninenzaka, which is an important preservation district for groups of historic buildings, including the Hokanji Temple (Yasaka-no-to), and which is located very near Kiyomizu-dera Temple. The latter temple, designated as a 'national treasure' along with many other Buddhist temples, is perhaps the most

Cultural policies of sharing in Kyoto and Osaka 55

popular of the temples in Kyoto and is a fixture of trips made by Japanese people (Takamura, 2012; Niglio, 2016a).

Recently in Kyoto, Professor Masato Tanaka of the Faculty of Regional Development Studies, Otemon Gakuin University Osaka, conducted important research in Ninenzaka, Higashiyama district, about the urban landscape with the participation of citizens' associations (Tanaka, 2017).

Ninenzaka district was built in 1929, and the designated World Heritage Site around Kiyomizu-dera Temple contains many traditional-style buildings (machiya) and other temples and shrines that are very important for both the Japanese people and foreign tourists, including Tofuku-ji, Kodai-ji, and Sanjusangen-do (Temple of the Thousand Buddhas).

In 2005 the municipality of Kyoto City proposed a landscape plan for this area but, more recently, the tourism sector in Ninenzaka district, located between Kiyomizu-dera Temple and Kodai-ji Temple, has greatly affected this district with major consequences for the loss of cultural identity. For these reasons, the aim of the project proposed by Kyoto City was not to prosper as a tourist destination but to maintain a local landscape.

Since 2001 citizens, with the support of academic institutions, have encouraged community meetings and workshops to discuss issues and problems local to Ninenzaka. The main issues have been conservation of the natural landscape; heritage education programmes for children and adults; voluntary activities for the conservation of places; development of projects and proposals by citizens; and the respect for diversity and *human heritage*, and thus people and community (Figure 3.3). These meetings produced many documents and proposals but primarily favoured cultural approaches and inclusion, even among people of different cultures living in the district. Their proposals have been analysed and included in the project for urban restoration. This citizen participation expressed three important points: (a) residents hope to maintain living environments and memories based on the history of Ninenzaka district; (b) they refuse to be involved in the political and economic movements of Kyoto City and/or temples while working to protect policies for the weakest citizens; (c) they seek protection of the cultural landscape while respecting their mutual urban identities.

In 2009 the general meeting of citizens decided to adopt landscape self-regulation in Ninenzaka district, which today continues to host important events, meetings, and courses for engaging young people with both tangible and intangible cultural heritage. In 2013 the landscape design committee was established based on a system of consultation with citizens, and today this committee has a very important role and encourages the study of heritage. Obviously the Ninenzaka district citizens' association is the fulcrum of this initiative. Today, Masato Tanaka affirms that the system of voluntary regulation in Ninenzaka district acquired legal status through the *Local*

56 Olimpia Niglio

Landscape Building Council Scheme. This has established a more secure system for prior consultation on any environmental changes proposed in the district and is thanks to the active participation of citizens and to collaboration with local institutions.

Kitakagaya District, Osaka

In Japan during the Edo period (1603–1867) Osaka was the centre of commercial activities. Feudal princes owned warehouses in Osaka to which they sent their native products to be sold. There was a regular freight service between Edo and Osaka, thereby facilitating the transportation of products from Osaka and nearby provinces to the Kantō region, or Eastern Japan. Products from all provinces were first assembled at Osaka and then distributed to all parts of the country by various routes. The development of communications and of exchange business between Edo (today Tokyo) and Osaka indicates that economic relations during the period were not locally isolated but instead closely connected.

Throughout the 20th century Osaka retained the role of an industrial city, but the great economic crisis that began in the 1980s marked the development of this city and its economic downsizing (Mori and Nishikimi, 2001; Mori and Smith, 2014).

Since the new millennium, this economic hardship has produced interesting urban participation projects, with programmes aimed at creating shared spaces for learning arts and local traditions. In recent years Osaka has also seen many educational and cultural initiatives open to foreign communities that have either immigrated or travelled to study in Japan. In fact, the main purpose of these projects is social inclusion.

In 2011, the Kitakagaya Creative Village Project (Figure 3.3) was launched, which aims to turn the Kitakagaya area of Osaka city, centred around the old Namura shipyard, into a creative and attractive place. In particular, as confirmed by Tomoko Kitamura of the Chishima Foundation for Creative Osaka, this project makes efforts to attract artists, art organizations, and creatives to Kitakagaya by providing cultural facilities, accommodation, and properties (vacant houses and factories) at reasonable rent in the hope that the area will become a centre of artistic activity.

The Chishima Foundation for Creative Osaka was founded in November 2011. As times have changed, Osaka's Kitakagaya district, once a prosperous shipbuilding area, has experienced continuous urban hollowing-out. Many factories have left the area, and empty lots and abandoned houses have increased in number due to the aging population. The local Chishima Real Estate company adopted the Kitakagaya Creative Village Project in 2009 in order to cultivate a base and build up a store of arts and culture. To fulfil this objective, the company decided to creatively repurpose some of its holdings, including disused factory sites and empty houses, most notably

Figure 3.3 Kitakagaya Creative Village, Osaka during a cultural event. © 2015 Chishima Foundation Osaka.

the former Namura shipyard, a designated site of Heritage of Industrial Modernization. On its 100th anniversary in 2011 the company established the Chishima Foundation.

Today the foundation aims to contribute to promoting arts and culture in the Kansai region, helping imbue the area with a new vitality and fostering urban development. When the foundation was established the financial situation for arts and culture in Osaka City and prefecture was declining, and there was little support for contemporary arts from private foundations. Therefore, the foundation launched a grant programme that contributes to the creative environment by using underutilized real estate and making these sites available to welcome artists' communities.

Despite being one of the largest cities in Japan, Osaka has no public theatre or museum for contemporary arts; instead, there are private galleries and theatres, although not on a large scale. Previously, some creative spaces were established in disused buildings and schools managed by Osaka City, but this project failed due to the financial difficulties that Osaka has experienced in recent years. Therefore, Creative Center Osaka—the cultural institution established by the real estate company—utilized the old Namura shipyard, which has become the only large-scale facility for contemporary arts in Osaka. It is managed under a unique policy of utilizing the old docks

58 Olimpia Niglio

and factories remaining on the 42,000-square-metre site as a space for creative activities almost as it is, in order to make full use of the potential of the industrial remains.

With the new millennium, contemporary arts events are well-practiced throughout Japan, regardless of city scale. This was considered an effective strategy for regional revitalization because in some large cities like Osaka, as the industrial structure changes, expectations for creativity are increasing as a new way to enhance the city's presence. This strategy is seen in many of the main industrial cities worldwide (Oevermann & Mieg, 2014, pp. 12–16); post-industrialization has imposed conversion and reuse projects, and in Japan this topic has been dealt with through the support of local citizens who have also contributed new ideas, and through public utility projects. These projects have enabled the reclamation of agricultural areas, creating new centres for culture, schools, and social housing.

These projects are also of interest to rural areas that are facing serious depopulation or industrial hollowing-out. Consequently, some of the art festivals are held not only for the economic effect of attracting customers, but also with the aim of establishing the identity of the local residents and to reinforce the knowledge of cultural heritage. Artists and visitors from outside the area can discover the originality and attractions of each region, which local people do not recognize.

In recent years cultural heritage has become an important depiction of Japanese society. There are many citizens' associations that work on the valorization of local heritage and ancient traditions. Management autonomy works positively for the cultural programmes, and the arts are an important key to resolving many kinds of social problems, such as assisting socially vulnerable groups and improving social inclusion, and so forth. Many artists regard it as a positive challenge to solve social problems with their creative activities.

At the national policy level, the Cultural Affairs Agency supports cultural institutions and theatres directly through grant programmes and subsidies, and indirectly runs certain cultural institutions. The Ministry of Economy supports many cultural industries (fashion, animation, etc.) and supports the development of local culture (Ministry of Economy, 2015).

Today in Japan many private companies are also active in supporting culture and the arts. These activities take many forms, for example establishing cultural foundations. Thanks to such financial assistance it was possible to create cultural enterprises that offered important opportunities to young people, both Japanese and foreign, to develop their creative activities. Each new company therefore utilizes its own resources to bring the community closer to the themes of culture. Within these cultural policies, the Chishima Foundation for Creative Osaka has a grant programme that subsidizes 15 projects either within Osaka prefecture or by Osaka-based artists involved in projects overseas. The individual economic value of each grant is not large, but the foundation supports challenging activities that create new artistic values, which are very important for cultural learning.

Furthermore, since 2014 the foundation has operated MASK (Mega Art Storage Kitakagaya), a large facility of approximately a thousand square metres that stores and exhibits large-scale artworks at no charge. It is difficult for artists to secure a large production site, and so they are often forced to reduce the scale of their works. Furthermore, because it is difficult to secure storage facilities after an exhibition has ended, artists are often compelled to dismantle or dispose of their works. Spaces such as MASK promote the development of the arts, and many young people can experience their skills in the arts and come to know their cultural heritage, which is also linked to agricultural traditions such as the cultivation of rice and tea (Hanes, 2002).

Encouragement to start inclusion projects

In Japan, many field studies and experiences have proved that only inclusion and meetings among different groups and generations can ensure securitization, respect, and transmission of cultural heritage.

The Japanese experiences in Kyoto and Osaka help bring us closer to new cultural methodologies in which the community and citizens are the main cultural heritage. Concepts of heritage and of value are also associated the *human heritage* described in this contribution, which demonstrates different approaches to securitization and securing heritage. In fact, the projects in Kyoto and Osaka both illustrate these issues. Gion Matsuri, the research by Masato Tanaka in Kyoto, and the experience of the Chishima Foundation for Creative Osaka refer to this Japanese approach. The examples demonstrate the participatory role of the community and the importance of this involvement in building an appropriate approach to heritage in a country where securitization is synonymous with knowledge and cultural appropriation.

We hope that, from the points where different lines of thought meet, will emerge new cultural projects in which diversity must contribute to inclusive growth and to the role that heritage can play in promoting social inclusion and economic growth for sustainable development. We must work to realize the theory of change as a visual representation of cultural heritage for inclusive growth, based on research and on respect for diversity.

References

Enders, S., & Gutschow, N. (1998). *Hozon—Architectural and urban conservation in Japan*. Stuttgart: Edition Axel Menges.

Fiévé, N. (2008). *Atlas historique de Kyoto. Analyse spatiale des systèmes de mémoire d'une ville de son architecture et de son paysage urbain* [Historical atlas of Kyoto. Spatial analysis of a city's memory systems from its architecture and urban landscape] Paris: Éd. de l'Amateur.

60 Olimpia Niglio

Hanes, J. E. (2002). *The city as subject: Seki Hajime and the reinvention of modern Osaka*. Berkeley, CA: University of California Press.

Inoue, N. (2018). Moderna e globale. Osaka e le sue trasformazioni urbanistiche. In M. Marchi (Ed.), *Città dell'Asia. Ricerche geografiche e storico-culturali* (pp. 175–199). Bologna: Bononia University Press.

Japan Ministry of Economy, Trade, and Industry (2015). *Cool Japan initiative*. Creative Industries Division Commerce and Information Policy Office. Retrieved from www.meti.go.jp/policy/mono_info_service/mono/creative/150706 CJInitiativeJuly.pdf

Kikuchi, Y. (2004). *Japanese modernisation and Mingei theory: Cultural nationalism and oriental orientalism*. London: Routledge Curzon.

Kikuchi, Y. (2005). Yanagi Sōetsu et l'artisanat traditionnel japonais [Yanagi Sōetsu and traditional Japanese craftsmanship]. *Dossier de l'Art, 118*, 62–71.

Mori, T., & Nishikimi, K. (2001). *Self-organization in the spatial economy: Size, location and specialization of cities*. KIER Discussion Paper 532 (pp. 1–39). Kyoto: Institute of Economic Research, Kyoto University.

Mori, T., & Smith, T. E. (2014). *On the spatial scale of industrial agglomerations*. KIER Discussion Paper 904 (pp. 1–50). Kyoto: Institute of Economic Research, Kyoto University.

Niglio, O. (2011). Architectural restoration: A comparison between Japan and Italy. In O. Niglio & T. Kuroda (Eds.), *Twelve houses restored in Japan and Italy* (pp. 7–15). Rome: Aracne editrice.

Niglio, O. (2012). Cultural petition in the preservation project. In S. Giometti, W. Lipp, B. Szmygin, & J. Štulc (Eds.), *Conservation turn—return to conservation. Tolerance for change, limits of change* (pp. 271–275). Firenze: Polistampa.

Niglio, O. (2013, May). *John Ruskin. The conservation of the cultural heritage*. Lecture, Kyoto University, Graduate School of Human and Environmental Studies.

Niglio, O. (2016a). *Avvicinamento alla storia dell'architettura giapponese. Dal periodo Nara al periodo Meiji* [Approaching the history of Japanese architecture. From the Nara period to the Meiji period] Rome: Aracne editrice.

Niglio, O. (2016b). Il Patrimonio Umano prima ancora del Patrimonio dell'Umanità. *Cities of Memory (COM), 1*(1), 47–52.

Oevermann, H., & Mieg, H. A. (2014). Studying transformations of industrial heritage sites: Synchronic discourse analysis of heritage conservation, urban development and architectural production. In H. A. Mieg & H. Oevermann (Eds.), *Industrial heritage sites in transformation* (pp. 12–27). New York, NY: Routledge.

Shimada, T., & Nishiyama, H. (2006). 写真で見る祇園祭のすべて [Kyoto Gion Matsuri Festival Photo Collection]. Kyoto: Mitsumura Oshikudoin.

Shirō Inouye, C. (2008). *Evanescence and form: An introduction to Japanese culture*. Basingstoke: Palgrave Macmillan.

Takagi, T. (1906). *The Great Gion Matsuri: Being the annual festival of the Gion Shrine of Kyoto*. Kobe: Tamamura.

Takamura, G. (2012). *Urban renewal from commons*. Kyoto: Minerva-shobo.

Tanaka, M. (2017). *Community-based landscape control planning practice in Kyoto City. Case of Ninenzaka district, Higashiyama ward* (manuscript). Faculty of Regional Development Studies, Otemon Gakuin University, Osaka.

Tanaka, M. (2019). The possibility of conserving and handing down urban landscape by means of participatory community building: A case of Ninenzaka District in

Higashiyama ward, Kyoto. *Bulletin of the Faculty of Regional Development Studies*, 4 (Otemon Gakuin University, forthcoming).

Tanibe, S. (2010). Festival to purify the town—Gion Festival. *Hersetec: Journal of Hermeneutic Study and Education of Textual Configuration*, 4(2), 77–93.

Yamada, H. (2013). On the sustainability of the intangible cultural heritage in Japan: The case of Kyoto Gion Matsuri Festival. *International Cultural Policy*, 9(4), 1–7.

4 Urban heritage, communities, and environmental sustainability

Dennis Rodwell

Introduction

The history of modern architectural conservation has been traced to the confluence of Christianity and humanism at the time of the Italian Renaissance, and to the simultaneous recognition of classical antiquity as being a vital aesthetic, historical, and educational resource and—significantly in the present context—a springboard for cultural continuity and creativity (Jokilehto, 1999). The monumentalization of heritage—alongside insistence on a dichotomy between what William Morris (1834–1896) termed *protection* (later *preservation*) and *restoration* "to treat our ancient buildings as monuments of a bygone art, created by bygone manners, that modern art cannot meddle with without destroying" (Morris, 1877)—owes itself to later stylistic controversies.

This dichotomy characterizes the fragmented view of time that evolved as a major determinant in modern heritage, architecture, and urban planning studies and practice. The insistent application of overly simplistic meanings to terms such as *authenticity*, *contemporary*, and *pastiche*, as just three linguistic examples focused on buildings and architecture, seeks to deny continuity. Likewise, notwithstanding certain aspirational charters and homologous documents dating from the 1970s onwards (Ripp & Rodwell, 2015: Appendix, pp. 263–271), the continuity of inhabitant communities does not feature in the generality of urban heritage studies and practice. The correspondence between safeguarding physical place and continuity in human space as a condition of access and securitization is not well advanced. Indeed, for urban heritage that is recognized and labelled as such, there is an implicit presumption of discontinuity and change.

This chapter examines:

- Heritage orthodoxy and the monumentalization of heritage;
- The distinctiveness and inclusivity of urban heritage;
- Relationships to environmental sustainability.

Heritage orthodoxy and the monumentalization of heritage

Once, there was nothing unusual about architectural conservation. Buildings were safeguarded and recycled, in the French sense of *patrimoine* for their intrinsic values of personal and collective inheritance, esteemed for their usefulness as well as their associations and memory, and accumulated and passed down without being destroyed in the process.[1] Conservation was the subconscious norm, and to destroy anything without careful thought or to build out-of-place were the exceptions (Zouain, 2000; Rodwell, 1999). The modern usage of *heritage* assigns temporal, extrinsically attributed cultural values to selected objects (tangible heritage) and manifestations (intangible heritage) that are largely independent of their continued functionality or correlation to everyday life.

In his seminal 1903 essay "*Der moderne Denkmalkultus. Sein Wesen und Seine Entstehung*" (The Modern Cult of Monuments: Its Character and Its Origin), the Austrian art historian Alois Riegl (1858–1905) speculated on the appeal of monuments in Western culture and distinguished three forms of memory value: intentional *commemorative* value and unintentional *historical* and *age* values (Riegl, 1903). Riegl foresaw *age* as the modern value and reinforced Morris's purist approach to the preservation of monuments as objects (Arrhenius, 2003).

Modern societies sustained major convulsions throughout the 20th century. Armed conflicts, civil wars, and revolutions spurred major intellectual transformations and outcomes, including the Modern Movement in architecture and urban planning. Collectively as well as individually, these ruptures signified a renunciation of the past, reinforced a fragmented view of history into discrete pasts relative to the present, and abandoned notions of social and cultural continuity. Patrimoine was transfigured into *heritage* and distanced from creative continuity.

The UNESCO World Heritage Convention (1972) displayed an essential inconsistency in its approach to cultural and natural heritage. Whereas cultural and natural heritage are both characterized as *properties*, the tripartite categorization of cultural heritage into monuments, groups of buildings, and sites is focused on historical objects; the categories of natural heritage, on the other hand, include threatened non-human habitats. This poses a challenge for living urban heritage, defined in the UNESCO Operational Guidelines under the category of groups of buildings as "historic towns which are still inhabited" (UNESCO, 2017, annex 3, para 14(ii)). Citizens in their communities, including marginalized sectors, whether threatened by tourism, gentrification, or other pressures, do not feature.

It is no coincidence that the only natural heritage site to have been deleted from the UNESCO World Heritage List is the Arabian Oryx Sanctuary in Oman (inscribed in 1994; delisted in 2007), on the elementary basis that the populations of Arabian oryx and other threatened species on the site had suffered irreversible decline (UNESCO, n.d.(a)). No equivalent decline in human population numbers or ethnic and socio-cultural mix of urban settlements has, to date, threatened the status of any cultural heritage property on the World Heritage List. Venice is a prime example: A city whose early-1970s population of just over 130,000 represented a balance between the number of households and the number of dwellings in the city, now counts less than 60,000 residents, mostly in peripheral areas of the city; the 20 million visitors in a year, averaging 55,000 a day, have assumed precedence (Kington, 2009; Figure 4.1).

In the interdisciplinary field of heritage studies, heritage is today understood as "a social and political construct" in which "heritage results from a selection process, often government-initiated and supported by official regulation" (Logan & Smith, 2006). Selection processes are top-down not bottom-up, and the protection of heritage is generally assumed to be atypical, largely determined by specialists, and expensive.

As Laurajane Smith (2006) argues, the dominant authorized heritage discourse "constitutes the idea of heritage in such a way as to exclude certain actors and interests from actively engaging with heritage", framing audiences as passive recipients of the authorized meaning of heritage and creating significant barriers to "the social and cultural roles that it may play".

Mainstream concepts of heritage confer value based on the perspective of an educated elite. With few exceptions, this excludes established low-income neighbourhoods. Conventional attitudes and perspectives have

Figure 4.1 Venice, inscribed on the UNESCO World Heritage List in 1987. The resident population has more than halved since the early 1970s. © Dennis Rodwell.

Heritage communities and sustainability 65

presumed that their residents disregard their own environments, lack heritage of their own, and need to be educated about the better parts of their cities and ancient monuments elsewhere (Kennet, 1972; Smith, 2006; Ripp & Rodwell, 2016).

Today's heritage community is dominated by historians, architects, and their homologues, and does not engage on equal terms with urban planners, sociologists, and environmentalists. This seriously prejudices both the perception of heritage—access—and its protection and transmission to future generations—securitization. The disconnection between urban heritage and the dynamics of human and urban geography is especially serious (Ripp & Rodwell, 2015).

As Sharon Zukin (2010) recognizes, *authenticity*—the cardinal term in the architectural and urban conservationist's lexicon, and interpreted with often obsessive enthusiasm to physical objects—is not applied in relation to the long-established communities and socio-cultural life of neighbourhoods in urban heritage areas. The complementary term *integrity*, defined in the UNESCO Operational Guidelines as "a measure of ... wholeness and intactness", is similarly circumscribed (UNESCO, 2017, para 88).

The 2011 UNESCO Recommendation on the Historic Urban Landscape—proclaimed as a paradigm "shift from an emphasis on architectural monuments primarily towards a broader recognition of the importance of the social, cultural and economic processes in the conservation of urban values" (UNESCO, 2011)—equally omits extending *authenticity* and *integrity* to embrace communities and neighbourhoods. Furthermore, its insistence on *layering*, a term signifying periodic superimposition, contrasts with Gustavo Giovannoni's emphasis on harmonious coexistence between the old and new quarters of cities and *use* value (Giovannoni, 1998; Rodwell, 2018).

The 2011 Recommendation repeats, albeit in moderated formulation, the mockery of stylistic continuity that is explicit in its predecessor document, the 2005 UNESCO Vienna Memorandum—"urban planning, contemporary architecture and preservation of the historic urban landscape should avoid all forms of pseudo-historical design, as they constitute a denial of both the historical and the contemporary alike" (UNESCO, 2005)—wording that ignores the multiple meanings embedded in the word *contemporary*,[2] and effectively disparages the Italian Renaissance and later stylistic revivals (all of which feature prominently in the UNESCO World Heritage List) as *pastiche*.

UNESCO has been described as having a "fetishism for making lists" (Askew, 2010). Narratives constructed to evidence *outstanding universal value* for the purpose of nomination and inscription in the World Heritage List constitute carefully edited variants of the authorized heritage discourse. They pose additional challenges for access to and securitization of urban heritage.

Taking the example of Suriname, which gained its independence from the Netherlands in 1975, the UNESCO description of the capital, the Historic

Figure 4.2 Paramaribo, Suriname, inscribed in the UNESCO World Heritage List in 2002, and monumentalized for its Dutch colonial heritage. © Dennis Rodwell.

Inner City of Paramaribo, concentrates on its Dutch colonial and Christian heritage (UNESCO, n.d.(c); Figure 4.2). An information website focuses on the wooden architecture of the houses of the colonial elite—which are inventoried as "monuments"—together with their constructional and ornamental details (InterAct Foundation, n.d.).

The complexity of the ethnic, religious, social, and cultural diversity of the historical as well as present-day communities in the inner city is not reflected in the UNESCO description; this ignores, for example, the main synagogue and the assemblage of Modernist buildings from the 1950s and 1960s (Strik & Lambert, 2018).

The inner city is currently under-occupied and in poor condition, lacking the animation that characterized its historical multifunctionality. There is a shortfall of support for the heritage of the country's colonial past in political and governmental circles, filtering through to omissions in heritage education, professional and craft skills training, and interpretation material for visitors to the city. The monumentalization of this World Heritage Site offers little access and renders it acutely insecure.

For dissimilar reasons, restriction of access in the financial sense, allied to loss of socio-economic balance in the community and diminution of security in the multifunctional sense, arise in the instance of branded urban heritage in the United Kingdom. In the early post–Second World War years, heritage designations were often perceived as a burden, deflating property values and rent returns. Today, the opposite is the case. Research conducted by the

London School of Economics and the real estate company Savills concluded that the added capital and rental value—labelled the *heritage premium*—of properties located in conservation areas can range between 25 and 50 per cent, fuelling gentrification and loss of community diversity (Ahlfeldt, Holman, & Wendland, 2012; Foord, 2016).

The distinctiveness and inclusivity of urban heritage

A central tenet of William Morris's thesis that monuments should be taken out of use unless they can be preserved unaltered, was echoed in a seminal publication from 1975 (declared European Architectural Heritage Year by the Council of Europe) in the affirmation that "the starting point in a historic town must be its historic quality and visual character, and not *secondary* [author's emphasis] social, economic, or even ecological arguments" (Cantacuzino, 1975). Such sentiments were typical of their time and ignored the truism that "a historic city is at one and the same time a physical place and a human space. Its authenticity is a compound of manmade and associated natural elements coupled with a complex mix of human activities" (Rodwell, 2012).

An essential attribute of unintentional monuments is that they were constructed to perform functions, individually and collectively—their *use* value, as Gustavo Giovannoni classified it. Protecting the material fabric of urban heritage cannot be dissociated from safeguarding its elemental purpose: to serve the complexity of interrelated activities in the collectivity of the urban environment. Historically, residential occupancy dominated these use functions: as human habitat comprising a typically broad spectrum of complementary ethnic and socio-economic urban communities.

Over a time span of more than five centuries, interest in historic buildings has expanded from its beginnings with the ruins of classical antiquity and the monuments of the early-Renaissance that they inspired, to encompass the Romanesque and Gothic periods and, progressively over time, the plurality of architectural variants and styles up to and including our own. From an initial focus on major individual monuments and ensembles this interest has spread to include historic gardens, domestic architecture, and the vernacular, the historic areas of cities, industrial archaeology, the Modern Movement, and later (Rodwell, 2007, pp. 1–22).

Over time, different periods have been disparaged and then returned to favour. In the United Kingdom, the neo-classical Georgian period (1714–1830) fell out of fashion between the third quarters of the 19th and 20th centuries. The built heritage of the subsequent Victorian period (1837–1901) suffered equal prejudice before returning to favour in the 1990s (Rodwell, 2017). Ambivalence remains with regard to the Modern Movement. In all instances, controversies have been dominated by the variability of extrinsically attributed cultural values allied to the hypothesis of selected survival through diverse formulations of protective designation. Considerations of

68   Dennis Rodwell

use value, especially in relation to the culturally unrecognized residential vernacular of industrial cities, have only come to the fore in recent decades.

Across the United Kingdom, lower-income inner-city housing was undervalued from the rupture of the First World War through to the third quarter of the 20th century for two main reasons. Firstly, under the pejorative term *slum*, a term applied in the vast majority of cases to housing stock that was structurally sound but required modernization. Secondly and more fundamentally, the emerging and soon dominant contemporaneous planning ethos of the Modern Movement was biased against urban residency, prioritizing instead the suburban lifestyle of the autonomous middle-class family over the mutually supportive extended family of the typical inner-city working-class community. Marcus Binney (1984), founding chairman of *SAVE Britain's Heritage*, described as a "sinister and draconian piece of social engineering", a 1963 UK governmental publication that stated:

> One result of slum clearance is that a considerable movement of people takes place over long distances, with devastating effect on the social grouping built up over the years. But, one might argue, this is a good thing when we are dealing with people who have no initiative or civic pride. The task, surely, is to break up such groupings even though the people seem to be satisfied with their miserable environment and seem to enjoy an extrovert social life in their own locality.
>
> (Burns, 1963, p. 93)

The scale of the 1960s clearance and dispersal programme of just one inner-city neighbourhood—the 125,000-strong community of the Everton district of Liverpool—has been described as being "of almost biblical proportions" (Rogers, 2010). The few buildings that were left standing included the listed Everton Library which, notwithstanding that it has lost the community it once served, is currently the subject of a multi-million-pound restoration scheme.

This example highlights ignorance both of the use value of inner-city neighbourhoods and of the communities themselves. Urban working-class culture in the United Kingdom did not lack initiative or civic pride: it was educationally highly advanced (Rose, 2010); likewise, the primordially self-supporting extended family (Young & Willmott, 1962). The dispersal of such communities in the name of slum clearance triggered housing shortages together with multiple social problems that continue to this day.

SAVE Britain's Heritage has fought and won many heritage battles since it was founded in 1975, including protecting from demolition and inspiring new uses for high-grade monuments such as country houses (Binney & Harris, 2014). In recent decades it has given parallel attention to low-grade urban vernacular. In 2003, residents in the Welsh Streets, an area of the Toxteth district of Liverpool comprising almost 500 terraced houses, were evacuated pending demolition under a latter-day slum clearance programme dubbed 'Pathfinder' (Wilkinson, 2006; Robinson, 2006; Hines, 2010; Figure 4.3).

Heritage communities and sustainability 69

Figure 4.3 Madryn Street, part of the Welsh Streets in the Toxteth district of Liverpool. The Beatles' drummer, Ringo Starr (Sir Richard Starkey) was born at 9 Madryn Street. © Dennis Rodwell.

Following a hard-fought campaign during which Liverpool City Council officials condemned the houses as "obsolete, unviable and in low demand", SAVE researched and successfully employed a heritage argument to save the area—but only after the established community had been dispersed. Strong competition, including from some former residents, resulted in the first of the remodelled streets being reoccupied immediately upon completion in August 2017 (Shennan, 2017, 27 August).

An earlier and equally successful campaign against the 'Pathfinder' programme prevented the planned clearance of the Whitefield district in the former mill town of Nelson, Lancashire, and pioneered its regeneration. Here, the terraced housing constructed for indigenous industrial workers— held in contempt in the 1963 governmental publication quoted above— has proved well adapted to the extended families of post-1945 immigrant communities from the Indian sub-continent (Lancashire Telegraph, 2004, 24 November). Understanding the dynamics of change in urban societies, whether from extended to nuclear families to single-person households, and irrespective of native or immigrant origin, is a vital part of securing survival and continuity in urban heritage.

The presumption underlying disdain for working-class urban vernacular highlights a disconnection between the monumental values espoused by Alois Riegl and the use value championed by Gustavo Giovannoni. It also highlights the disconnection between the academically grounded heritage world and today's global agenda of sustainable development (United Nations, 2016), which embraces wider societal, cultural, and environmental

70   Dennis Rodwell

issues and recognizes a spectrum of complementary values beyond the authorized heritage discourse. Japonica Brown-Saracino (2010) has partially picked up on this in her articulation of "social preservation".

The notion of one-way cultural outreach that one finds today in certain historic cities where selected areas have been inscribed in the World Heritage List, and citizens in the hinterland are perceived as requiring education about the culture and cultural heritage that relates solely to the inscribed parts,[3] is anathema to any ambition "to adopt a general policy ... to give the cultural and natural heritage a function in the life of the community and to integrate the protection of that heritage into comprehensive planning programmes" as provided for in the World Heritage Convention (UNESCO, 1972, Articles 5 and 5a); or to moderate heritage values in any given community.

A starting point for moderation is to affirm that culture and cultural heritage, whether categorized as tangible or intangible, are no more a product that should be selectively identified, packaged, and branded than are nature and natural heritage. The underlying generic concept of *culture* embraces what any given society *has* (material possessions and objects), *thinks* (traditions and beliefs), and *does* (behavioural patterns, including recreational activities) together with how it relates to and interacts with its natural and manmade environment: no more and no less (Williams, 1981; 1988; Eagleton, 2000).

This resonates with the broad definition of culture articulated by UNESCO (1982):

> In its widest sense, culture may now be said to be the whole complex of distinctive spiritual, material, intellectual and emotional features that characterize a society or social group. It includes not only the arts and letters, but also modes of life, the fundamental rights of the human being, value systems, traditions and beliefs.

Isaiah Berlin (2013) expressed the characteristics of *cultural distinctiveness* as follows:

> The ways in which men live, think, feel, speak to one another, the clothes they wear, the songs they sing, the gods they worship, the food they eat, the assumptions, customs, habits which are intrinsic to them—it is these that create communities, each of which has its own 'lifestyle'. Communities may resemble each other in many respects, but the Greeks differ from Lutheran Germans, the Chinese differ from both; what they strive after and what they fear or worship are scarcely ever similar.

Physical and intellectual access and ownership of *culture* is not delimited and exclusive. In this over-arching sense, there is no greater degree of *culture* in a historic city centre, especially where overtaken by tourism and/or gentrification, than in a socially stable but statistically deprived post-industrial inner-city district. Urban heritage should not be considered an elite brand that can only be credited to monumental ensembles.

Heritage communities and sustainability 71

Successive European Capitals of Culture have displayed a series of inclusive interpretations of culture—innovative or shocking, depending on one's point of view: from Liverpool, UK (2008), the culture of sport (especially football), popular music and entertainment; through Turku, Finland (2011), the culture of work; to the programme for Plovdiv, Bulgaria (2019), involving the vibrant culture of the Romani district of Stolipinovo (ECOC, 2014). Such broadening interpretations challenge the differentiation between high and low culture that is implicit in orthodox discourses on culture.

Following from an inclusive comprehension of culture is moderation between academia and everyday citizens in the matter of urban heritage. This is especially relevant when it comes to definitions including both *heritage* and *heritage values*. The terms themselves are not ones that citizens in the generality of urban communities use in their daily lives to describe the things that are important to them about the places in which they live or the daily interactions they most value in their surroundings and with fellow citizens. The community values of a place and its academically constructed heritage values will have commonalities, but their starting points are distinct and need to be moderated effectively to secure a commonality of understanding and respect—the prerequisites of common ownership and responsibility; of access and securitization.

The process of top-down/bottom-up moderation of heritage values in a community involves (Ripp & Rodwell, 2016):

- Asking different sectors and age groups (children, youths, parents, the retired) in any given community what is important to them about their place—and heeding their responses;
- Not pre-judging the outcome by using academically loaded terms such as *heritage* and *heritage values*;
- Anticipating that most of the responses will focus on friends, family, community, and familiar landmarks or lowly objects that have personal or collective meaning. These are the keys to establishing common ground;
- Comprehending that *heritage* and *culture*, in the widest sense but not enunciated as such, are an integral part of the everyday social exchanges within a community and valued instinctively as such;
- Not representing top-down and essentially selective understandings until after citizens have first represented the values that are important to them;
- Building from the bottom up in order to establish common ground;
- Showing respect for the values articulated by the community as an indispensable foundation for soliciting their respect for yours.

At its simplest, no one in the cultural heritage sphere should anticipate respect for their own interests and enthusiasms until they first listen to and respect those of others.

Two target groups, amongst the least considered hitherto, are especially important:

72   Dennis Rodwell

First, school children, a sector of the population that has multi-generational extended family relationships and influence, and is open-minded, highly creative, *and* represents the future.

Early in 2006 a campaign was launched in the historic centre of Sibiu, Romania, aimed at informing and persuading residents not to use polyvinyl chloride (PVC) as a substitute for the traditional joinery of doors, windows, and shutters, including for environmental reasons (Rodwell, 2007, pp. 168–170; 2010). It was a campaign that included engaging with school children through a competition in which they were invited to submit written work, artwork, and performance. The level of involvement and the standard of the entries were such that the mayor hosted a celebratory barbecue in the main square and himself took part in the cooking. Klaus Iohannis—an inspirational figure in the local and national community, first elected Mayor of Sibiu in 2000 and since 2014 the President of Romania—spearheaded the anti-PVC campaign, including signing the promotional leaflets and attracting widespread media coverage.

Second, a sector of the population that is often regarded as one of the most challenging to access: youths with poor educational qualifications in post-industrial urban communities where unemployment levels are high and often three- or four-generational.

Also, in 2006 a government minister in the United Kingdom Department for Culture Media and Sport solicited a visit to Liverpool—a city that consistently features at the top of official indices of deprivation—and requested to see 'the good, the bad, and the ugly'. Part of her programme included a visit to a youth centre in a disadvantaged neighbourhood. In the centre, unemployed youths presented what the city meant to them. The minister was so impressed with the civic pride and articulateness she witnessed that she cancelled parts of the subsequent official programme in the town hall, on the premise that "These are the real people of Liverpool; these are the people I have come to see".

Applying the appropriate techniques of communication and moderation are key to winning audiences for the appreciation of all types of cultural heritage. Urban heritage, whatever its academically esteemed historical or age value, will be the most familiar to citizens, whatever their level of education, ethnicity, or socio-economic background. Animating their pride in their own environments is a vital step to sharing and escalating pride in both the designated and unrecognized urban heritage.

The concept of *stakeholder* in relation to urban heritage also needs to be clarified. For example, does it:

- Comprise only those who have a direct and significant governmental and/or financial interest in a place? Or,
- Comprise all who have physical and intellectual access to a place?

This author would open with the second of these.

Or, as Tania Ali Soomro (2015) has articulated, should the concept be divided into

- Primary stakeholders: direct users—the local community;
- Secondary stakeholders: indirect users—incoming traders, consumers, and tourists, service providers, and other work-related categories;
- Tertiary stakeholders: influential—governmental, non-governmental, academia, and outside investors.

This tripartite classification is the inclusive one, placing citizens to the fore.

A practical case with which this author has been closely involved is Asmara, the capital of Eritrea in the Horn of Africa. It is summarized here as indicative of the range of real-life issues for which an inclusive attitude to culture and cultural heritage can advance the cause of preserving heritage at the scale of an entire historic city. It subsumes indications of the range of partnerships that the heritage community needs to consolidate in order to position itself at the heart of a holistic approach to the management of urban heritage.

The objective of a 2004 assignment, which took place immediately antecedent to the launch of the UNESCO historic urban landscape initiative, was to prepare over-arching urban planning guidelines for what was known as the "historic perimeter" of Asmara—covering an area of approximately four square kilometres—in the context of the city as a whole (the historic perimeter represents about 5 per cent of the total area of the city), and co-ordinating specialist studies already prepared and in hand, all with the objective of promoting an integrated approach to heritage protection and sustainable urban development (Rodwell, 2004(a); 2004(b)). The mission was undertaken within the framework of the Cultural Assets Rehabilitation Project (CARP), an initiative of the Eritrean government and people, supported by the World Bank. A major determinant was understanding and respect for Asmara's complex, interrelated and evolving tangible and intangible cultural-heritage traditions, embracing indigenous cultures, the colonial and Modernist eras, and the city's status as the capital of a re-emerging nation.

The factors embraced by this mission included:

- Water supply and sanitation;
- Food supply and markets;
- Housing supply and quality serving the city's diverse communities and varied lifestyles;
- Traffic and transportation within the historic perimeter and across the metropolitan area;
- Land and building uses, building heights, urban morphology, and design issues appropriate to different locations in the historic perimeter and wider city;

74 *Dennis Rodwell*

- Incompatible land and building uses (summarized as large-scale office buildings and hotels, retail stores and shopping complexes, depots and warehouses, and large-scale workshops, factories, and heavy industry);
- Vacant land and underused plots and buildings, and their suitability for development, including for recreational, other community uses, and public art.
- Over-arching historic building conservation guidelines allied to the need for training and related capacity-building initiatives;
- Identification of the need for an integrated city–region masterplan together with subjects for ongoing detailed studies, including socio-economic data collection; review of legislative, regulatory, and administrative systems; support for community engagement; and the city's tourism potential.

A main driver for this assignment was to position basic human needs alongside social processes, considerations of tangible and intangible cultural heritage in their inclusive definitions, and relationships with the wider natural environment, promoting what Patrick Geddes (1968) formulated as an evolutionary and sociological approach to the city in its entirety as an *urban ecosystem*.

The assignment animated ongoing reflections by the Eritrean government and the Municipality of Asmara. It was immediately followed by the drafting of the Tentative List submission to UNESCO and informed the nomination and management plan for the inscription of "Asmara: A Modernist City of Africa" at the 2017 session of the World Heritage Committee (UNESCO World Heritage List, n.d.(b)).

Relationships to environmental sustainability

The examples cited above, of the Welsh Streets in Liverpool and the Whitefield district of Nelson, both rhyme with what have become known as '*the three Rs*' of sustainability: reduce, reuse, and recycle.

Urban Splash, founded in 1993, soon established itself as a leading heritage rescue company in industrial cities in the northeast of England, refunctioning redundant historic warehouses and mills and moving on to numerous other building types, including terraced housing. As co-founder Jonathan Falkingham writes:

> I hope that one thing we have demonstrated over the last 20 years is that it is all too easy to give up on old buildings—and that if we apply some creativity and lateral thought we can reinvent and repurpose them for another generation to enjoy. I also believe that in this age of sustainability, before coming to convenient conclusions about demolition, our first obligation is to give serious thought to reuse—this may take a bit more time and effort, but continually knocking down our heritage (in all its forms) is quite simply unsustainable [...] It's often the same people

who are worrying about plastic bags who are happy to tear down perfectly good buildings.

(Urban Splash, 2011)

One of Urban Splash's most imaginative schemes at the scale of urban heritage has been the plan-form inversion of the 318 mostly 'two-up two-down' houses (with two rooms upstairs and two downstairs) at Chimney Pot Park, Salford, Greater Manchester: practical, from the perspective of providing natural light to the new upper floor living rooms; and symbolic (Figure 4.4).

A compendium of the values that citizens attribute to urban heritage, reinforced by 21st-century agendas of environment sustainability and climate change, can be encapsulated as follows:

- *Community*: All social values and relationships, especially everyday ones esteemed by inhabitants. Tools of cognitive mapping reinforce these relationships (Smith, J., 2010);
- *Resource*: In multiple senses, including the environmental capital/ embodied energy of exploited natural resources as well as financial;
- *Use*: Including ongoing adaptability and creative reuse. Together with *resource*, this relates to the *three Rs* of sustainability;
- *Culture*: Broadly defined; especially as recognized and appreciated by inhabitant communities through meaning and processes of engagement rather than just *things* (Smith, L., 2006).

Figure 4.4 Chimney Pot Park, Salford, Greater Manchester. The plan-form inversion of the houses has the symbolic objective of turning people's perceptions of non-elite industrial urban heritage upside down. © Dennis Rodwell.

76   Dennis Rodwell

Tangible cultural heritage, which may be considered a subset of both resource and culture, constitutes the physical backdrop in this summation, focused as it is on citizens in their communities, not on external interests and visitors.

Conclusion

Cities are at one and the same time physical places and human spaces: places of historically continuous human habitation animated with a diversity of complementary communities and multifarious social, cultural, and economic activities. Heritage orthodoxy disassembles the complexity of established cities, focusing on exemplar historic areas—in some cases entire cities—as *urban heritage*, without regard to their historical purpose. In our urbanized world, urban heritage—whether high- or low-grade in the classification of its tangible heritage—is the norm not the exception.

In the composite of their tangible and intangible heritage, and applying generic rather than the academically delimited meanings assigned by heritage academics and their homologues, there is as much culture and cultural heritage in a demographically stable, low-income inner-city neighbourhood as in a delimited historic quarter, especially where the latter has been given over to tourism or repopulated through gentrification. Currently, the values attributed to urban heritage are circumscribed by a heritage orthodoxy whose roots were nourished by conventions, charters, and declarations in the third quarter of the 20th century. Now, well advanced through the first quarter of the 21st century and under the umbrella of sustainable development, international agendas have moved on from the selective survival of tangible and intangible heritage vestiges to comprehend community, resource, and use values.

As the norm rather than the exception, the need today is to invest in and apply inclusive not exclusionist definitions and techniques of understanding to reflect this new canvas: to assure mutual respect and common ownership of the underlying commonalities between what have hitherto been regarded as high- and low-grade urban heritage; and as a precondition of mutually responsive intellectual access and applied securitization by the community at large.

Notes

1 An analysis of the origins and evolution of the concept of *patrimoine* is to be found in Zouain (2000), writing as deputy director of the UNESCO World Heritage Centre. See also Rodwell (1999).
2 The multiple meanings of *contemporary* include: living or occurring in the same period; existing or occurring at the present time; conforming to modern ideas in style and fashion; and having approximately the same age.
3 For example, Liverpool Maritime Mercantile City and the Old and New Towns of Edinburgh World Heritage Sites.

References

Ahlfeldt, G. M., Holman, N., & Wendland, N. (2012). *An assessment of the effects of conservation areas on value*. London: London School of Economics and Political Science. Retrieved from https://content.historicengland.org.uk/content/docs/research/assessment-ca-value.pdf

Arrhenius, T. (2003). The fragile monument: On Alois Riegl's modern cult of monuments. *Nordisk Arkitekturforskning: Nordic Journal of Architectural Research 16*(4), 51–55. Retrieved from http://arkitekturforskning.net/na/article/view/296

Askew, M. (2010). The magic list of global status: UNESCO, world heritage and the agenda of states. In S. Labadi & C. Long, (Eds.), *Heritage and globalisation* (p. 32). London: Routledge.

Berlin, I. (2013). *The proper study of mankind* (p. 10). London: Vintage. Retrieved from http://assets.press.princeton.edu/chapters/s9983.pdf

Binney, M. (1984). *Our vanishing heritage* (p. 193). London: Arlington Books.

Binney, M. & Harris, J. (2014). *Forty years on*. London: SAVE Britain's Heritage.

Brown-Saracino, J. (2010). *A neighborhood that never changes: Gentrification, social preservation, and the search for authenticity* (pp. 80–103). Chicago, IL: University of Chicago Press.

Burns, W. (1963). *New towns for old: The technique of urban renewal* (p. 93). London: HMSO.

Cantacuzino, S. (Ed.) (1975). *Architectural conservation in Europe* (p. 4). London: Architectural Press.

Eagleton, T. (2000). *The idea of culture*. Oxford: Blackwell.

European Capital of Culture (ECOC). (2014). *Selection of the European capital of culture in 2019 in Bulgaria: The selection panel's final report*. Sofia: ECOC. Retrieved from https://ec.europa.eu/programmes/creative-europe/sites/creative-europe/files/files/ecoc-2019-report-bulgaria_en.pdf

Foord, G. (2016). *Interactive map: The value of our built heritage*. London: Savills. Retrieved from www.savills.co.uk/blog/article/211355/residential-property/interactive-map--the-value-of-our-built-heritage.aspx.

Geddes, P. (1968). *Cities in evolution* (with an introduction by Percy Johnson-Marshall). London: Ernest Benn.

Giovannoni, G. (1998). *L'urbanisme face aux villes anciennes* (with an introduction by Françoise Choay). Paris: Seuil.

Hines, M. (2010). *Reviving Britain's terraces: Life after Pathfinder*. London: SAVE Britain's Heritage.

InterAct Foundation (n.d.). *City of Paramaribo: World heritage*. Retrieved from http://cityofparamaribo.com/read/worldheritage

Jokilehto, J. (1999). *A history of architectural conservation*. Oxford: Butterworth-Heinemann.

Kennet, W. (1972). *Preservation*. London: Temple Smith.

Kington, T. (2009, 1 March). Who can now stop the slow death of Venice? *The Guardian*. Retrieved from www.theguardian.com/world/2009/mar/01/venice-population-exodus-tourism

Lancashire Telegraph. (2004, 24 November). Residents tell hopes and fears to planners. *Lancashire Telegraph*. Retrieved from www.lancashiretelegraph.co.uk/news/5807239.Residents_tell_hopes_and_fears_to_planners/

78   Dennis Rodwell

Logan, W., & Smith, L. (2006). *Urban heritage, development and sustainability: International frameworks, national and local guidance* (p. xii, series editors' foreword). London: Routledge.

Morris, W. (1877). *Manifesto of the Society for the Protection of Ancient Buildings*. London: SPAB.

Riegl, A. (1903). *Der moderne Denkmalkultus. Sein Wesen und seine Entstehung*. Vienna. English translation: (1982). The modern cult of monuments: Its character and its origin (transl. Forster & Ghirardo). *Oppositions 25*, 21–56.

Ripp, M., & Rodwell, D. (2015). The geography of urban heritage. *Historic Urban Environment: Policy and Practice, 6*(3), 240–276.

Ripp, M., & Rodwell, D. (2016). The governance of urban heritage. *Historic Environment: Policy and Practice 7*(1), 81–108.

Robinson, E. (Ed.) (2006). The Victorian terrace: An endangered species again? *The Victorian 21* (special issue).

Rodwell, D. (1999, February). *Que veut dire 'patrimoine'?* A reflection drafted preparatory to missions on behalf of the UNESCO world heritage centre, March through June 1999. Retrieved from www.academia.edu/35994135/_Que_veut_dire_patrimoine_The_concept_of_heritage_reflection_1999_02

Rodwell, D. (2004a). *Over-arching urban planning and building conservation guidelines for the historic perimeter of Asmara, Eritrea*. Asmara: Cultural Assets Rehabilitation Project.

Rodwell, D. (2004b). Asmara: Conservation and development in a historic city. *Journal of Architectural Conservation 10*(3), 41–58.

Rodwell, D. (2007). *Conservation and sustainability in historic cities*. Oxford: Blackwell.

Rodwell, D. (2010). Comparative approaches to urban conservation in Central and Eastern Europe: Zamość, Poland, and Sibiu, Romania. *Historic Environment: Policy and Practice 1*(2), 116–142.

Rodwell, D. (2012). The social aspect of urban revitalisation. *Biuletyn Informacyjny 19*(4), 27. Retrieved from www.icomos-poland.org/pl/biuletyn-informacyjny-pkn-icomos.html

Rodwell, D. (2017). The values of heritage: A new paradigm for the 21st century. In M. Rossipal (Ed.) *The 6th Baltic Sea Region Cultural Heritage Forum: From Postwar to Postmodern*. Stockholm: Riksantikvarieämbetet.

Rodwell, D. (2018). The historic urban landscape and the geography of urban heritage. *Historic Urban Environment: Policy and Practice, 9*(3–4), 180–206.

Rogers, K. (2010). *The lost tribe of Everton & Scottie Road* (p. 7). Liverpool: TrinityMirror Media.

Rose, J. (2010). *The intellectual life of the British working classes* (2nd ed.). New Haven, CT: Yale University Press.

Shennan, P. (2017, 27 August). Revamped homes in Welsh Streets snapped up in 24 hours. *Liverpool Echo*. Retrieved from www.liverpoolecho.co.uk/news/liverpool-news/revamped-homes-welsh-streets-snapped-13518004

Smith, J. (2010). Marrying the old with the new in historic urban landscapes. In R. van Oers & S. Haraguchi (Eds.), *Managing historic cities* (World Heritage Papers 27, pp. 95–52). Paris: UNESCO.

Smith, L. (2006). *Uses of heritage*. London: Routledge.

Soomro, A. T. (2015, March). *The revival of the surroundings of Empress Market and adjoining areas of Saddar Bazaar*. Presentation at How to Assess Built

Heritage communities and sustainability 79

Heritage? ICOMOS theory and philosophy international scientific conference. Florence, Italy.

Strik, F., & Lambert, A. (2018). *Paramaribo: De Modernistische Architectuur van ir. Peter J Nagel*. Volendam: LM Publishers.

UNESCO. (n.d., a). *Arabian oryx sanctuary*. World Heritage List online. Retrieved from http://whc.unesco.org/en/list/654

UNESCO. (n.d., b). *Asmara: A modernist city of Africa*. World Heritage List online. Retrieved from http://whc.unesco.org/en/list/1550

UNESCO. (n.d., c). *Historic inner city of Paramaribo*. World Heritage List online. Retrieved from http://whc.unesco.org/en/list/940

UNESCO. (1972). *Convention concerning the protection of the world cultural and natural heritage*. Paris: UNESCO. Retrieved from https://whc.unesco.org/archive/convention-en.pdf

UNESCO. (1982). *Mexico City declaration on cultural policies*. Mexico: UNESCO. Retrieved from www.culturalrights.net/descargas/drets_culturals401.pdf

UNESCO. (2005). *Vienna memorandum on world heritage and contemporary architecture—Managing the historic urban landscape* (Para 21). Paris: UNESCO. Retrieved from http://whc.unesco.org/archive/2005/whc05-15ga-inf7e.pdf

UNESCO. (2011). *Recommendation on the historic urban landscape* (Introduction, Para 4). Paris: UNESCO. Retrieved from https://whc.unesco.org/uploads/activities/documents/activity-638–98.pdf

UNESCO. (2017). *Operational guidelines for the implementation of the world heritage convention*. Paris: UNESCO. Retrieved from https://whc.unesco.org/en/guidelines/

United Nations. (2016). *The sustainable development agenda*. Retrieved from www.un.org/sustainabledevelopment/development-agenda/

Urban Splash. (2011). *Transformation*. London: RIBA Publishing.

Wilkinson, A. (2006). *Pathfinder*. London: SAVE Britain's Heritage.

Williams, R. (1981). *Culture*. London: Fontana.

Williams, R. (1988). *Keywords: A vocabulary of culture and society* (revised and enlarged edition, pp. 87–93). London: Fontana.

Young, M. & Willmott, P. (1962). *Family and kinship in East London* (3rd ed.). London: Penguin Books.

Zouain, G. (2000, 8–11 November). *Le rôle du patrimoine dans l'économie locale*. A study prepared for the Séminaire européen sur la gestion des quartiers historiques, Granada.

Zukin, S. (2010). *Naked city: The death and life of authentic urban places*. Oxford: Oxford University Press.

Part II

Technology, heritage, and access

5 Securitization through digitalization and visualization

Piotr Kuroczyński

Introduction

The 21st century is characterized by urbanization, digital change, and connectivity. Ever more people are moving to cities and thus changing their place of residence during the course of their lives. The preservation of social contacts is increasingly supported by digital information and communications technologies, while the outsourcing of other aspects of one's everyday life to the digital world increases the demand for authenticity and the extension of its definition. City administrations and citizens increasingly perceive cities as stone-built testimonies to our society, and built space as both an identity-creating moment and an economic locational factor.

The importance of access to urban space as a cultural place of remembrance—against the background of a fluctuating, multicultural, and digitally networked population—plays an important role in the mediation and appropriation of the city. At a time in which we are "citizens of a place no longer primarily qua birth, but via history" (Flachenecker, 1993), we increasingly notice that interested and digitally networked citizens themselves write and mediate the history of their city. The emancipated inhabitants of the city see themselves as part of the city's history and want to interpret, document, and help to shape it. Today, such individuals have at their disposal new forms of access which, in a first step, can lead to sensitization towards lost and preserved cultural sites and, in a second step, to a multi-perspective development and sustainable safeguarding of their heritage—whether of a virtual or real nature may be left open for now.

We currently witness how the Internet increasingly becomes the third *cultural memory* (Assmann, 1992). The Internet, as a digital repository of our information society, opens and confronts us with new, virtual spaces of memory, the effects of which on our perception and on the current debate about historical authenticity remain to be explored (Sabrow & Saupe, 2016). Against the background of new audiovisual experiences as a result of augmented reality (AR) and virtual reality (VR), Benjamin's 'aura' of a place as the "unique appearance of distance, as close as it may be" (Benjamin, 2012) receives a new meaning that will affect the authenticity

84 *Piotr Kuroczyński*

of urban cultural sites. How can new digital access help to secure cultural heritage sites? The question will be discussed using the example of the city of Kaliningrad in today's Russian enclave of Kaliningrad Oblast.[1]

New approaches and access to the city as cultural heritage

Since the 1990s, the rapid development of information and communications technologies through the spread of the Internet has led to a second democratization of knowledge following the invention of printing [with moveable type] by Johannes Gutenberg over five hundred years ago. Above all, Web 2.0, also called the participatory or social web, enabled the networking of interest groups and their participation in the creation of information. Open Internet portals for the active processing and documentation of the city as a shared place of remembrance (such as *dolny-slask.org.pl* for the region of Lower Silesia in Poland) offer a comprehensive tool for geo-referenced confrontation with and participation in a complex and difficult-to-read cultural space. Users take part in the development of information and its mediation in the sense of citizen science, which brings with it new qualities, particularly for the appropriation of a culturally foreign space. In contrast to established, analogue city guides, which in the past often postulated a politically motivated view of the city and of its appropriation (Schäfer, 2008), Internet-based platforms allow for documentary multi-perspectivism and for individual access to content in accordance with the personal preferences and interests of users (Kuroczyński, 2011). The power of the participatory concept of knowledge creation is exemplified by the free online encyclopaedia *wikipedia.org*, where anyone can post and edit articles and images under a Creative Commons license. The driving force behind it is the Wikimedia Foundation with its vision of a world "in which everyone can share, use and multiply the knowledge of mankind" (Wikimedia Deutschland, 2018).

With the introduction of the idea of the Semantic Web (also called Web 3.0) almost ten years after the introduction of the World Wide Web, an invitation was issued to structure knowledge on the Internet in a human- and machine-readable form (Berners-Lee, Hendler, & Lassila, 2001). The aim is to better evaluate, with the help of machines, the constantly increasing volumes of information on the Internet; to file the meanings of digital data in ways that are intelligible to humans and machines; and to link data together. The desire to make knowledge about our cultural heritage accessible on the Internet became the open science concept, and it is primarily promoted by the Open Knowledge Foundation. One of its initiatives is openGLAM, which pursues the free provision of digital resources by galleries, libraries, archives, and museums. The basis for open, networked, and interoperable data sets is the formalization and structuring of data, which is pursued as Linked (Open) Data by the networking of information across institutions and disciplines (Kailus & Stein, 2018).

Security, digitalization and visualization   85

This type of open access—to high-quality, semantically indexed, person- and geo-referenced as well as unique data sets—enables a wide range of applications in the field of cultural heritage. Knowledge from the cultural sector, which is openly available, can generate novel approaches to cultural heritage in the form of publicly organized cultural hackathons[2] which are, in turn, funded by various organizations in the form of Creative Industries. The added value of open and structured data is also discovered by science. Pioneering projects such as the Venice Time Machine show a view in which heterogeneous data sets from Venetian archives can merge into a networked four-dimensional (4D, where the fourth dimension is time) information model (Schughart & Kaplan, 2017). This view reveals a new dimension of information exploration, mediation, and extraction that may be attributed to a web-based cultural memory.

Since the 1990s, we have observed the steady development of computer graphics, which has led to, among other things, the broad application of virtual reconstruction (Messemer, 2016). Using the example of virtual reconstruction of the German synagogues destroyed during the *Kristallnacht* in 1938, this visualization technique was able to demonstrate a sensitization for lost cultural heritage (Grellert, 2007). To date, we have observed continuous growth in virtual reconstructions that increasingly suggest the photorealistic representation of past times in documentary films and museum exhibitions, such as the *Popes* exhibition (2017) at the Reiss Engelhorn Museum, Manheim (Courtial, 2017).

Today, the maturing generation of 'digital natives' displays a natural ability to handle these new media and at the same time has high expectations of the entertainment value of digital offerings. The breathtaking computer-supported image sequences and interactive adventures produced by the film and computer game industries condition users from an early age. Who does not know ancient Rome after the Hollywood production of *Gladiator*? And who, after days of playing *Assassin's Creed Unity*, published by Ubisoft, would not claim to know what the streets of Paris smelled and looked like in July 1789? Closer examination reveals that the film and games sectors are less concerned with historical authenticity than with the emotional impact that provides these industries with their billion-dollar businesses. In our consumer and experiencer society, so-called 'edutainment' does not seem to have achieved a balance between education and entertainment. The hyper-realistic virtual worlds create a new *virtual fictitious authenticity* that nevertheless convinces many users, who do not question the presented imagery or narrative.

The leading games manufacturers have only started to discover the potential of their breathtaking *virtual worlds* for a growing, emancipated clientele—one more interested in exploring the smallest details of (re)constructed scenery and of a scholarship-based story than in an adrenaline-packed 'ego-shooter experience'. This demand is met by a new kind of offering that enables interactive exploration of virtual cultural sites, such as

86   Piotr Kuroczyński

ancient Egypt in *Assassin's Creed Origins*. In a special discovery-tour mode, players can virtually visit the wonders of the world, admire everyday crafts being produced in the streets, and access scientifically researched information about cultural sites and everyday life (Ubisoft, 2018).

The intensification of the experience—the proverbial immersion in virtual worlds—is enhanced by VR technology. The visual reference to a real space (one's real surroundings) is interrupted by a VR headset providing aural and visual inputs, so that the user is 'transported' into an interactive virtual world. The availability of the software for integrating virtual reconstructions within a VR application, and the shrinking cost of VR devices, have led to popularization of the technology. Spectacular usage can be observed within archaeological excavations, such as during a virtual tour through the *Domus Aurea* in Rome, or during a historical presentation of the small town of Arnswalde/Choszczno in present-day Poland, which was severely damaged during the Second World War. In the latter example, today's inhabitants of Choszczno can travel a hundred years into the past and take a virtual walk through the physically non-existent cultural heritage of former Arnswalde (Odyssey, 2015). The immersive experience of a 'completely reconstructed' place touches young people more directly and more deeply than the elaborate and incomplete study of well-known picture albums from series like *Königsberg—Then and Now* (Scharloff, 1982).

In addition to the triumph of the Internet, the increase in computing power, and the improvement of computer graphics, the spread of mobile interfaces, particularly of smartphones, are among the major phenomena of digital change. In Germany alone, in 2018 more than 57 million people used a smartphone, and the trend is increasing (Bitkom Research, 2018). The potential for high-performance devices to provide forms of virtual and augmented access to cultural sites is increasingly presented at tourism trade fairs. In March 2018, the city of Mainz presented the new *Mainz app* at the International Tourism Exchange in Berlin (Virtuelles Mainz, 2018, March 6). In addition to service functions, the app contains a virtual-reality module called *Roman Theatre*, which allows visitors to enjoy a Roman theatrical performance from a range of positions and perspectives in today's ruins. For this purpose, the Roman theatre was virtually reconstructed, and contemporary actors from the Mainz State Theatre were recorded in front of a Green Screen and then superimposed onto the ancient scenery to create the audiovisual impression that they had taken the place of a Roman citizen. The smartphone, inserted into a *cardboard frame* and placed on the bridge of one's nose, thus becomes a pair of VR glasses that take the viewer on a journey through time and—in Walter Benjamin's words concerning aura—evoke an "unique appearance of distance, as close as it may be" (Benjamin, 2012). Inspired by the well-known and popular smartphone game *Pokémon Go*, the Mainz app also includes a playful element, in that users may collect various artefacts from a representation of Gutenberg's print shop. In the form of a digital treasure hunt, users search for Gutenberg's working

Security, digitalization and visualization 87

materials with the help of *augmented reality* technology through which a virtual component is added to captured real images.

In addition to this nonmaterial documentation and mediation, by means of virtual reconstruction, of cultural sites that no longer exist, the physical rematerialization of digital data sets with the help of rapid-prototyping processes represents an exciting approach that will be widely applied in the near future. This technology from mechanical engineering employs diverse additive (e.g. printing) or subtractive (e.g. cutting) processes that enable digital 3D renders to be reproduced as physical 3D models. The progress of this technology was recently demonstrated by the media-effective restoration of the *Arch of Triumph* that was destroyed by Islamic State militia in Palmyra, Syria. The demolished architecture was virtually reconstructed by computer from numerous overlapping photographs of the Arch of Triumph, using a method termed *structure from motion*. The resulting 3D data were then passed to a robotic manufacturing system that cut a replica of the arch from Egyptian marble. The topicality of cultural heritage that is threatened by war and destruction led to the #*NewPalmyra* project, which took up the idea of participatory open access to cultural heritage. The non-profit 3D community, which makes its 3D reconstruction models available through a *Sketchfab* 3D repository, acts as an important pillar of the project and had 1.5 million registered users and 2.5 million 3D models by mid-2018. Web-based 3D visualization is progressing, and in February 2018 #*NewPalmyra*'s virtual reconstruction of the *Asad Al-Lat* statue became the first 3D model to be published on Wikimedia Commons. As a result, a steady increase in 3D models can be expected on Wikipedia.

Case study: Kaliningrad

The city of Kaliningrad, formerly Königsberg, looks back on a long German (Prussian) and a short Russian history. The Prussian coronation, trading, and university city was founded in the mid-13th century by the Teutonic Knights and finally became the capital of the East German province of East Prussia. The city was severely damaged during the Second World War, in particular by massive air raids in August 1944, and the later siege and capture of the city (declared a fortress in January 1945) by the Red Army. Following Germany's surrender, it was agreed at the 1945 Potsdam Conference that the northern part of East Prussia and its capital would be transferred to the control of the Soviet Union. In 1946, the city was renamed Kaliningrad, and a gradual population exchange took place. With the flight and expulsion of the remaining German population, the city experienced a further deep erosion of its cultural heritage. To use the words of Jan Assmann (1992): Within a very short time, the "communicative" as well as a large part of the built "cultural memory" disappeared from the then-Russian Königsberg. The void was provisionally filled by new settlers from all over the Soviet Union, who found a strange city during its reconstruction phase. The difficulty experienced by

88   Piotr Kuroczyński

these new settlers in mentally appropriating the city was evident from the fact that, in contrast to the Polish territories that were regained by the Soviet Union, these Soviet citizens had no historical connection with Königsberg. During Poland's reconstruction of regained cities such as Wrocław (Breslau), it was possible to recall the medieval foundation of the cities as a kind of Polish mythical primeval period (Thum, 2003). Kaliningrad could not refer to a Russian primeval period and was therefore destined to become a future-oriented socialist city; above all it was to be an important military base as the only Russian Baltic Sea port that is free of ice year-round. The city was meant to renounce its ideologically and culturally foreign past, even though certain continuities can be observed with regard to modernity in socialist urban and housing construction (Podehl, 2012).

The context of access to Königsberg as a cultural site is characterized by the treatment of the historic centre, which suffered severe destruction in 1944–1945. As the nucleus of a German city, the ruins of Kneiphof Island were levelled, and a park was established on the site, which is touched by the multi-lane Lenin Street in a north–south direction. With the collapse of the Soviet Union and the independence of the Baltic States in 1991, and since the eastward enlargement of the EU in 2005, Kaliningrad Oblast has been an exclave of the Russian Federation on the eastern periphery of the EU. The collapse of communist ideology and the totalitarian state led, as in other former Eastern Bloc countries, to an interest in the German vestiges of the city (Thum, 2003; Zalewski & Drejer, 2014). After decades of tabooing and demonizing its German cultural heritage, interest in the now *shared cultural heritage* was awakened so that, for example, during the period of perestroika: (1985–1991) there was renewed discussion about the future of the destroyed Königsberg Cathedral on Kneiphof Island—ultimately reconstructed between 1992 and 1998 with financial support from Germany.

The rediscovery of the German Königsberg in the middle of Kaliningrad is reflected by Avenir P. Ovsyanov who, in 1957 at the age of 20 had actively supported the destruction of the *German spirit in town*, for example, by blowing up the remains of Königsberg Castle. Since the political change, he elected to write about the city's German cultural heritage and to communicate it to younger generations (Myers, 2002). In the 1970s, the construction of the House of the Soviets had begun on the site of the demolished castle. The building could not be completed due to construction defects and, as a striking phantom building of a bygone era, it developed into a thorn in the side of Kaliningrad's present-day inhabitants, who increasingly yearn for re-historization of various fallow areas in the middle of the city. This desire is expressed in projects such as the Fischdorf tourist quarter near the restored Königstor, where old-German architecture is used in an imaginative mix of styles.

The rebirth of the vanished city of Königsberg in popular history books and in picture albums, as well as that of the Fischdorf, was accompanied by the establishment of the Museum Friedländer Tor (МАУК, 2015). The museum

Security, digitalization and visualization   89

is located in an entrance gate to the extensive 19th-century fortifications and maintains a meticulous collection of everyday German objects such as beer bottles, jugs, street signs, and municipal rubbish bins. The central exhibit is dedicated to the streets of Königsberg, which are presented as a projection on the bricked-up archway. Visitors sit on the cobblestone pavement and are taken on a journey by means of historical film and photographic recordings from Königsberg.

Just how serious the interest in Königsberg is in today's Kaliningrad was demonstrated by an international symposium in 2005 on the aims of inner-city development on the occasion of the 750th anniversary of the city's founding, and by the announcement of an investment project two years later at the MIPIM international real estate fair in Cannes. In 2007, the governor of Kaliningrad Oblast announced in Cannes the rebuilding of Kneiphof, located on the eponymous island in the Pregel river and one of the three founding towns (along with Altstadt and Löbenicht) of medieval Königsberg. For the Kaliningrad architect, Arthur Sarnitz, the international symposium and the prospect of reconstructing the historic city centre prompted a virtual reconstruction of Königsberg. Its aim was to arouse and sharpen interest in— and, above all, the imagination of—Kaliningrad's inhabitants regarding the historical buildings, in order to protect the long-outstanding development of the city centre, which is the consequence of inappropriate reconstruction proposals. At his own expense, Sarnitz's architectural studio meticulously researched historical materials and created a building-by-building picture database. On the basis of this material, to date more than two thousand houses and buildings have been virtually reconstructed, as far as historically possible, as digital 3D models. While the governor's words were not followed by action, Sarnitz's virtual *Altstadt Projekt in Königsberg* (City Centre project in Königsberg) was created to become known beyond the city's borders and to convey a picture of the future city centre in numerous film animations (Sarnitz, 2018). The impact of this historical visualization was demonstrated in the open international architectural competition for the redesign of the historic centre of Kaliningrad, launched in 2014 under the title *Post-Castle*, starting from the site of the former Königsberg Castle (Попадин & Крамень, 2015). Among the 49 proposals presented to the public at Kaliningrad's Art History Museum in September 2015, the submission prepared by the Arthur Sarnitz architectural office, which had projected the large-scale reconstruction of the city's pre-war condition, received a special prize from the jury (Figure 5.1). The implementation of the winning proposal was prevented by the economic and political situation in Russia (e.g. economic sanctions imposed) following its 2014 annexation of Crimea.

Securitization through digitalization and visualization

The new approaches to cultural heritage listed at the beginning of this chapter, and the current debate about the redesign of the historical city

Figure 5.1 Visualization for the competition "Post-Castle" submitted by Arthur Sarnitz. © 2015 Arthur Sarnitz.

centre of Kaliningrad, lead to considerations of how information and communications technologies can help in the process of securing cultural sites that are no longer physically present. The following thoughts derive from experience of a project in computer-aided research and from the development of a 'virtual museum' using the example of demolished East Prussian baroque-era castles (Kuroczyński, Hauck, & Dworak, 2016). The aim of the project was to bring together fragmented sources, to make them accessible, and to scientifically document the virtual 3D reconstruction of lost cultural sites by using the example of the former East Prussian royal castles.

Between 2013 and 2016, digital reconstructions were created of Schloss Friedrichstein (now Kamenka in Kaliningrad Oblast), and Schloss Schlodien (now Gładysze in Poland). The project presented the prototype of a web-based virtual museum that enables visitors to interactively tour Schloss Schlodien and access, with the click of a mouse, information stored behind the 3D models. The focus was on the scientific traceability, sustainability, and free availability of the data sets as Linked (Open) Data, as well as on investigating new, virtual research spaces for the history of art and architecture (Kuroczyński & Schelbert, 2017).

The new perspective is reflected in the digital 3D models, which are seen as a scientific information model that combines architectural and art historical as well as socio-cultural knowledge. The models provide barrier-free access to knowledge that can be conveyed in a variety of formats, from individual perspectives and film animations to interactive games and virtual reality. In addition, the models provide an anchor for spatial- and temporal-related information storage. The status of 3D or 4D information models is underpinned by the linking of geo-referenced and chronologically dated models with structured data on sources, actors, research activities, and historical events. The data structuring follows the Linked (Open) Data requirements within a Virtual Research Environment (VRE), which serves the project's web-based interdisciplinary co-operation as well as the visualization and publication of the results. Data processing in the VRE enables the mapping of uncertainties and hypotheses in the source-based reconstruction, to ensure the traceability and scientific character of the results. As a result, it is possible to test the authenticity of visual perception during the reception of the visualization. Current challenges concern the lack of digital infrastructure and the need to clarify copyright issues in order to ensure the continued availability of such semantic 3D/4D information models. In addition, most virtual reconstructions lack the financial resources that are a prerequisite for sustainable documentation. The medium has typically tended to be regarded as a supporting visualization and not as an independent, mature information medium.

In the case of Kaliningrad, Sarnitz's virtual reconstruction of Königsberg can represent a solid foundation for the sustainable preservation of lost cultural heritage on the Internet, the 'third cultural memory'. The combination of individual 3D models with socio-cultural contexts as well as the illustration of hypothetical variants and versions can be developed into an interactive 4D city-model that will enable 'time travel' to places of remembrance, illuminated by multiple perspectives. In a first step, the sources and historical context within a VRE ought to be opened up, followed by scientific documentation of the source interpretation, and 3D reconstruction. Web-based visualization of the models within the VRE could be ensured by integrating the services of 3D repositories such as Sketchfab or Wikimedia Commons. The development work, data modelling, and structuring, as well as the 3D reconstruction, can be achieved as part of teaching and research within the emerging discipline of the Digital Humanities. In autumn 2017, the association History and Computers in co-operation with the Kant University in Kaliningrad organized a conference in the city to strengthen digital research methods in the humanities. This collaboration is envisaged as crossing disciplines and borders and is supported by German–Russian funding programmes.

'Immanuel Kant Year' in 2024 (commemorating the 300th anniversary of Kant's birth) will be an important milestone, especially in view of the cross-border commitment to safeguard the shared German–Russian cultural heritage. On the German side, the *Ostpreußisches Landesmuseum* (East Prussian State Museum) in Lüneburg, which opened its newly designed permanent exhibition in August 2018, secures a large part of the cultural heritage of Königsberg. In the run-up to Kant's tercentenary, consideration is being given to creating an extension of the museum with a haptic city-model of Königsberg as the central exhibit.

92 Piotr Kuroczyński

The extension of a 4D city-model to include the Königsberg of Immanuel Kant, the conquered Königsberg, the Soviet Kaliningrad, and the Kaliningrad of the 21st century is particularly appropriate as a project to safeguard the shared cultural heritage. German and Russian project partners ought to be involved in the 3D reconstruction and contextualization of knowledge that was decimated and dispersed as a result of the Second World War, and thus manage to popularize and employ it scientifically in a broad context as Linked (Open) Data. The virtual reconstruction as a source-based digital 3D reconstruction of former buildings comprehensively confronts participants with the objects and existing sources. The reconstruction process itself offers a holistic view (access) and a novel understanding (grasp) of the properties and characteristics of cultural sites (Favro, 2012). The interpretation of the sources and the accompanying 3D digital reconstruction places those involved in the role of the old master builders, since one first has to understand the building in its entirety in order to be able to reproduce it spatially.

The construction of digital city models and related databases enables a variety of applications that can incorporate the potential of social networks in addition to the VR technologies mentioned above. Using smartphones and other mobile interfaces, geo-referenced 3D models and the knowledge associated with them can be accessed on-site. Access to history is thus available at the authentic location via the touch gestures and speech recognition provided by personal digital devices. Computer-aided mixing and expansion of the real place with virtual reconstructions creates a new dimension for Benjamin's (2012) aura of a location, as a "unique appearance of a distance, as close as it may be". The surviving witnesses to the new beginning in Kaliningrad after 1945 could add their memories to the 4D city model and thus convey the equally threatened Soviet heritage. To this end, the VRE would have to be expanded to include interactive visualization, in which visitors could intuitively mark the 3D models and enrich them with annotations. Experiences from crowdsourcing projects, such as the social tagging project *Artigo*[3], or the *Berliner Großstadtgeschichten*[4] prove the added value of playful, Internet-based involvement of users in the development of knowledge, as well as active participation in the historiography of the city chronicle.

Finally, rapid prototyping processes can provide haptic 3D models of selected periods of Königsberg's history for museum communication. One obvious approach is to employ projections as a means of playing on materialized (printed) *white city models*. City installations and individual objects can be highlighted in a didactic concept; relationships and movements can be depicted; and dramaturgical staging (e.g. of air raids and destruction) can be developed. Three-dimensional printed models can represent materialized 'plaster casts' of a virtual Königsberg/Kaliningrad and would be the heart of a dynamic–hybrid, partly material/partly virtual

Security, digitalization and visualization 93

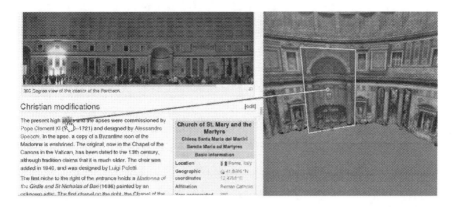

Figure 5.2 3D Wikipedia: Using online text to automatically label and navigate reconstructed geometry. © 2013 Scientific paper: 3D Wikipedia.

exhibition. The easy reproducibility of digital data sets allows city segments to be printed as needed, updated, and included in other exhibitions, as well as placed as souvenirs in our own homes. Similar to a QR code, printed 3D models can be used as trackers for augmented reality applications. The captured image of the model is recognized by the software as a tracker and superimposed by the virtual reconstruction. Interactive tracking allows pre-defined sections to offer in-depth insights from a pedestrian perspective, and spatial contextualization from a bird's-eye view, as ably demonstrated by the applications *AR Mail from Harbin* (Nagakura, Sung, & Li, 2017) and *kARtka z Synagogą* (Kuroczyński, Dworak, & Jara, 2018).

Virtual reconstruction is the means to an end. It serves the indexing and mediation of knowledge. As an information model, it ensures access to digital cultural heritage and can be used in the preservation of historical monuments. Innovative projections allow interactive group-tours in three-dimensional space. In contrast to individual perception within personal VR environments, the concept behind the project *photo portals* enables several people to have an interactive experience of virtual worlds (Kunert, Kulik, Beck, & Froehlich, 2014). Within the application (developed at Bauhaus-Universität Weimar), meetings and group tours can be organized within the virtual reconstruction for spatially separated persons by means of video tracking. VR glasses greatly limit the unconstrained movement of a user disconnected from the real space, whereas *photo portals* allow the movement of all users in front of a screen, and natural viewing of the 3D projection from individual angles, thereby creating the impression of natural access to digital representations of cultural sites. However, due to the high costs and human resources currently required to operate interactive 3D projections, this type of group experience is not yet widely

94   Piotr Kuroczyński

available. At this point, it is intended to demonstrate the possibilities of undisturbed group perception parallel to established VR technologies, which can soon be used in teaching and research and, in future, in users' own home cinemas.

Conclusion

Cultural memory (Assmann, 1992) is shifting to the Internet, which is moving from Web 1.0 and Web 2.0 towards Web 3.0. However, according to the UNICEF report *Children in a Digital World* (2017), lack of access to digital information in some communities remains a cause for concern. For example, in Africa 60 per cent of adolescents aged 15–24 are offline, compared with 4 per cent in Europe. Today, more than half of all websites are in English. Consequently, even when adolescents have access to the web, they often cannot understand the content or cannot find topics related to their lives (UNICEF, 2017).

Cultural and educational institutions are digitizing their collections, structuring and networking their data in the spirit of Linked (Open) Data and Open Science. With regard to web-based 3D visualization, new technologies (such as WebGL) are emerging that ensure easy access to 3D models. The importance of 3D models in the World Wide Web, particularly in the context of cultural sites, is currently showing strong growth. A variety of 3D technologies allows us to create spatial representations of our environment, bringing with them realistic experiences of materiality and geometry. Due to the visual language of 3D models, linguistic and age barriers play a lesser role in the reception of the information and contribute to the mentioned democratization of knowledge. With a kind of *virtual fictitious authenticity*, the virtual worlds captivate the generation of digital natives. The games industry, as a visual trendsetter of virtual worlds, shows new possibilities for conveying history and cultural heritage by means of new offerings such as discovery tours. However, these virtual journeys of discovery through time and space can only be as good as their scientific processing and contextualization of content allow. Access to cultural heritage can only take place on the basis of source cataloguing and information processing adapted to the requirements of monument preservation (documentation) and the individual needs of recipients (mediation/dissemination). If we speak of safeguarding cultural heritage through digitization and visualization, then standardized, sustainable data preparation and curation (data curation) play a central role that should be based on broad citizen participation (citizen science) à la Wikipedia, due to the amount of work involved. The scientific paper *3D Wikipedia* initiated an award for multilingual Wikipedia articles on the theme of built cultural heritage, which resulted in the direct visual annotation of interactive 3D visualizations of such buildings (Figure 5.2). This approach shows us what access to and understanding of cultural sites could

Security, digitalization and visualization 95

look like in the sense of Open Science (Russell, Martin-Brualla, Butler, Seitz, & Zettlemoyer, 2013).

Wikipedia ergo sum!

Notes

1 Oblast can refer various types of administrative divisions, but in this case is approximately equivalent to a federal region.
2 https://codingdavinci.de/
3 https://www.artigo.org/
4 Cosmopolitan histories: www.grossstadtgeschichten-berlin.de

References

Assmann, J. (1992). *Das kulturelle Gedächtnis: Schrift, Erinnerung und politische Identität in frühen Hochkulturen.* München: Verlag H. C. Beck.

Benjamin, W. (2012). *Das Kunstwerk im Zeitalter seiner technischen Reproduzierbarkeit: drei Studien zur Kunstsoziologie* (1. Aufl., [Nachdr.]). Frankfurt am Main: Suhrkamp.

Berners-Lee, T., Hendler, J., & Lassila, O. (2001). *The Semantic Web—A new form of web content that is meaningful to computers will unleash a revolution of new possibilities.* Retrieved from www-sop.inria.fr/acacia/cours/essi2006/Scientific%20American_%20Feature%20Article_%20The%20Semantic%20Web_%20May%202001.pdf

Bitkom Research. (2018). *Anzahl der Smartphone-Nutzer in Deutschland in den Jahren 2009 bis 2018 (in Millionen).* Retrieved from https://de.statista.com/statistik/daten/studie/198959/umfrage/anzahl-der-smartphonenutzer-in-deutschland-seit-2010/

Courtial, J. (2017). *Die Päpste und die Einheit der lateinischen Welt/Making of Imperial Rome.* Retrieved from www.youtube.com/watch?time_continue=1&v=UrUcgAuAP44

Favro, D. (2012). Se non e vero, e ben trovato (If not true, it is well conceived): Digital immersive reconstructions of historical environments. *Journal of the Society of Architectural Historians, 71*(3), 273–277. https://doi.org/10.1525/jsah.2012.71.3.273

Flachenecker, H. (1993). Stadtgeschichtsforschung als Akt der Selbstvergewisserung. *Zeitschriftenband* (1993), 128–158.

Grellert, M. (2007). *Immaterielle Zeugnisse: Synagogen in Deutschland: Potentiale digitaler Technologien für das Erinnern zerstörter Architektur.* Bielefeld: Transcript.

Kailus, A., & Stein, R. (2018). Besser vernetzt: Über den Mehrwert von Standards und Normdaten zur Bilderschließung. In P. Kuroczyński, P. Bell, & L. Dieckmann (Eds.), *Computing art reader—Einführung in die digitale Kunstgeschichte.* Heidelberg: arthistoricum.net.

Kunert, A., Kulik, A., Beck, S., & Froehlich, B. (2014). *Photoportals: Shared references in space and time.* CSCW '14: Proceedings of the 17th ACM conference on computer supported cooperative work & social computing (pp. 1388–1399). ACM Press. https://doi.org/10.1145/2531602.2531727

96 Piotr Kuroczyński

Kuroczyński, P. (2011). *Die Medialisierung der Stadt Analoge und digitale Stadtführer zur Stadt Breslau nach 1945*. Retrieved from http://nbn-resolving.de/urn:nbn:de:101:1-201511284234

Kuroczyński, P., Dworak, D., & Jara, K. (2018) *kARtka z Synagogą*. Retrieved from https://arvr.hs-mainz.de

Kuroczyński, P., Hauck, O., & Dworak, D. (2016). 3D models on triple paths—new pathways for documenting and visualizing virtual reconstructions. In S. Münster, M. Pfarr-Harfst, P. Kuroczyński, & M. Ioannides (Eds), *3D research challenges in cultural heritage II* (Vol. 10025, 149–172). Cham: Springer. https://doi.org/10.1007/978-3-319-47647-6_8

Kuroczyński, P., & Schelbert, G. (2017). *3D Digital Heritage—Exploring Virtual Research Space for Art History* [conference website]. Retrieved from http://3d-digital-heritage.info/

Messemer, H. (2016). The beginnings of digital visualization of historical architecture in the academic field. In S. Hoppe & S. Breitling (Eds.), *Virtual palaces, part II—Lost palaces and their afterlife. Virtual reconstruction between science and media* (Vol. 3). Heidelberg: arthistoricum.net.

Myers, S. L. (2002, August 13). Kaliningrad journal; A Russian city digs up its past and finds Germany. *The New York Times*. Retrieved from www.nytimes.com/2002/08/13/world/kaliningrad-journal-a-russian-city-digs-up-its-past-and-finds-germany.html

Nagakura, T., Sung, W., & Li, D. (2017). *AR Mail from Harbin*. Retrieved from https://armailfromharbin.netlify.com/

Odyssey. (2015). *Arnswalde—architecturel reconstruction in VR*. *Odyssey*. Retrieved from www.youtube.com/watch?v=aaj1yXYHEFY&t=207s

Podehl, M. (2012). *Architektura Kaliningrada: wie aus Königsberg Kaliningrad wurde*. Marburg: Herder-Institut.

Russell, B. C., Martin-Brualla, R., Butler, D. J., Seitz, S. M., & Zettlemoyer, L. (2013). 3D Wikipedia: Using online text to automatically label and navigate reconstructed geometry. *ACM Transactions on Graphics*, 32(6), 1–10. https://doi.org/10.1145/2508363.2508425

Sabrow, M., & Saupe, A. (Eds.). (2016). *Historische Authentizität*. Göttingen: Wallstein Verlag.

Sarnitz, A. (2018). *Website zum Altstadt Projekt (Königsberg)*. Retrieved from https://altstadt.ru/

Schäfer, B. (2008). Die Präsentation von Erinnerungsorten im Reisefürher am Beispiel der Stadt Poznań (Posen) 1870–1939. In *Erinnerungsorte, Mythen und Stereotypen in Europa: [… internationale und interdisziplinäre Nachwuchstagung zum Thema "Erinnerungsorte und Mythen in Europa. Das Beispiel Schlesien"]* = *Miejsca pamięci, mity i stereotypy w Europie* (pp. 27–45). Wrocław, Atut.

Scharloff, W. (1982). *Königsberg damals und heute*. Rautenberg Verlag.

Schughart, A., & Kaplan, F. (2017). Venice time machine: Aus Geschichte muss dringend Big Data werden! Retrieved from www.wired.de/collection/science/venice-time-machine-frederic-kaplan-ca-forscari-university-venice-polytechnique

Thum, G. (2003). *Die fremde Stadt: Breslau 1945*. Berlin: Siedler.

Ubisoft. (2018). Assassin's creed origins—Entdeckungstour-DLC. Retrieved from www.youtube.com/watch?v=9dZa9tgvTcs

UNICEF. (2017). *Children in a digital world*. New York, NY: UNICEF.

Security, digitalization and visualization   97

Virtuelles Mainz. (2018, March 6). Stadt und Tourismusakteure entwickeln offizielle App mit Virtual und Augmented Reality-Inhalten. Retrieved from www.mainzplus.com/presse/pressemeldungen/nachrichtendetails/news/virtuelles-mainz-stadt-und-tourismusakteure-entwickeln-offizielle-app-mit-virtual-und-augmented-rea/?no_cache=1&tx_news_pi1%5Bcontroller%5D=News&tx_news_pi1%5Baction%5D=detail&cHash=ec748d71508d146488976094fdc59dff

Wikimedia Deutschland. (2018). Website of Wikimedia Deutschland. Retrieved from https://wikimedia.de/

Zalewski, P., & Drejer, J. (Eds). (2014). *Kulturerbe und Aneignungsprozesse in deutsch-polnischen Kontakträumen. Motivationen, Realitätet, Träume* (Vol. Band IX = tom IX). Warszawa/Frankfurt (Oder): Instytut Sztuki Polskiej Akademii Nauk; Europa-Universität Viadrina.

МАУК, М. Ф. ворота. (2015). *Website of the Friedländer Tor museum*. Retrieved from http://fvmuseum.ru/

Попадин, А., & Крамень, Л. (2015). Пост-замок—итоговый альбом открытого международного архитектурного конкурса на объёмно-планировоч- ное решение Историко-культурного комплекса на территории бывшего орденского замка Кёнигсберг в Калинин- граде. Май-сентябрь 2015. Kaliningrad: Издательство П икторика.

6 Documenting modernity

Torben Kiepke and Hans-Rudolf Meier

Introduction

In the year 2000 Ulrich Müther, architect of Berlin's so-called Maple Leaf, led a group of students through the building in anticipation of its demolition. This large restaurant, built in the early 1970s on Berlin's Fischerinsel (Fisher Island), was named for its roof, which comprised five hyperbolic concrete bowls arranged in the shape of a maple leaf. Asked whether he was somewhat disappointed to see the building torn down, Müther answered: "You know, it does make me sad, but an architect is always dependent on new construction. This building is now being documented for posterity." (Ulrich Müther, personal communication, 22 January 2000).[1] Although the documentation of a condemned building is not unusual in heritage preservation, widespread media coverage of the images in this particular case sparked a great deal of public interest (see Figure 6.1). "The demolition of the Maple Leaf saved me from oblivion", Müther is quoted as saying in 2003, after some two hundred articles had appeared on the Maple Leaf and its impending demolition (Michel, 2003). Modernist buildings of the 1970s were forced into the public eye by this loss, directly contradicting what Hans Stimmann, former director of urban planning and construction for the Berlin Senate, had once predicted: That no-one would take up the cause of "ugly buildings" (Stimmann, 2000).

The reaction to images of the Maple Leaf being torn down was not the first time that coverage of a demolition brought about a turn in the appreciation of modern architecture. In 1972, an image depicting the demolition of a social housing block in the Pruitt Igoe district of St. Louis (Missouri) was provocatively titled by Charles Jencks as "The day modern architecture died" (Jencks, 1977, p. 9). Jencks thus introduced—in distinct contrast to the concerns of the actors of the 2000s—a critique of modernist buildings and, thus, also a revisionist view of the functionalist avant-garde within a post-modern architecture. That image of the Pruitt Igoe demolition has been repeatedly exploited as a poster child representing the failure of modern construction (Schlüter, 1997; Freidrichs, 2011). The demolition—and

Figure 6.1 Demolition of the Ahornblatt/Maple Leaf, Berlin. © August 2000 Friedrich May.

thus the broadly promulgated interpretation of the image—figured as a strategy of last resort in the restoration of public safety within a problematic neighbourhood. In comparison, images of the Maple Leaf's demolition had relatively limited impact, but—more importantly—had the opposite effect for Pruitt Igoe, giving rise to debate concerning the value and conservation of buildings of the 1960s and 1970s. Buildings of the *Ostmoderne* (Modernism of the East)[2] began to find defenders of all sorts, who catalogued, investigated, and documented them. The images of the Maple Leaf demolition and its implied impending loss of the built heritage of an entire historical period, thereby served in Germany as a wake-up call to attend to the construction legacy of the German Democratic Republic (GDR) and to confront the question of its significance. The interim has witnessed increasing public attention to such images, particularly those of the Palace of the Republic in former East Berlin, but also to documentary images exemplifying so-called GDR-Modernism, of modernist buildings in the western states of today's Federal Republic of Germany, and in Europe generally. The concurrent development of digital media, and the emergence of social networks and image-sharing platforms have further accelerated a process otherwise largely driven by institutional research (cf. Eckardt et al., 2017; *Big Beautiful Buildings*, n.d.[3]).

100 *Torben Kiepke and Hans-Rudolf Meier*

New media mobilize new actors and generate a new store of accessible information. Never before has such a copious informal inventory of buildings been generated in so short a time, such that an official charged with inventory at the Berlin Monument Authority admitted that, in his daily work of describing and assessing historical monuments, he consults open-access images from the Internet more often than institutional image archives (Kohlenbach, 2015). This informal and unsystematic documentation of modernist buildings, now accessible online, has considerable influence on both institutional research and the buildings' assessment within heritage preservation.

Three points of interest arise in this context with regard to securitization: On the one hand, the basic principle still applies: That public awareness of objects and knowledge about them are indispensable to the work of preservation, as recognized in the 19th century by William Morris (cf. the introduction to this volume) and many others. This is also true—even more so—for modern buildings, since the need to preserve them is less obvious and thus more requires in need of explanation than do buildings of earlier periods. When something has been documented, it also excites attention and therefore cannot be clandestinely removed. On the other hand, as elaborated with reference to Bandarin and van Oers in the introduction to this book, urban heritage is constituted in part by public access. Online documentation creates new means of access and new actors as 'caretakers', and thus also contributes to the protection of urban heritage. A third aspect of the question relates to the understanding of protection as security design: to what extent freely available information about objects actually makes them more susceptible to criminal attack—an argument against open access to documentation that is frequently raised by public officials.

Also pertinent in this regard is the recent vigorous debate over the Digital Humanities, and in particular the significance of online documentation in the history of art and architecture (Drucker, 2013), as reflected in a call for papers that appeared in August 2018 in the *International Journal for Digital Art History*, to address the question of how digitalization is changing institutions (of art history) (http://dah-journal.org). There is also the issue of participatory archives (which has been under discussion for some time in the fields of archival studies and museology), and thus fundamental questions regarding the possibilities (and limitations) of participatory research (Huvila, 2008; *Audience+: Museen und das partizipative Web*, n.d.).

New heritage actors and web documentation

Since the year 2000, for instance, numerous efforts have been made in European countries to record the building stock of the second half of the 20th century for purposes of heritage preservation and to bring it before the public eye through print publications, exhibitions, and increasingly via online databases. But, to date, there are also great differences regarding

Documenting modernity 101

the legal consequences of listings, tentative lists, and even publicly accessible documentations in different countries. One main problem of listing and documenting buildings from the latter part of the 20th century is in general the large number of buildings. Another challenge is the fact that redevelopment and reconstruction, as well as rapidly growing demands for energy efficiency, are threatening these buildings before society is even aware of their cultural value. Nevertheless, it is remarkable that a variety of actors can be identified, who are publishing lists of buildings and documentation on the building stock of the second half of the 20th century. On the one hand there are governmental or institutional actors such as heritage preservation offices and research groups, and on the other hand private networks of highly diverse organization. In the present-day Federal Republic of Germany, five of the eighteen state Monument Authority offices have so far made their databases available online. Of these, five offices are also co-operation partners of the German Digital Library (DDB), through which their data can be linked to further databases, archives, and so forth (*Denkmale in Brandenburg; Denkmaldatenbank Berlin; Denkmaldatenbank Bremen; Geoportal BayernAtlas; Kulturdenkmäler in Hessen*). The non-governmental actors are, for the most part, grouped locally or at national level and rely on social networks as a means of dissemination. Above all, groups that focus on the late-modern building stock of their city, on the work of a single architect, or on a modern style such as Brutalism or Post-Modernism, are commonly found in regions where state-organized heritage preservation efforts have not yet registered the buildings in question (thus resulting in an immediate need), and/or in societal contexts in which the same buildings are unlikely to find any appreciation. These activists see their work as mediation between the public and the built environment in an attempt to awaken greater public interest in buildings that, at first glance, may not readily appeal to aesthetic judgement. Such initiatives, which document buildings and raise awareness based on interest rather than on systematic criteria, exist in countless variations, though it is often difficult to determine whether such a group is still active or not. In most such cases, however, a documentary footprint persists on the Internet independently of the lifetime of a particular group, in the form of collections of buildings, accounts of personal experiences, photos, and at times even blueprints or plans—all these often remain accessible on the Internet indefinitely. Other collections and documentation disappear almost as quickly as they were first assembled—such as when a webpage is no longer hosted, work on a project is abandoned, or when interest wanes in the buildings concerned. Furthermore, only a small selection of these documentation sites meets the standards for scientific research, so while they may encourage and enhance heritage research they cannot replace it.

As collections of material, these initiatives remain valuable for preserving personal impressions of the building stock of this period. They show us what was important to the actors in question and what information and

102 Torben Kiepke and Hans-Rudolf Meier

data were accessible to them. As examples of bottom-up approaches to architectural heritage, they testify to a public interest in the preservation of these buildings that is not juridically defined, but rather articulated through practical action. Where some heritage preservation officials find this interest problematic, others have long since learned to use the existence and knowledge of these groups as arguments for the work of preservation. Conversely, in preparing their exhibition for the Frankfurt Architecture Museum in 2018, the online campaign SOS-BRUTALISM could rely on detailed official lists of protected buildings that had been compiled by the Working Group on Inventory of the Association of State Monument Preservationists (DAM, 2018). Wikipedia has also adopted the monument numbering system employed by the state Monument Authorities and provides links to their databases (Liste der Baudenkmale in Potsdam/B, n.d.).

The emergence of such special-interest groups and their documentary platforms also makes it possible to draw conclusions on the status of heritage inventory in a given country (VDL, 2005; Meier, 2015). For example: Are published registers of state-protected monuments generally available, and do they also include justifications? To what extent do such inventories include contemporary building stock? While in some European countries—the Netherlands, for instance, and certain cantons of Switzerland—the inventory process is well advanced, others present a very different picture. Even where no minimum building age has been legally stipulated for heritage classification, efforts to register the building stock may be all but non-existent. The reasons are at times political and at others administrative in nature. Where the inventory of building stock is well advanced, special-interest groups may sooner focus their databases and social-media efforts on topics of limited scope, whereas in countries where the building stocks of this period have not yet received attention, such groups are concerned with fundamental groundwork and raising public awareness. According to information from the state heritage preservation offices in Bulgaria, for instance, only three urban sites have been registered for the post-war period in Dimitrovgrad, and the most recent listed monument dates from 1979. Thus, although the period after 1945 brought forth a great "number of new building typologies in Bulgarian architecture", no widespread registration of buildings of this "neglected period" is yet foreseen (Kaleva, 2015). It is nevertheless the case that here as well, outside the purview of state institutions, private initiatives are emerging with a focus on the building stock of the second half of the 20th century. These are once again organized through online social networks, so that in the case of Dimitrovgrad as elsewhere, discussion forums and image documentation are being collected and redistributed.[4]

The public impact of a database initiative is demonstrated by the 'Unwritten' project that took place in Latvia in 2014.[5] Here a group posed the provocative question of whether the country in fact possessed no modern building worthy of preservation, as at the time hardly any such monuments had been listed—the vast number of extant buildings from the period notwithstanding. The objective of the initiative was to spur research on the subject and to seek an echo within society. A database was established on Facebook that assembled a remarkable collection of buildings from the second half of the 20th century, the first-ever collection of such buildings in Latvia. The initiators called for contributors to post photographs, descriptions, and evaluations, and thus over a period of only five months documented 450 buildings. The project description explains that the members of Un-written sought to achieve a scientifically valid answer to their original question, namely by first documenting relevant buildings in the form of an expandable collection with basic information on each building's identification, its location, and address, including a photograph. Second, they invited experts, contemporary witnesses, preservationists, and architects to submit essays on the documented buildings. In a third step, on "how to absorb", they attempted to address the question of the proper handling of these buildings. In this case, the structured collection and documentation of modernist buildings had a thoroughly positive impact on the public discussion and produced tangible results in that a number of the collected buildings were ultimately listed as historical monuments.

In summary, it can be stated that the longevity and standards of these—by all measures supra-local—initiatives and projects are variable, and that in this regard a certain interdependence is the rule. Online archival initiatives mirror the level of awareness and progress of inventories in their respective countries: As a rule, the more specialized the intervention of the groups, the greater is the public awareness and the more advanced the work of the responsible officials. Where informal actors make use of opportunities for greater external exposure (as in case of the Un-written project, which formed the Latvian contribution to the 2014 Venice Biennale of Architecture), their impact can be considerably enhanced. Even taking into account unsuccessful projects that recede entirely from public view, it cannot be denied that the overall contribution of such online documentation to the mobilization of actors and interested parties is considerable, and that they thereby constitute an essential factor in rescuing the architectural heritage of modernity.

Informal provisional listing as a protection instrument

The situation is somewhat different in countries where a minimum age applies for the listing of historical monuments. A recent inquiry, extending almost worldwide, has shown that relatively few countries require such an explicit minimum age. (cf. Carughi & Vissone, 2017). In the Federal Republic of Germany (and in many other countries) no numbers are specified in the laws on heritage preservation; in practice, however, a consensus applies that monuments should be from a period that has reached closure. Where an explicit minimum age is in force, there is often—as in Italy, for instance—awareness that while the law all but prohibits the protection of buildings dating from after 1960, such buildings nonetheless exist that merit

104 *Torben Kiepke and Hans-Rudolf Meier*

protection. As a result, in Italy this building stock is at least investigated and documented in a publicly accessible database, so that through monitoring a certain degree of protection is achieved (Architetture del secondo 900, n.d.; Kiepke, 2015). Current Italian law excludes buildings less than 50 years old; for publicly funded buildings, a minimum of 70 years is required before they can benefit from legal protection. The reason why such an exclusion applies in the country with the largest number of historical monuments in Europe may, in the case of the 50-year minimum, partly be found in the legislation on monument preservation, which dates from 1937 and is therefore itself historic. That the minimum age for publicly funded buildings was raised by the Berlusconi government to 70 years may be seen as an act of desperation over Italy's notoriously empty public coffers, or as further evidence of vandalization in Italian cultural policy (Stella & Rizzo, 2011). The intention, which can only be called short-sighted, would seem to be a sizable reduction of public building stock, so that fewer buildings are even eligible for consideration as monuments. That a similarly crude form of selection might threaten buildings eligible after only 50 years becomes self-evident. Listing for protection as historic monuments is now possible for these buildings if constructed in or after 1968; one of the most recent buildings to benefit from such listing is the Fiat production hall in Turin. The building was placed under protection immediately upon reaching the minimum age, which raises the question of whether and to what extent a provisional list in fact exists in which likely candidates for monument status are classified in advance, and which serves in itself as a crucial argument for protection once the minimum age has been reached. In this case, the responsible office was apparently well prepared. While the hands of the Ministry for Cultural Heritage and Activities (MiBAC) are effectively bound when it comes to prematurely assigning monument status to buildings from the second half of the 20th century, a procedure has nevertheless emerged in recent years that has proven effective in achieving de facto early protected status. Every ten years, the ministry calls upon all regions to identify buildings especially worthy of protection and to place these on provisional lists.

To this end, committees are formed in the individual regions, comprised of representatives of the regional heritage protection office, the *sopraintendenze* (regional organs of MiBAC), and representatives of the research community from the regional universities. The region of Campania serves to illustrate this process, where a catalogue of more than 500 buildings dating from post-1945 has been compiled; for the city of Naples alone the total is approximately 190. The committee regards the list as open, so that later additions remain possible. The selection is publicly accessible and can be consulted online. Also documented are the criteria by which the collected buildings were selected (Architetture del secondo 900, n.d.). The attributes that determine selection have been standardized across all Italian regions and include, above all, an assessment of national and international specialist literature. The database contains indications of construction year, architect(s), address, function, contractor, and partial archive materials such as photographs and blueprints (in low resolution) as well as relevant literature; each object is additionally situated on a city map in a geodatabase (Elenco opere, n.d.).

The region of Veneto has gone further and established connections to other important databases that facilitate the selection of buildings for heritage protection. Thus, the University of Venice has published a collection of buildings that, by reason of technical characteristics in building construction, are of national significance. The selection is based on intensive research in periodicals and monographs and was the work of a research team in historical construction techniques (Atlante dell'architettura italiana degli anni '50 e '60, n.d.).

The presentation of the modernist building stock in Italy through databases stands as a highly transparent procedure, which serves to invite the public to comment on the selection and to suggest potential additions. Overall, however, this advance preparation through 'pre-listings', well-structured databases, and broad public interest in the buildings of late modernity must avoid raising suspicion that the maintenance of provisional lists is merely a way of circumventing the legal minimums for official listing.

That reservation notwithstanding, the comprehensive publicly accessible documentation on Italy's modernist building stock exhibits the essential value of such collections: on the one hand to mediate between modernity and the interested public (general contextualization), and on the other to present and catalogue specific content, such as construction methods (catalogue of construction elements, modernist construction typology).

These examples make two aspects of our inquiry especially clear: They show how, particularly in the area of modernism, collaboration between state institutions and new actor groups, whether formal or informal, makes new options available for registration and monitoring and thus also contributes to the protection of this imperilled group of buildings. At the same time, these new informal registers are inherently process-bound, and none of them allows comprehensive or complete coverage. Interest in the heritage value of individual objects thus reaches the public eye before a great number of others that also need to be registered, and thus too much time may be lost to ensure the protection of imperilled structures.

Documentation versus security design?

The previous example constitutes very liberal handling of the plans and photographs of buildings, and is the exception; after all, aspects of security in the traditional sense of crime prevention, or those already described in the introduction as security design, require consideration. As a result, such generous provision of open-access documentation is rarely found in other European countries. For example, the Berlin Monument Authority maintains a far more extensive heritage database so far as the textual description of objects is concerned, yet it contains no representations of floorplans

106 Torben Kiepke and Hans-Rudolf Meier

(Denkmaldatenbank Berlin, n.d.). In general, state institutions are far more restrictive in publishing building-specific data than their more carefree counterparts on the Internet, whose datasets are, however, more coincidental in composition. Detailed information on the building stock is often omitted due to concerns for the security of owners or users, and as a protection against criminal violation.[6] Information is often limited to the basics, such as location, time of construction, and architect, at times accompanied by an often-antiquated photograph. Such security-driven restrictions are not specific to the buildings of modernity, but rather apply to the entire constructed domain and, in particular, to objects of political or cultural significance.[7] Certain categories of buildings are the focus of particular security concerns—for example single-family dwellings which, compared to the general building stock, are already under-represented in the inventory and registering of monuments, and for which the protection of privacy is of particular significance. In the context of a purported increase in the threat of terrorist attacks, higher levels of security apply above all to state buildings. By way of example, one might cite an administrative building in the government quarter of Oslo: Following the terrorist incident of 2011, the building's security was questioned due to its location directly on a street. In this case, even demolition was considered.[8] The transparent building structures and open floorplans of many modernist buildings may indeed constitute particularly attractive targets for potential attack, and there are numerous cases in which the installation of security checks and barriers has deprived buildings from this period of their original spatial concepts. This not only robs the buildings of an essential formal aspect—which as a rule itself constitutes an element of heritage—but also weakens their value as programmatic expressions of an open, democratic society. The construction of any public building today occurs in collaboration with security advisors, as is apparent in recently emerging spatial arrangements (cf. Balthasar, 2017). This makes the buildings of that more optimistic period (epitomized by Willy Brandt's slogan, "dare to be more democratic"[9]) all the more worthy of documentation and protection.

In practice, it is questionable whether public access to information on modernist buildings directly contributes to security risks.[10] The world has not been made more dangerous through the publication of building collections and databases; the sharing of architectural values does not constitute a security risk, but should instead be understood as a process of social consolidation, a broad-based appropriation without physical or digital safeguards, and as a contribution to security through the informed and committed participation of citizens.

Conclusions and outlook

In recent years, state-run institutions for heritage preservation have begun to make their documentation partially available to the interested public. At the same time, highly diverse groups of actors interested primarily in the built heritage of later modernity have placed informal collections of information online, which they use as a matter of course. The quality of collaboration between heritage preservation institutions and these citizen groups is variable; the two complement and profit from each other. The visibility of documentation on the Internet in itself makes clear that heritage preservation is neither a form of nostalgia dictated from on high nor merely an additional bureaucratic hurdle in the construction process, but rather, to refer to Laurajane Smith quoted in the introduction to this book, a cultural process with various actors. This process includes the users of databases that are affiliated with neither state offices nor activist groups. Google and Facebook doubtless know a great deal about these users, while the scientific community still knows very little, since few user studies have yet been undertaken on behalf of archives or museums. These reveal how the structure of user groups and their behaviour are changing (cf. Huvila, 2008). The institutions will also change, however, as is currently under discussion in contributions to archival science within the Digital Humanities, where the step from a digital archive to a participative archive has been attempted (ibid.). The documentation of modernism can form a first step in this direction within the field of heritage preservation. The (well-documented) destruction of key buildings from this period fuelled public interest, producing an overall positive influence on the listing process. Linked to the importance of documentation are the surrounding actors whose documentation work often forms a basis for the inventories of national or local heritage institutions and illustrates the significance of *informal provisional listings as a protection instrument.* Releasing specific information via publicly accessible documentation and databases raises questions concerning what kinds of documentation or inventory information can and should be published, or whether this represents a contradiction: documentation versus security design? On the one hand, such knowledge should be shared with the public to enable appropriation of such heritage; on the other hand, the publication of sensitive information may represent an additional hazard in terms of security risks. Documenting modernity is a complex cultural process between new stakeholders and traditional institutions, new methods of placement, and public access that is in development and requires further discussion.

Acknowledgement

Thanks go to Ralph Paschke, Uwe Schwartz, and Katja Hasche for their suggestions, and to Morgan Powell for the translation into English.

Notes

1 Ulrich Müther, during a tour of the building as part of a seminar on structural design taught by Prof. Pichler, University of the Arts Berlin; the demolition was documented by Pichler Engineers, Berlin.

108 Torben Kiepke and Hans-Rudolf Meier

2 Buildings of the post-war modern period in the GDR have been referred to as 'Ostmoderne' since Butter and Hartung (2005).
3 Further information on referenced projects and websites is presented at the end of the chapter.
4 In Bulgaria an initiative has formed around Zhivka Shishkova, committed to the preservation of buildings in Dimitrovgrad. Dimitrovgrad is a planned city from the 1950s with Eisenhüttenstadt and Nova Huta as partner cities. The initiative, which dates from 2005, does not have its own website, but forums exist devoted to collecting material on Dimitrovgrad (SkyscraperCity, 2011–2015).
5 The "Un-written" project was completed and exhibited as the Latvian contribution to the 2014 Venice Biennale of Architecture.
6 The cited public databases of the German federal states each also have an Intranet section containing further data that are not publicly accessible.
7 In central Germany, for example, there exist no publicly accessible inventories of church assets because of fear of theft and vandalism.
8 The proposed demolition of the so-called Y-Block, built by the architect Erling Viksjø in 1969, prompted reactions from ICOMOS (2016) as well as Europa Nostra (2015).
9 www.willy-brandt.de/fileadmin/brandt/Downloads/Regierungserklaerung_Willy_Brandt_1969.pdf
10 Pictures of buildings that were destroyed in the government quarter of Oslo in the terror attack in July 2011, for instance, were consulted more frequently after their destruction than had ever been the case before (cf. Heath-Kelly, 2017, pp. 114ff.).

References

Balthasar, D. (2017). *Kann man Sicherheit entwerfen?* Retrieved from www.baumeister.de/kann-man-sicherheit-entwerfen/
Butter, A., & Hartung, U. (2005). *Ostmoderne: Architektur in Berlin 1945–1965.* Berlin: Dt. Werkbund Berlin e.V.
Carughi, U., & Vissone, M. (Eds.). (2017). *Time frames: Conservation policies for twentieth-century architectural heritage.* Abington: Routledge.
DAM (Deutsches Architekturmuseum). (2018). *SOS BRUTALISMUS—Rettet die Betonmonster!* Retrieved from http://dam-online.de/portal/de/Ausstellungen/Ausstellungen2018/1596/2597/88170/mod2246-details1/1594.aspx
Drucker, J. (2013). Is there a "digital" art history? *Visual Resources, 29,* 3–13.
Eckardt, F., Meier, H-R, Scheurmann, I., & Sonne, W. (Eds.). (2017). *Welche Denkmale welcher Moderne? Zum Umgang mit Bauten der 1960er und 70er Jahre.* Berlin: Jovis.
Europa Nostra. (2015, June 22). *Europa Nostra's delegation visit Y-Block in Oslo.* Retrieved from www.europanostra.org/europa-nostras-delegation-visit-y-block-oslo
Freidrichs, C. et al. (Producers) & Freidrichs, C. (Director). (2011). *The Pruitt-Igoe myth* [Motion picture]. United States: Unicorn Stencil Documentary Films.
Heath-Kelly, C. (2017). *Death and security: Memory and mortality at the bombsite.* Manchester: Manchester University Press.
Huvila, I. (2008). Participatory archive. Towards decentralised curation, radical user orientation, and broader contextualisation of records management. *Archival Science, 8,* 15–36.

Documenting modernity 109

ICOMOS (International Council on Monuments and Sites). (2016, September 28). *International Heritage Alert Launched by ICOMOS*. Retrieved from www.icomos-isc20c.org/pdf/final pressreleaseforinternationalha forgovernmentbuildingsosloicomosisc20cseptember2016.pdf

Jencks, C. (1977). *The language of post-modern architecture*. New York, NY: Rizzoli.

Kaleva, E. (2015). Survey regarding the status of second half of 20th century listed buildings within the research project: *Welche Denkmale welcher Moderne?* National Institute of Immovable Cultural Heritage, Sofia (Grey Literature).

Kiepke, T. (2015). Zwischen Institution und Initiative: Erfassungsstrategien für Bauten der späten Moderne in Süd- und Osteuropa. *Die Denkmalpflege, 73,* 119–122.

Kohlenbach, B. (2015, October 13). Konzepte zur Erfassung und zum Schutz der Nachkriegsmoderne in Berlin. In Austrian Federal Monuments Authority and WDWM. *Nachkriegsmoderne in Österreich* [Colloquium]. Mauerbach.

Liste der Baudenkmale in Potsdam/B. (n.d.). *Wikipedia*. Retrieved from https://de.wikipedia.org/wiki/Liste_der_Baudenkmale_in_Potsdam/B

Meier, H.-R. (2015). *Das Denkmalinventar*. In W. Augustyn (Ed.), *Corpus— Inventar—Katalog: Beispiele für Forschung und Dokumentation zur materiellen Überlieferung der Künste* (pp. 117–130). München: Zentralinstitut für Kunstgeschichte.

Michel, K. (2003). Nach der Utopie. *Brandeins, 9,* 138–145.

Schlüter, G. (1997). Pruitt-Igoe—Die Dritte. *Wolkenkuckucksheim, Internationale Zeitschrift für Theorie und Wissenschaft der Architektur, 1.* Retrieved from www.cloud-cuckoo.net/openarchive/wolke/deu/Themen/971/Schlueter/schlueter_t.html

SkyscraperCity. (2011). *Dimitrovgrad: Monument of culture* [Online discussion board]. Retrieved from www.skyscrapercity.com/showthread.php?t=1294731

Stella, A. G., & Rizzo, S. (2011). *Vandali. L'assolto alle bellezze d'Italia.* Milan: Rizzoli.

Stimmann, H. (2000, July 22). Für hässliche Gebäude wird sich niemand engagieren (R. Haubrich, Interviewer). *Die Welt.* Retrieved from www.welt.de/print-welt/article524423/Fuer-haessliche-Gebaeude-wird-sich-niemand-engagieren.html

VDL (Vereinigung der Landesdenkmalpfleger in der Bundesrepublik Deutschland). (2005). *Arbeitsblatt 24: Inventarisation der Bau- und Kunstdenkmäler.* Retrieved from www.vdl-denkmalpflege.de/fileadmin/dateien/Arbeitsbl%C3%A4tter/Nr24.pdf

For further information regarding specific projects, please refer to:

Architetture del secondo 900: http://architetturecontemporanee.beniculturali.it/architetture/index_metodologia

Atlante dell'architettura italiana degli anni '50 e '60: http://atlante.iuav.it

Audience+: Museen und das partizipative Web: https://blog.hslu.ch/audienceplus

Big Beautiful Buildings: https://bigbeautifulbuildings.de

Denkmale in Brandenburg: http://ns.gis-bldam-brandenburg.de/hida4web/search?smode=advanced

110 Torben Kiepke and Hans-Rudolf Meier

Denkmaldatenbank Berlin: www.stadtentwicklung.berlin.de/denkmal/liste_karte_datenbank/de/denkmaldatenbank/index.shtml

Denkmaldatenbank Bremen: www.denkmalpflege.bremen.de/denkmal_digital/denkmaldatenbank-37984

Elenco opere (Architetture dal 1945 ad oggi a Napoli e provincial): http://na.architetturamoderna.it/post.html

Geoportal BayernAtlas: https://geoportal.bayern.de/bayernatlas/?lang=de&topic=ba&bgLayer=atkis&catalogNodes=11,122

Kulturdenkmäler in Hessen: http://denkxweb.denkmalpflege-hessen.de

Un-written: https://issuu.com/nrja/docs/unwritten (p. 20)

7 Urban nuclear reactors and the security theatre

The making of atomic heritage in Chicago, Moscow, and Stockholm

Anna Storm, Fredrik Krohn Andersson, and Eglė Rindzevičiūtė

Accessing the nuclear past

A group of excited visitors follows their guide, who is dressed in a white laboratory coat, to an inconspicuous door at the rear of an ordinary university campus building. Neither written or symbolic signs nor architectural features prepare them for the enigmatic site, located 25 metres below ground. In fact, the everyday and anonymous character of the built environment contributes to the visitors' excitement. They are to explore a hidden treasure: an underground nuclear facility imaginatively loaded with a mixture of scientific utopian visions of the 1940s and 1950s, and dystopian fears of radioactive catastrophes and contamination. There is no longer any reactor in the rock cavern, and the facility has been cleared of radioactive material. Still, a lingering sense of danger heightens the visitors' perceptions of the materiality of the site when descending the stairs, moving through thick metal doors at the end of winding corridors, and entering the impressive reactor hall that measures 12 metres from floor to ceiling. The guide reminds the group about the non-sensory qualities of radiation: It cannot be seen, heard, or smelled by human senses unaided. This circumstance further contributes to an atmosphere of authenticity that is irresistible to the visitors, being some of the lucky ones to gain access to the site.

During and immediately after the Second World War, physicists and engineers in several countries worked intensively and in competition to develop nuclear weapons and to control the chain reaction creating nuclear energy. An experience of urgency and a sense of revolutionary future promise permeated their activities and, as we will see, largely outweighed the risks as they were calculated at the time. As a result, small experimental reactors were built at research institutes or universities relatively close to city centres and densely populated areas—the key localization factor being the physicists' own geography. The 1940s and 1950s saw the creation of

112 *Storm, Krohn Andersson, and Rindzevičiūtė*

about 20 such experimental 'atomic piles'. Successively, and in parallel to the expansion of large-scale nuclear weapon facilities and commercial nuclear power plants, many countries continued to develop experimental reactors. Today, we count about 840 such small reactors in 71 countries, many of which are located in urban settings and about 200 of which are still operational (IAEA, 2018).

This chapter focuses on three of the early pioneering urban reactors, located in Chicago, Moscow, and Stockholm, and which were all symbols of national prowess as humanity was entering the nuclear age and which later became objects of heritage processes. In what follows, we will scrutinize the establishment of these reactors as well as the making of atomic heritage, through the conceptual lens of the 'security theatre'. The analysis will revolve around paradoxes of actual and imagined danger and safety, of intentional and unintentional architectural anonymity, and of varying physical access to the sites.

The security theatre

The "security theatre" (Schneier, 2003) refers primarily to security measures taken to counteract terrorism, such as scanning bodies and luggage at airports—measures that in many cases do not actually improve security but only the experience of security. In that way, it is not real but rather a "theatre" of improved safety. However, the function of the security theatre must not necessarily be understood as a way to cheat the ignorant masses, but rather—more positively—as a means to calibrate the concordance between, on the one hand, calculable risk and security and, on the other hand, perceived risk and security. Schneier argues that in some cases we tend to exaggerate risks, such that the security theatre may then help to adjust feelings and reactions to match the calculable level of threat. In other cases, the risks are greater and the security lower than we recognize; the reason for this might be traced to performances of a security theatre that is an expression of power abuse—that is, to actually disguise risks (Schneier, 2007, 2009). In an attempt to unveil the security theatre, Amoore and Hall explored how routinized and thereby invisibilized security rituals enacted at border controls can be interrupted by artistic interventions, rendering the "security practice [...] strange", with the result that "existing conditions are discovered or alienated". One of their examples is the artist Marcos Ramirez's installation of a ten-metre-high wooden horse with two heads, which in 1997 straddled a US/Mexican border crossing and thereby created a "space of confusion" (Amoore & Hall, 2010, pp. 301–302).

For us, the security theatre will provide a point of departure to explore: firstly, the anonymous architecture of *operational* urban nuclear reactors as an expression of masking risks and, secondly, the architectural features, guided tours, and artistic interpretations of *heritagized* reactors as performing an exaggerated experience of risk which, in turn, enhance heritage attraction. That is, we will argue that, in the case of urban nuclear reactors, the security theatre in fact almost never worked to calibrate calculable security with perceived security, but rather to either disguise or exaggerate the risks of the nuclear site.

This chapter is based on historic and contemporary written and visual sources in combination with interviews and on-site visits.

Atomic heritage

Heritage is generally seen as a positive-affirmative resource for identity formation and community strength—that is, heritage "invoked as a positive quality" (Harrison, 2013, p. 7). Atomic heritage confirms this understanding in two ways: first, through stories of what are seen as remarkable scientific and technological achievements and, second, through stories of dark and difficult pasts that should never be repeated—that is, by extension, as a sign of contemporary progress.

Stories of scientific achievements

The stories of scientific and technological achievements in the nuclear field are populated by intelligent, brave, and assiduous pioneers, and convey future visions built on the many promises of atomic power. The focus is often to highlight the 'firsts' of the 1940s, 1950s, and 1960s, such as: the Manhattan Project in the US with the development of the first atomic bomb (AHF, 2018; Molella, 2003); the Obninsk plant in Russia, which was the first nuclear reactor in the world to produce electricity for the grid (Schmid, 2015); the Zoé reactor, which was the first nuclear reactor in France (Boudia & Soubiran, 2013); Calder Hall power station, which was the world's first large-scale commercial nuclear power plant (NDA, 2007); the Dounreay plant, which developed so-called fast-breeder reactor technology (CHM, 2018; J. B. Gunn, personal communication, 15 December 2017); and Ågesta, the first nuclear plant in Sweden (Tafvelin Heldner, Dahlström Rittsél, & Lundgren, 2008; see also Krohn Andersson, 2012; Storm, 2014). By their heritagization these sites tell an overall utopian story of techno-scientific progress and boundless future energy, omitting negative consequences and risks. For instance, nuclear weapons development is dissociated from casualties, while nuclear power production is disconnected from the history of environmentalist anti-nuclear movements and public nuclear fear (Molella, 2003).

The three urban reactors in our focus here correspond to this emphasis on nuclear firsts—the Chicago reactor (CP-1) was the very first reactor where a self-sustaining chain reaction was artificially achieved, and thus counts as the birthplace of controlled nuclear energy; the Moscow reactor (F-1) was the first in Eurasia to repeat the CP-1 achievement; and the Stockholm reactor (R1) was the first nuclear reactor in Sweden.

114 *Storm, Krohn Andersson, and Rindzevičiūtė*

In the afterlife of urban reactors, a heritagization process might appear to be both alien and provocative, given that today the risks of radiation are well known. However, a positive-affirmative heritage approach has obvious forerunners when it comes to nuclear technology, likely paving the way for heritagization. The promises of the atom, its utopian energy and supposed peace-building qualities, were already on display in the 1940s and 1950s at World's Fairs, national fairs, and in the exhibitions of science and technology museums (see, for example, Forgan, 2003; Laucht, 2012). In addition, many nuclear sites later featured museum-like information centres that were constructed and managed by the nuclear industry and generally focused on technical descriptions. The move from displaying nuclear power as a promising object of the future or a potent technology of the present, to an object of heritage value in terms of scientific achievements is therefore not as big a step as one might imagine.

Stories of disastrous pasts

In contrast to this optimistic heritagization driven by the nuclear industry, stories of disastrous pasts occupy other heritage arenas. The UNESCO World Heritage list includes two sites (out of almost 1,100) directly related to nuclear power, both of which focus on the devastating effects of nuclear bombings: the Hiroshima Peace Memorial in Japan, and the Bikini Atoll Nuclear Test Site in the Marshall Islands. Moreover, the listed Kakadu National Park in Australia includes abandoned as well as operational uranium mines (uranium being a critical component for both military and civilian nuclear uses). However, the mines are not regarded as industrial or atomic heritage but rather as a threat to the natural-cultural heritage of the park through "physical and radiological hazards" (UNESCO, 2018). In this way, the World Heritage list limits the nuclear past to the nuclear bomb and its consequences, framed as a nuclear dystopia of human and environmental disasters. Hence, atomic heritage here emerges as difficult and dark (Logan & Reeves, 2009; Macdonald, 2009), a public warning and a deterrent: Nuclear power led to disaster, but now it is over, and society must make sure it will not happen again (for another approach to difficult heritage, see Macdonald, 2015).

In parallel to the official heritage deterrents, emerging tourism practices seek to explore a wide range of former nuclear sites as part of a more adventurous interest in dark heritage, for example the Chernobyl exclusion zone and the evacuated 'atomic city' of Pripyat; Three Mile Island; and various nuclear test sites (Hooper & Lennon, 2017; see also Dark Tourism, 2018). Such dark nuclear heritage sites are normally remote and visually stunning in their combination of grandeur and decay—a clear contrast to the early experimental reactors in urban settings, to which we will now turn in more empirical detail.

Urban reactors in Chicago, Moscow, and Stockholm

Chicago: CP-1

The Chicago Pile 1 (CP-1) was part of the Manhattan Engineer District, commonly known as the Manhattan Project. The role of the reactor was primarily to explore plutonium production, needed for an atomic bomb. Experiments were first scattered across a number of universities (Rhodes, 1988, pp. 399–400) but became concentrated at Chicago because one of the leading physicists was based there (Hewlett & Anderson, 1962, pp. 55–56). From 1942, what was named the Metallurgical Laboratory was located in the northern part of Chicago University campus, close to other laboratory buildings and to university sports facilities. Experiments were conducted in a former racket court situated beneath the neo-Gothic west stand building of Stagg Field, a football field that had stood more or less unused since 1939. The interior space was 18 metres long, 9 metres wide, and 8 metres high, sunk half below street level (Rhodes, 1988, p. 401).

Here, the physicist Enrico Fermi and his team constructed a number of intermediary atomic piles prior to the final test to actually achieve a self-sustaining chain reaction. It was planned to conduct the final test in a forest about 30 kilometres southwest of the campus, but for various reasons CP-1 was ultimately assembled on the same spot as the intermediary versions. It consisted of 45,000 blocks of graphite, six tons of uranium metal, and 50 tons of uranium oxide, and the process was controlled by cadmium rods. The pile was formed as a sphere and sealed within a large balloon of rubberized canvas. It was planned to fill the balloon with carbon dioxide instead of air but this eventually proved unnecessary (Rhodes, 1988, pp. 429–431; Seaborg, 1977, pp. 333–347, 390).

The dangers of experimenting in an urban location were later emphasized by one of the team members, in a detailed, diary-like, report: "It was a dreadful decision [...]. If the chain-reaction could not be bound, the whole campus might be destroyed by the explosion, or at the very least, radioactive fission products would be spread far and wide" (Seaborg, 1977, p. 343). Nevertheless, the test was carried out and in December 1942, a month ahead of schedule, the reactor achieved so-called criticality—a moment which thus counts as the birth of controlled nuclear energy.

After the successful test, by February 1943 CP-1 had already been shut down, disassembled, and transported to the forest (today known as Red Gate Woods) as initially planned. Here, the reactor was essentially rebuilt and named CP-2 (Hewlett & Anderson, 1962, p. 200). This new incarnation was somewhat larger, surrounded by a concrete shield, and operated between 1943 and 1954 (US DoE, 1978, p. 5). In 1954, nuclear research activities were to be moved to yet another site, located 10 kilometres away, but this time CP-1/CP-2, along with a later CP-3 reactor, would not follow. Instead, the fuel was

116 *Storm, Krohn Andersson, and Rindzevičiūtė*

sent to a nuclear facility in Oak Ridge, Tennessee, and the remaining reactor containments were filled with concrete. A 12-metre-deep hole was dug on-site and, with the aid of explosives, the reactors were tumbled into it. The hole was then covered with debris from other contaminated items (US DoE, 1978, p. 9). The decision to bury the reactor remnants on site was likely influenced by the continuous dumping of radioactive waste nearby. Since 1943, building debris, clothing, contaminated equipment, air filters, and other radioactive and hazardous materials had been buried in trenches only 500 metres from the reactors (US DoE, 2017, p. 2). From 1948 the waste was put in steel bins, which were dug up in 1949 and transported to the new Argonne National Laboratory site, but the waste buried prior to 1948 was left in the ground.

Already in 1947, a bronze plaque was mounted on the wall next to the Stagg Field entrance (CCHAL, 1971) stating in capital letters: "On December 2, 1942 man achieved here the first self-sustaining chain reaction and thereby initiated the controlled release of nuclear energy". Ten years later the Stagg Field west stand was demolished and, after a few years, representatives of the University of Chicago commissioned a sculpture to occupy the empty space. Their vision was a full-scale monument and "not just a simple bas relief" (Katzive, 1973), and the commission was awarded to the world-renowned sculptor Henry Moore (Boal, 2003). The choice of Moore seems reasonable, since his abstract style promised to strip the monument of unwanted connotations of danger and death. The bronze sculpture *Atom Piece* was inaugurated in 1967, on the 25th anniversary of the successful CP-1 experiments, and placed in the middle of what then appeared as a small plaza (Figure 7.1). At the close of the ceremony, one of the speakers addressed the future: "May this place, in fact and deed, be holy ground, to us and our successors, generation after generation, as long as men survive and know enough to reverence landmarks from the human past" (CCHAL, 1971).

Despite the expectations of a largely apolitical, abstract monument to scientific achievements, contemporary readings of the sculpture ranged from a skull to a mushroom cloud (Boal, 2003). Furthermore, Moore's title of *Atom Piece* phonetically alludes to "atom peace"—a potentially politically invested title. Perhaps to mitigate negative connotations, official narratives renamed the sculpture *Nuclear Power* (CCHAL, 1971).

In conjunction with the inauguration of the sculpture in 1967, the bronze plaque from 1947 was mounted on a low block of granite beside the sculpture, together with three other plaques. One declared that the site had been registered as a National Historic Landmark in 1965 and the two others described the sculpture. In 1971, a fifth plaque was added, on the back of the granite block and facing the monument, which declared that the site had also been designated a Chicago Landmark. As of 2017, the site is an important stop on the campus walking tour undertaken by new students and, in parallel, a continuous flow of tourists photograph themselves in front of the 1947 plaque and the sculpture.

A commemoration also took place at the Red Gate Woods forest site, which was finally abandoned in 1956. In that year, an irregularly shaped block of

Figure 7.1 In 1947, only five years after the first successful experiment worldwide to control nuclear energy, a bronze plaque was installed to commemorate the event and to indicate its location on the University of Chicago campus. © 2017 Authors.

natural stone was placed at the spot where the reactors were buried, bearing the inscription: "The world's first nuclear reactor was rebuilt at this site in 1943 [...] and the U.S. Atomic Energy Commission then buried the reactor here". At the nearby site of the trenches containing various radioactive leftovers, a more elaborate cube of stone bears the inscription: "Caution—Do not dig. Buried in this area is radioactive material from nuclear research conducted here 1943–1949". Today, the forest area appears as a picturesque landscape garden, with serpentine paths beneath leafy trees. The pastoral setting plays upon the theme of the allegorical tomb as a place for sublime contemplation of the vanity and transience of life (Charlesworth, 2013).

Moscow: F-1

Directly following the successful CP-1 experiments of 1942, Joseph Stalin established a secret 'Laboratory 2', headed by the physicist Igor Kurchatov, to catch up with US advances in developing nuclear weapons. The laboratory was located in a rural area about 12 kilometres northwest of central Moscow. The location was retrospectively described as a "potato field" by participating scientists, but soon developed a suburban character with numerous scientific research institutes (Larin, 2007). Similarly to CP-1, the first experimental reactor at Laboratory 2 was preceded by several intermediate atomic

118   Storm, Krohn Andersson, and Rindzevičiūtė

piles, or "atomic cauldrons" as they were called in Russian (*atomnyi kotel*), which were successively assembled in a large tent while awaiting a proper reactor building (Moscow Manege, 2015, p. 8). The work involved a team of some thirty scientists, a quarter of whom were women (Larin, 2007).

After three years, in 1946 the "first physical" (*fizicheskii-pervyi*) reactor, F-1, achieved criticality. Its primary aim was to produce plutonium for nuclear weapons (Moscow Manege, 2015, p. 8), but the experience gained from F-1 was also crucial in designing, for example, the Obninsk reactor, which since 1954 provided electricity to the grid (Josephson, 2005; Schmid, 2015, p. 45). F-1 was housed in a one-storey building with neoclassical features, designed by the *Akademproekt* bureau, where many flagship buildings for the Soviet Academy of Sciences were designed in a signature neoclassical style. Inside there was an underground pit of 10 metres diameter and 7 metres depth that contained the spherical atomic cauldron, which was accessible only through a labyrinth of corridors (Holloway, 1994, p. 181). In order to produce plutonium, F-1 ran at high power (24 kW). Elevated radiation levels were indicated by a red warning light on the roof of the building, and to protect the staff the control centre was situated 500 metres away. Indeed, the Soviet government itself had to be educated about the dangers of radiation: At one point, Kurchatov had to stop Lavrentiy Beria, the chief of security, from rushing into the reactor hall to see for himself the chain reaction taking place (Holloway, 1994).

Laboratory 2 was renamed several times, and since 1960 has been known as the Kurchatov Institute (Schmid, 2015, pp. 43–44). It was the pioneering research unit that brought the Soviet Union into the nuclear age (Voinova, Verny, Zenkova, Strelnikova, & Yasitsishina, 2015, pp. 115–117; Morozova, Buras, Mikheenkov, Sviridov, & Kharat'ian, 2012), but the work was also fuelled by internal competition within the Soviet nuclear physics community (Schmid, 2015, p. 98). For example, a similarly secret Laboratory 3, today known as the Alikhanov Institute of Theoretical and Experimental Physics, also in Moscow, was established in 1945 to develop a more expensive and less stable heavy-water nuclear reactor. Overall, 12 Soviet and later Russian research reactors were concentrated around Moscow, eight of them at the Kurchatov Institute (Arkhangelsky et al., 2004).

Unlike CP-1, F-1 was not shut down following successful initial experiments but instead continued operations (Figure 7.2). Its uses changed, for example towards testing neutron fluxes and, in parallel, it was also beginning to be heritagized as part of the Kurchatov Institute, thus becoming an important part of the growing nuclear exhibition complex in Soviet Russia (Rindzevičiūtė, 2016). In the 1950s, the institute established an archive that later accumulated a rich collection of audio-visual materials and, when Kurchatov died in 1960, his wife initiated a memorial house museum. In 1967, a mock-up of F-1 was exhibited at the Polytechnical Museum in Moscow (Moscow Manege, 2015, p. 8); in 1971 a five-metre-tall bronze head of Kurchatov was installed in a square and, in 1975, Kurchatov's luxury

Figure 7.2 The neoclassical architecture of the F-1 reactor building with surrounding woods emphasize the exclusive working and living environments for nuclear physicists and engineers in Moscow during the Soviet period. © Mid-1980s Nikolai Kuznetsov. Courtesy of the Memorial House-Museum of the Academician Igor Kurchatov.

villa, located within the institute, featured in a film about the Soviet atomic project. The suburban area of the research institutes, the Shchukino District, was generally characterized by government-funded exclusive housing for the elite scientists adjacent to their workplaces, expressed in bourgeois villas surrounded by gardens and orchards, special hospitals, and areas of green parkland (Josephson, 2005, p. 18).

While the military uses of nuclear technology were criticized by Soviet physicists (Josephson, 1996), civilian nuclear energy was not questioned (despite fatal accidents, for example at the Kurchatov Institute in 1971) in the Soviet Union prior to the Chernobyl disaster of 1986, which is often seen as a turning point contributing to the break-up of the union (Dawson, 1996). During the turbulent years of the late 1980s, F-1 still continued operations. In 1991, however, Moscow City Council decided to shut down all nuclear reactors within the city, and the prevailing practice of extending the operation of urban research reactors was also publicly criticized by environmental NGOs (Kuznetsov, 2002). The title of an article in the main

120   *Storm, Krohn Andersson, and Rindzevičiūtė*

daily *Kommersant* put it ironically: "*A Nuclear Tip is our Home Sweet Home*" (Shvarts, 1992). At the same time, the nuclear character of the Shchukino District was generally neither a secret, nor seen as a drawback. Indeed, in 2005, the district council adopted a coat of arms that boasts an image of the atom; squares and streets are named after nuclear celebrities; and a public radiation information sign shows live data for the district and for Moscow on average. Furthermore, in the aftermath of the Fukushima accident of 2011, the vice director of the Kurchatov Institute reassured Muscovites that "Kurchatov's reactors" did not pose any risk, since F-1 would simply stop should there be an earthquake (Interfax, 2011). A survey revealed that 83 per cent of the Russian public considered nuclear power "relatively safe" (Black, 2011). However, concerns were also voiced by the local population, including about the state of contaminated soil depositories, several of which were still located in the area of the institute (Ozharovskii, 2012).

In 2016, F-1 was finally shut down after 70 years of operation. However, it was not decommissioned, and the fuel remained in the reactor. A journalist enthusiastically commented that F-1 had "enough fuel for hundreds of years and can be restarted any time" (Iudina, 2016). Nevertheless, immediately after the shutdown, F-1 was listed as a monument to science and technology and, in December 2016, an F-1 museum was opened, complementing the Kurchatov Institute museum, which had opened a few years earlier (Voinova et al., 2015, p. 117). As of 2018, the institute thus houses one archive and three separate museums with an overall focus on atomic research and its founding fathers, and particularly targets school children. At the same time, the institute is closed territory—a complex of buildings surrounded by high security walls, continuously classified as a nuclear site with special restrictions. It is nested in a popular residential area dominated by high-rise apartment buildings with high social status thanks to the presence of research institutes, greenery, and good metro connections to the centre.

Stockholm: R1

R1 stands for reactor number one, that is, the first nuclear reactor in Sweden. It began operation in 1954, decidedly later than CP-1 in Chicago and F-1 in Moscow, but it was constructed when the nuclear physics knowledge of the two superpowers was still highly secret and not available to other countries. Similarly to other experimental reactors, R1 was small with an initially envisaged effect of 5 kW, eventually built for 300 kW, and with some adjustments to the cooling system the effect was successively increased to 1 MW (Pershagen, 2017, p. 30). The reactor was based on heavy-water technology and used natural uranium as fuel. The design was chosen to meet Sweden's ambition to increase energy independence, since natural uranium was a domestic resource—an ambition that was highly topical due to recent experiences of wartime shortages. Furthermore, the design combined efforts

Urban nuclear reactors and security theatre 121

to increase knowledge of both the civilian and military usages of nuclear energy, as this type of reactor could also produce plutonium.

After the US bombings of Hiroshima and Nagasaki in 1945, the Swedish Defence Research Agency (FOA) suggested that the Swedish Government form a committee to "investigate the existing national atomic research and propose necessary measures" (Larsson, 1987, p. 125). Soon, a new company, AB Atomenergi, was created to handle the applied parts of the research that were foreseen as leading to the construction of atomic piles. AB Atomenergi was majority-owned by the state and also included more than 20 power companies and industrial firms (Lindström, 1991, p. 92). Two locations were discussed for the first atomic pile: Gåshaga on the island of Lidingö, about 12 kilometres from Stockholm city centre; and the so-called 'science city' directly connected to a Royal Swedish Academy of Engineering Sciences (IVA) research station, located adjacent to the Royal Institute of Technology (KTH) campus about three kilometres from Stockholm city centre. The risks for the populations living near the two sites were compared with regard to reactor casualties (Larsson, 1987, p. 133), with Gåshaga being a sparsely built area facing the Stockholm archipelago, whereas the science city had 35,000 residents within a one-kilometre radius (Larsson, 2008, p. 29). Due to a range of factors, it was decided to use the more centrally located science city site, in combination with the construction of an underground cavern for the reactor. Nevertheless, at the time there was almost no public debate concerning either the location or the very existence of the reactor (Fjæstad, 2000, p. 23).

The reasons for placing the reactor underground seem to be manifold and overlapping. Among the articulated motives were that the aboveground location next to the existing research station in the science city was already planned for other uses and therefore unavailable; that in case of sabotage, the surrounding rock would contain potential radiation leakages (and therefore the reactor did not need a special containment building); that the cavern could be used as a bomb shelter for nearby residents (Larsson, 2008, p. 29; B. Pershagen, personal communication, 21 September 2018); and, furthermore, that the first CEO of AB Atomenergi had previously been CEO of the company Nitroglycerin AB. Consequently, he was well acquainted with rock-blasting and caverns, and also suggested the underground option (B. Pershagen, personal communication, 18 September 2018).

Soon, the proximity to the Royal Institute of Technology (KTH) proved most beneficial for both parties. Various departments at KTH were able to carry out laboratory activities at R1, and numerous students were directly recruited to work on the reactor as there was a shortage of skilled personnel. Around 1950, the average age of the employees was less than 30 (Larsson, 1987, p. 134), which probably contributed to the overwhelming enthusiasm expressed by the project team. One of the young engineers retrospectively described the work at R1 as a "paradise" and recounted how "[l]ife in the Swedish atomic project was exciting and meaningful" (Larsson, 2008, p. 45).

122 *Storm, Krohn Andersson, and Rindzevičiūtė*

The decision to build R1 was made in 1949 and, in 1954, the reactor went critical for the first time, and so "[t]he Swedish Columbus of our time had launched its ship" (Larsson, 1981, p. 108). The reactor was placed in a cavern hall 24 metres long, 12 metres wide and with an arched ceiling reaching 12 metres. The hall was painted in blue with numerous spotlights covering the ceiling, giving "the illusion of a never changing star sky" (Larsson, 1981, p. 116). One of the walls housed 12 office spaces in three floors, called the 'swallow nests', connected with a spiral staircase and exterior corridors. The control room was located next to the reactor hall and visually linked through a large window. Two aisles connected the hall with two vertical shafts containing elevators and stairs. At ground level, the only indication of any underground activity was a high ventilation stack. The buildings aboveground, belonging to the research station of the Royal Swedish Academy of Engineering Sciences, were of a non-spectacular 1940s modernist vernacular, located behind fences and a locked gate to prevent unauthorized access.

Central to the "Atoms for Peace" campaign, launched by US president Dwight D. Eisenhower in 1953, was a massive release in 1955 of previously classified information from both the US and Soviet Union. Suddenly, R1's role as a key Swedish source of knowledge generation in the field was outdated. The employees struggled to demonstrate the continued relevance of the reactor, in competition with a succession of new reactors built at other locations. Despite the benefits of having a reactor available in the city centre—for example, the possibility of transporting short-lived isotopes to nearby hospitals (Fjæstad, 2000, p. 53)—in the 1960s there was an increasing debate on the costs of operating R1 and the questionable siting of a reactor so close to residential areas (Handberg, 2008, p. 125). Finally, the reactor was closed down in 1970.

At the time of the closure, some R1 engineers suggested to the Swedish prime minister that the reactor should be preserved as part of Swedish scientific heritage, but growing anti-nuclear public sentiment ultimately precluded a monument to atomic research (L. Handberg, personal communication, 4 October 2018). Instead, R1 stood empty for over a decade until it was decommissioned and dismantled in the early 1980s. The highly radioactive fuel rods were stored in a nuclear research facility in Studsvik, about a hundred kilometres south of Stockholm, while the rest of the debris was transported 150 kilometres north to Forsmark and a final repository for low- and medium-level nuclear waste (Handberg, 2008, p. 126). The control panel was given as a gift to the Swedish National museum of Science and Technology, but for some reason it also ended up in Studsvik (L. Handberg, personal communication, 4 October 2018).

After dismantling the reactor, the cavern was cleared of radioactivity and again stood empty for more than a decade, and in the early 1990s the ventilation stack was knocked down. The location was generally not well known (Figure 7.3), but anyone who happened to know about it and which doors to enter could reach the cavern simply by descending stairs and passing

Figure 7.3 In the early 1980s, the R1 reactor was removed from its underground location on KTH campus, and the cavern decontaminated of radioactivity. The hole in the ground and the numbered grid from measuring radioactivity in the ceiling serve as reminders of what is no longer there. © Anna Gerdén, Tekniska museet/National Museum of Science and Technology, Sweden.

through doors that were unlocked during daytime. Some KTH students used this opportunity to illegally arrange parties in the reactor hall (L. Handberg, personal communication, 4 October 2018).

In the late 1990s, a group of KTH faculty 'discovered' the abandoned reactor cavern and found it a perfect place for creating an experimental

124 *Storm, Krohn Andersson, and Rindzevičiūtė*

stage. They arranged multimedia events, offered guided visits, and invited dancers, actors and musicians to perform in R1. Early on, the music video for *Nothing Really Matters* by Madonna was filmed in the premises (Handberg, 2008, p. 128), which gained the site some reputation. Over the years, several films have used the premises, where the "raw environment, the location and the history has inspired and been utilized in different ways" (Handberg, 2008, p. 136). In parallel to the artistic work, the faculty enthusiasts worked on historicizing the place through exhibitions, video recordings of former R1 employees, and by reinstating the control panel in its original place with the approval of the National Museum of Science and Technology.

In the early 2000s, an external commercial organization asked to take over the premises in order to rebuild it as an indoor climbing facility. However, the then-owner, a real estate company specializing in campus areas, gave priority to KTH in this matter, and since 2007 KTH has been the formal tenant of what is still called R1. The latest negotiation on the future of R1 took place during 2017 and 2018. The Swedish Defence University, located since 2005 on the KTH campus close to R1, secretly worked on behalf of the Swedish Civil Contingencies Agency (MSB) to establish an interception-proof site for training Swedish authorities through war games, and was very keen to transform R1 into such a site (L. Handberg, personal communication, 4 October 2018). When the plans were leaked, the KTH faculty as well as parts of the nuclear industry mobilized in order to maintain R1 as an experimental and publicly open stage. Their efforts were eventually successful, and the MSB is said to have dropped the plans to use R1 as its training facility. It is suggested that perhaps the agency's representatives were also moved by the special "aura" of the reactor cavern, and did not want to change it (Handberg, 2008, p. 128; L. Handberg, personal communication, 4 October 2018).

Temporalities of the security theatre

As demonstrated by the three case studies, the security theatre of urban nuclear reactors has undergone great changes over time. In fact, we argue that its characteristics were reversed between the period of establishment and early operations compared to that of later and contemporary heritagization processes.

That is, during the establishment period the calculable risk was comparatively high, while the perceived risk was very low, or at least trumped by an experience of urgency and spirit of enthusiasm at the time. This is conveyed in the choice of reactor locations in or near densely populated areas, as well as in the conventional architecture that conveyed no signals of potential risk. The neo-Gothic racket court reused as a reactor hall in the midst of the bustling Chicago University campus; the purpose-built neoclassical reactor building in the Moscow district of suburban research institutes; and the hidden cavern below the unremarkable institutional buildings of

Stockholm's science city all speak about downplaying the potential risks associated with conducting experimental nuclear activities in urban settings.

A possible exception to this is the red warning light installed on the F-1 building, although this is probably best understood as internal communication for staff, connected to the remotely located control centre, and not as a warning to nearby residents. In subsequent decades, additional warnings were added that addressed the public, such as the radiation information sign at the entrance of the Kurchatov Institute and the inscribed stone cube in Red Gate Woods that exhorts passers-by "Do not dig", which nevertheless do not change our overall interpretation in any fundamental way.

Thus, the security theatre of the establishment period did not perform any calibration between calculable and perceived risk; instead, the risks were decisively downplayed or even disguised. However, as already mentioned, this is not primarily to be interpreted as the intentional risk exposure of employees and the public from the decision-makers' side, but rather as an expression of perceived urgency and also enthusiasm for the new technology, which were allowed to outweigh the potential dangers of the nuclear experiments and research.

In practice, during the period of heritagization the calculable risk at the original CP-1 and R1 sites was zero, since all radioactive material had been removed. Nevertheless, there was definitely a perception of risk at R1, which was articulated through the partly limited and also ritualized access: the visitors' thrill and excitement when actually entering the facility, a heightened experience of being in an authentic place loaded with potential dangers, reinforced by the anonymous architecture perceived as a means of concealing what is located inside. At CP-1 the perceived risk was also high but in a delayed sense. That is, the astonished question: "How could they have carried out such experiments at this place?!" which may linger long after the dangers have been removed; combined with a struggle to perceive the site as authentic as it is stripped of all original fittings and appointments.

Furthermore, the site offers no pointers to the reincarnation of CP-1 as CP-2 in the forest, and certainly no elaboration concerning what happened to the radioactive materials. We argue that the delayed experience of risk is instead largely triggered by the sculpture, which places the explicit story of scientific achievements into an imaginative context of nuclear disasters, in an example of how artistic interventions may render the security theatre 'strange'. Thus, in the period of heritagization at CP-1 and R1, the security theatre exaggerates the perceived risks instead of calibrating them to what is fundamentally now a non-risky environment. This risk exaggeration is critical, as we will argue below, for the attraction of atomic heritage.

At F-1, the calculable risks were continuously high in parallel to the heritagization processes, not only because reactor operations ceased only in 2016, but also because of nuclear waste stored on-site. The initial downplaying of the risks also continued as heritagization successively shaped the story of scientific achievements in harmonic co-existence with

126 *Storm, Krohn Andersson, and Rindzevičiūtė*

elite luxury living and working environments, through founding-father monuments, nuclear-related street names, and architectural and environmental beauty.

In sum, the security theatre of early urban reactors shows a paradoxical change over time: Initially the calculable risk was high but downplayed; later on, the calculable risks were low but exaggerated. (However, in the case of F-1, the initial phase was instead continued.) Thus, the two key temporalities of the security theatre of urban reactors have at no point provided a calibrating function but have instead reinforced tensions between calculable reality and perceived reality.

Atomic heritage attraction

As previously mentioned, our three cases unquestionably belong to the category of nuclear firsts, and through this status they gain basic and easily communicated heritage value. Like other heritagized nuclear firsts, the three cases show a main framing story of scientific achievement within an overarching positive-affirmative heritage understanding. However, this essentially utopian message is interwoven with slightly worrying elements facing visitors. In the case of CP-1, the *Atom Piece* sculpture performs an interpretative flexibility that is not wholly in accordance with the message of the plaques but is instead a reminder of the consequences following the successful experiment, primarily in terms of atomic bombings. At F-1, despite the solid security theatre, the worrying element takes the shape of public concerns about safety, expressed in ongoing debates in the press. At R1, finally, the descent below ground, the 'raw' and rough environment and the series of radioactivity measurement notes covering the reactor hall since its decommissioning, along with artistic installations that make the environment 'strange'—these all cause visitors some unease.

By themselves, such unsettling elements would certainly not be very worrying. Instead, we argue that a prevalent public understanding, at least in a former Western context, of nuclear power as not only utopian—and not even primarily utopian, but dystopian—triggers the worrying elements as meaningful beyond themselves. The sense of remaining risks is well substantiated by a broader public imaginary of nuclear and radioactive dangers and disasters, and urban reactors are thereby brought into a category of difficult heritage and dark tourism practices.

As a consequence, we argue that the contemporary visitor's experiences of our three cases therefore provide a rare space in which both utopian and dystopian understandings of the nuclear past are ambivalently blended. The result is atomic heritage attraction combining, on the one hand, a fascination with scientific future utopias of the past, and on the other hand, a heightened sense of invisible or delayed radioactive danger. However, the sense of danger does not contain a repelling message of actual, substantial, and acute risks; instead, the attraction derives from a tension between the site's present demonstrable safety versus underlying dread of its historical risks—the delayed danger just provides a precise level of adventurous thrill. In some ways it might resemble the excitement of the physicists and engineers who originally populated the early urban reactors, in the societal context of their time.

What are not part of the atomic heritage attraction are the dis-localized actual dangers; that is, the radioactive substances moved elsewhere, out of sight. The forest where CP-1/CP-2 was buried; the temporary and controversial depositories of radioactive waste from the F-1 site; and the leftovers of R1, technically invisibilized by being stored hundreds of kilometres away: These materially connected sites of continuous contamination originating from the early urban reactors show another, much less attractive, story.

The authors thank Paul Josephson, Arne Kaijser, Tatiana Kasperski, Sarah May, and Andrei Stsiapanau for their help and valuable comments on earlier versions of this chapter.

References

AHF. (2018). *Atomic Heritage Foundation*. Retrieved from www.atomicheritage.org/

Amoore, L., & Hall, A. (2010). Border theatre: On the arts of security and resistance. *Cultural Geographies, 17*(3), 299–319.

Arkhangelsky, N. V., Cherepnin, Yu., Gabaraev, B. A., Khmelshchikov, V. V., Kuznetsov, Yu. N., & Tretiyakov, I. T. (2004, October 5–8). *Current trends in and prospects for development of Russian research reactors*. Proceedings of the Third Eurasian Conference: Nuclear Science and its Application. Tashkent, pp. 19–30.

Black, R. (2011, November 25). Nuclear power "gets little public support worldwide". *BBC News*. Retrieved from www.bbc.co.uk/news/science-environment-15864806

Boal, I. A. (2003). Ground zero: Henry Moore's Atom piece at the University of Chicago. In J. Beckett & F. Russel (Eds), *Henry Moore: Critical essays* (pp. 221–256). Aldershot: Ashgate.

Boudia, S., & Soubiran, S. (2013). Scientists and their cultural heritage: Knowledge, politics and ambivalent relationships. *Studies in History and Philosophy of Science Part A, 44*(4), 643–651.

CCHAL. (1971). *Summary of information on the site of the first self-sustaining controlled nuclear chain reaction*. Chicago, IL: Commission on Chicago Historical and Architectural Landmarks.

Charlesworth, M. (2013). Types of gardens. In S. Bending (Ed.), *A cultural history of gardens: In the Age of Enlightenment* (pp. 51–72). London: Bloomsbury.

CHM. (2018). *The history of the Dounreay Nuclear Research establishment*. Caithness Horizons Museum. Retrieved from www.caithnesshorizonsmuseum.com/the-history-of-the-dounreay-nuclear-research-establishment/

Dark tourism. (2018). Retrieved from www.dark-tourism.com/

Dawson, J. (1996). *Eco-nationalism: Anti-nuclear activism and national identity in Russia, Lithuania and Ukraine*. Durham, NC: Duke University Press.

Fjæstad, M. (2000). *Sveriges första kärnreaktor: från teknisk prototyp till vetenskapligt instrument*. Stockholm: SKI.

128 Storm, Krohn Andersson, and Rindzevičiūtė

Forgan, S. (2003). Atoms in wonderland. *History and Technology, 19*(3), 177–196.

Handberg, L. (2008). R1ro, som i retro: Från experimentreaktor till experimentscen. *Dædalus: Tekniska museets årsbok. Årg. 76*, 122–137.

Harrison, R. (2013). *Heritage: Critical approaches.* Abingdon: Routledge.

Hewlett, R. G., & Anderson, O. E., Jr. (1962). *The new world, 1939/1946: A history of the United States Atomic Energy Commission, vol. I.* University Park, PA: The Pennsylvania State University Press.

Holloway, D. (1994). *Stalin and the bomb: The Soviet Union and atomic energy, 1939–1956.* New Haven, CT: Yale University Press.

Hooper, G., & Lennon, J. J. (2017). *Dark tourism: Practice and interpretation.* Abingdon: Routledge.

IAEA. (2018). *Research reactor database.* International Atomic Energy Agency. Retrieved from https://nucleus.iaea.org/RRDB/RR/ReactorSearch.aspx?filter=0

Interfax. (2011, March 17). *Kurchatovskie reaktory nikomu ne ugrazhaiut. Interfax.* Retrieved from www.interfax.ru/russia/181701

Iudina, A. (2016, December 27). *Otkryt muzei v chest' iadernogo reaktora F-1v NITs 'Kurchatovskii institut'.* Retrieved from www.scientificrussia.ru

Josephson, P. (1996). Atomic-powered communism: Nuclear culture in the postwar USSR. *Slavic Review, 55*(2), 297–324.

Josephson, P. (2005). *Red atom: Russia's nuclear power program from Stalin to today.* Pittsburgh, PA: Pittsburgh University Press.

Katzive, D. H. (1973). Henry Moore's nuclear energy: The genesis of a monument. *Art Journal, 32*(3), 284–288.

Krohn Andersson, F. (2012). *Kärnkraftverkets poetik: Begreppsliggöranden av svenska kärnkraftverk 1965–1973.* Stockholm: Stockholms Universitet.

Kuznetsov, V. M. (2002). *Bezopasnost' iadernykh issledovatel'skikh ustanovok Rossiiskoi Federatsii.* Retrieved from www.seu.ru/programs/atomsafe/books/Kuznecov/Doclad3.htm

Larin, I. (2007). Reaktor F-1 byl i ostaetssia pervym. *Nauka i zhizn', 8.* Retrieved from https://mipt.ru/dppe/science_articles/reactor_F-1.php

Larsson, K.-E. (1981). Kärnreaktorn R1—ett stycke högteknologisk pionjärhistoria. *Dædalus: Tekniska museets årsbok. Årg. 50*, 105–120.

Larsson, K.-E. (1987). Kärnkraftens historia i Sverige. *Kosmos, 64*, 121–161.

Larsson, K.-E. (2008). Ett gyllene årtionde—1950-talet i retrospekt. *Daedalus: Tekniska museets årsbok. Årg. 76*, 23–47.

Laucht, C. (2012). Atoms for the people: The Atomic Scientists' Association, the British state and nuclear education in the Atom Train exhibition, 1947–1948. *British Journal for the History of Science, 45*(4), 591–608.

Lindström, S. (1991). Hela nationens tacksamhet: Svensk forskningspolitik på atomenergiområdet 1945–1956 (Dissertation). Statsvetenskapliga institutionen, Stockholms Universitet.

Logan, W. S., & Reeves, K., (Eds). (2009). *Places of pain and shame: Dealing with "difficult heritage".* Abingdon: Routledge.

Macdonald, S. (2009). *Difficult heritage: Negotiating the Nazi past in Nuremberg and beyond.* London: Routledge.

Macdonald, S. (2015). Is "difficult heritage" still "difficult"? *Museum International, 67*(1–4), 6–22.

Molella, A. (2003). Exhibiting atomic culture: The view from Oak Ridge. *History and Technology, 19*(3), 211–26.

Urban nuclear reactors and security theatre 129

Morozova, S., Buras, M., Mikheenkov, A., Sviridov, A., & Kharat'ian, K. (2012). (Eds.) *Politekh*. Moscow: Fond razvitiia Politekhnicheskogo muzeia.

Moscow Manege. (2015). *"70 let atomnoi otrasli: Tsepnaia reaktsiia uspekha"* ("70 years of the nuclear industry: Chain reaction of success"). Exhibition held at the Moscow Manege, 1–29 September 2015. Moscow City Department of Culture/Rostatom.

NDA. (2007). *Calder Hall nuclear power station feasibility study*. Nuclear Decommissioning Authority. Retrieved from https://tools.nda.gov.uk/publication/nda-calder-hall-nuclear-power-station-feasibility-study-2007/

Ozharovskii, A. (2012, 18 April). *Kurchatovskii institut: moshchnost' dozy gamma-izlucheniia v norme, no avarii ne iskliucheny*. Bellona. Retrieved from http://bellona.ru/2012/04/18/kurchatovskij-institut-moshhnost-dozy/

Pershagen, B. (2017). *Blågul atom: Sveriges väg till fossilfri elproduktion*. Fri tanke.

Rhodes, R. (1988). *The making of the bomb*. London: Penguin.

Rindzevičiūtė, E. (2016). Nuclear energy in Russia: From future technology to cultural heritage. *The Bridge*, 6(2), 15–20.

Schmid, S. (2015). *Producing power*. Cambridge, MA: MIT Press.

Schneier, B. (2003). *Beyond fear: Thinking sensibly about security in an uncertain world*. Berlin: Springer.

Schneier, B. (2007, January 25). In praise of security theater. *Wired*. Retrieved from www.wired.com/2007/01/in-praise-of-security-theater/

Schneier, B. (2009, December 29). Is aviation security mostly for show? *CNN*. Retrieved from http://edition.cnn.com/2009/OPINION/12/29/schneier.air.travel.security.theater/index.html

Seaborg, G. T. (1977). *History of Met Lab section C-I, April, 1942 to April, 1943*. Lawrence Berkeley Laboratory Report PUB112. Berkley: University of California.

Shvarts, I. (1992, October 25). Iadernaia svalka nash dom rodnoi. *Kommersant*. Retrieved from www.kommersant.ru/doc/186540

Storm, A. (2014). *Post-industrial landscape scars*. New York: Palgrave Macmillan.

Tafvelin Heldner, M., Dahlström Rittsél, E., & Lundgren, P. (2008). *Ågesta: Kärnkraft som kulturarv*. Stockholm: Tekniska museet, Stockholms läns museum, Länsstyrelsen i Stockholms län.

UNESCO. (2018). *World heritage list*. United Nations Educational, Scientific, and Cultural Organization. Retrieved from https://whc.unesco.org/en/list/

US DoE. (1978). *Formerly utilized MED/AEC sites remedial action program. Radiological survey of Site A, Palm Park Forest Preserve, Chicago, Illinois*. Washington, DC: United States Department of Energy. Retrieved from www.osti.gov/servlets/purl/6869820

US DoE. (2017). *Fact sheet Site A/Plot M, Illinois, decommissioned reactor site*. Grand Junction, CO: United States Department of Energy, Office of Legacy Management. Retrieved from www.lm.doe.gov/sitea_plotm/Sites.aspx

Voinova, S., Verny, A., Zenkova, Y., Strelnikova, N., & Yasitsishina, Y. (2015). *Principles of display structuring in the modern corporate museum and the use of multimedia in the display on the example of the Kurchatov Institute museum*. II International Conference Corporate Museums Today on the 70th Anniversary of the Nuclear Industry (pp. 115–119). Moscow: Boslen.

Part III
Securing urban heritage in time and space

8 Fences and defences
Matters of security in City Park, Budapest

Juli Székely

Budapest's City Park (Városliget)—formerly known as Ökrösdűlő, then City Forest—is in all probability one of the most multifaceted heritage sites in Central Europe. Once a marshland on the outskirts of the city, during the 19th century it gained significance in a double sense. On the one hand, this desolate area was redeveloped as the first urban public park in Europe, and as such began to function as a prominent green area. On the other hand, with the creation of the UNESCO World Heritage sites of Andrássy Avenue and Heroes' Square, it was turned into a central place of culture and entertainment. While several of the park's inner areas are now protected by heritage law, it has also become "the living room of Budapest" (Liget Budapest+, 2014) among the city's residents, including for the author.

Even though the history of City Park could easily be narrated through the various (mis)uses of the park itself, lately the question of who has the right to the place (Lefebvre, 1996) returned with a new élan. There was no doubt that the park—with its cracked sidewalks and overcrowded areas—needed renovation, but ordinary visitors witnessed the beginning of another story. A growing number of prefabricated fences appeared. One of these held an oblique board into the sky showing a fabulous building with wonderful clouds. Another presented an image of an ethereal structure with trees in the background: "The grove is to be renewed", we read. However, in reality, the planks are about to fall apart, the posters are already worn, and there is even a mysterious message attached to the fence that asks: "Are there any more cordons?" There is now a tangible tension within City Park.

In 2016 the park was not only redefined as a construction site for an urban mega project but, as a result, also began to function as a demonstration site. The Liget Budapest Project, which envisions a museum quarter within the territory of City Park, became one of the most debated development plans in Budapest. The park remains a conflict zone in which the parallel and permanent presence of security guards and grove defenders dominates, who all try to protect the same area through fences and barricades. City Park—also occasionally referred to as the Hungarian Gezi Park[1]—now represents a Central European episode in the history of urban

134 *Juli Székely*

Figure 8.1 Hacking the advertisement of the Liget Budapest Project. © Juli Szekely.

redevelopment projects that have led to urban protests (e.g. Kaufer, 2016; Illés, cited in Horváth, 2016).

The history of European urban public spaces records a complex interplay between openness and fortification. As Molotch and Coe (2015a, p. 1) argued, "Cities are populated by mechanisms of security. [...] The beginning of cities is virtually synonymous with the rise of apparatuses for exclusion and collective inclusion, the ancient city walls being the prominent exemplar". Although the issue of security—understood as a repertoire of control—is indeed essentially linked to urban life, the current experience of security regimes gave yet another stimulus to scholarly studies (e.g. Bell, 2011; Simon, 2007; Wacquant, 2008; 2010). These discussions, which lately talk about the "militarization of urban space" (Davis, 1992), the "culture of control" (Garland, 2001) or the trend of a "new punitiveness" (Pratt et al., 2005) address political, social, and economic practices while leaving the aspect of materiality largely unexamined. However, as Molotch and Coe (2015a, p. 5) emphasized, "security involves the whole 'world' in which it resides", which necessitates the close examination of "people", "ideas" *and* "things" together. Reintroducing the aspect of materiality to scholarly thought, they made a radical call to turn our attention towards the objects of urban security. Following their line of thought, this chapter discusses how matters of security have changed throughout the history of City Park.

In order to understand how the first supposedly public park in Europe became synonymous with a battleground between inclusion and exclusion, the chapter is framed by a comparative analysis. Within the framework of this comparison, the initial conditions of City Park, discussed through Heinrich Nebbien's development plan (1815) and the Hungarian Millennial Exhibition (1896), are examined alongside current developments as provoked by the master plan for the Liget Budapest Project (under construction). Throughout the chapter, the seeming contrast between 19th- and 21st-century practices are thoroughly re-examined through the approach introduced by Molotch and Coe (2015a, 2015b). Focusing on the triple notion of people, ideas, and things, the various sections of the chapter first study the primary actors of securitization; second, their vision of (in)accessibility; and third, the artefacts themselves as they enforce or facilitate other actors' behaviours. Ultimately, the three sections shed light on how objects of security are also embedded in a wider context of political structures and social relations.

Actors of security

According to Molotch and Coe (2015a, p. 1),

> Deliberately or by happenstance, the presence of large numbers of diverse people in small spaces opens the way for collision. People need to be allocated to particular spaces in specific ways, either by force or guidance through more general manoeuvre.

Similarly to the fact that "urbanism entails security", the issue of security is not a simple "add-on" in the case of the construction of gardens (Molotch & Coe, 2015a, p. 1). Planners are inevitably also the primary actors of security.

The transformation of City Park from an abandoned place into one of the most significant sites within the region was first and foremost brought about through a plan by the Embellishment Commission, founded in 1808 by Archduke Joseph, the Palatine of Hungary and the official representative of the king. In 1805 Joseph (cited in Siklóssy, 1931) emphasized in a letter to Franz Joseph I that:

> experiences in the past, but most of all in the present revealed that the borough council of the town of Pest—partly as a result of its tasks piled up, partly because of the impotence, ignorance or egoism of particular members—not only fails to contribute to the beautification and regulation of the city, but also prevents the improvements attempted, or wastes a significant amount of money without any profits. [...] Being aware of these experiences and examples, I cannot suggest trusting the borough

136 *Juli Székely*

council of the city with the accomplishments of recent matters. I believe that an Embellishment Commission needs to be established, which will be independent from the borough council of the city.

With the aim of transforming Pest into one of the most important cities of the Austrian Monarchy, the Embellishment Commission was indeed established with a double sense of independence. On the one hand, the committee—whose members included an architect, an engineer, a bricklayer, a carpenter, the chief of police, moreover three elected councillors, and citizens—had relative freedom over the execution of its own projects. On the other hand, the persons commissioned no longer had to be responsible to a single private client (which was still predominantly the case during that time) but only to the Embellishment Commission. Yet, since the commission had some reporting obligations to Palatine Joseph, one also suspects that the idea of independence could not be realized to its fullest extent. This impression is also underlined by the very timing of City Park project itself: Even though the development plan for the City Forest occupied only 24th place on the commission's list of tasks, in 1813 it announced a competition for the establishment of a public park—a plan very much dear to the heart of Palatine Joseph.[2] Thus, most certainly, Joseph as a representative of political authority did have some influence on the work of the commission that signified primarily, but not exclusively, the "knowledge-based authority" (Brint, 1990, p. 363) of experts.

This condition was also reinforced by Heinrich Nebbien's winning application of 1816, which put forward the idea of transforming the area of City Park into a "Volksgarten" (Nebbien, 1981). As Nehring (1985, p. 270) argued:

> This initiative show[ed] how in the early 19th century, bourgeois consciousness in the form of civic pride was consolidated inside the town community and linked to the idea that projects, for which citizens themselves could be held responsible, should be taken away from the town administration.

As many authors emphasized (e.g. Gyáni, 1994; Nehring, 1985; Ligetfalvi & Majkó, 2017), in contrast to other European gardens of that time, which in general were formerly owned by aristocrats, City Park was meant to be developed by the city (represented by the Embellishment Commission) for the city, on its own land and at its own expense. The budget—which was initially set at 700,000 forints, but later decreased to 300,000 forints after omitting certain features from the plan—was partly raised by the public: Besides Heinrich Nebbien foregoing his own prize of 200 forints and taking on the commission pro bono, a further 45,000 forints was 'crowd funded', among which Palatine Joseph himself gave approximately 6,000 forints, the bourgeoisie approximately 27,000, and the aristocrats approximately 12,000.

Fences and defences: City Park of Budapest   137

These distinctive features, as social historian Gyáni (1994, p. 89) argued, also mean that throughout the 19th century and even up to the present day, City Park was and has been the only public park in Budapest that can be compared to other well-known European urban gardens such as Hyde Park and Regent's Park in London or the Tiergarten in Berlin.

In contrast to the primacy of experts in the development plan for City Park, the project of the Hungarian Millennial Exhibition appeared as a political project par excellence of the Austro-Hungarian Empire. Even though—as reflected in the newspaper articles of that time (Vezsenyi, 2011)—there was a general social interest in celebrating the millennial anniversary of Hungary's foundation, it was the Hungarian Parliament that officially took up the issue. After consulting the Hungarian Academy of Sciences about the exact date of the Hungarian Settlement, in 1890 Parliament set the date for the celebration in 1895 and also entrusted the prime minister, and the ministers of education, finance, and trade, with the preparations for the programme. In 1891, Minister of Trade Gábor Baross presented their suggestions to the Council of Ministers and, as a result, the Parliament enacted a law in 1892 that once again, now in a juristic sense, reinforced the 1895 organization of the Hungarian Millennial Exhibition in City Park, which was subsequently postponed to 1896 due to the long-running preparations for various subprojects.[3] Also in 1892, Parliament ordered the establishment of the Hungarian Millennial Committee, to be headed by Kálmán Széll (formerly minister of finance, later prime minister) and including members from the Ministry of Trade, Ministry of Finance, and Ministry of Agriculture. It was this—very much political—body that announced an application for the architectural design plan of the Hungarian Millennial Exhibition in 1893 and that also chose the winning application, combining the design plans of Flóris Korb, Kálmán Giergl, Albert Shickedanz, Károly Gerster, Géza Mirkovszky, and Károly Neuchloss with a budget of approximately 10 million forints.[4]

If the original development plan for City Park and the organization of the Hungarian Millennial Exhibition could primarily be understood through the domination of expert or political knowledge, the present-day Liget Budapest Project is peculiar because it mobilizes a complex web of political *and* professional actors. This duality was already present at the very origin of the project: While Museum of Fine Art Director László Baán—along with aesthete Péter György—was a long-time proponent of combining the collections of the Hungarian National Gallery and the Museum of Fine Arts, the actual idea of a museum quarter was first articulated by István Tarlós in 2009, at that time a candidate and now the Mayor of Budapest. In 2011 László Baán and Undersecretary of Culture Géza Szőcs jointly announced a plan to transform the area stretching from the Castle District to Heroes' Square into a 'cultural axis', which covered approximately 10–15 development plans, including the idea of a 'Grove of Museums'. In 2012, Baán and László L. Simon (Szőcs's successor) narrowed down the idea of the Andrássy

138 *Juli Székely*

Quarter to the development plan for a Museums Quarter that at its core envisioned uniting the collections of the Hungarian National Gallery and the Museum of Fine Arts. In 2013 these preparations culminated in the project—by then branded as Liget Budapest—being enacted by the Hungarian government.[5] On the one hand, the state approved the various elements of the development plan, most importantly the joint building of the New National Gallery and the Ludwig Museum, the Museum of Ethnography, the House of Hungarian Music, the Museum of Hungarian Photography, and the Museum of Hungarian Architecture.[6] On the other, it also decreed the establishment of Városliget, Ltd., a special-purpose vehicle run by a three-member board of directors comprising former State Opera House Managing Director István Mozsár (who also served as CEO), Museum of Fine Arts Director Baán László, and Századvég Foundation Deputy Chairman Kristóf Szalay-Bobrovniczky. In subsequent years the state-owned Városliget, Ltd., announced various applications, including a competition on the inner structure of the Museum Quarter (2013), an international tender on the architectural design plans of the buildings (February 2014, October 2014, January 2016), and a call for landscape architecture plans for City Park (2015). In all these cases, the winners were chosen by a panel of (inter)national experts.[7]

This seeming balance between expert and political authorities, however, was disturbed by several factors. First of all, the Liget Budapest Project repeatedly faced the problem of high turnover among team members, which art historian Edina Nagy (2015) even labelled as the soap opera of Hungary. Not only did Péter György, who served as an official consultant to Baán between 2015 and 2016, abrogate his contract due to professional disagreement, but in 2017 Mozsár also left Városliget, resulting in Undersecretary of State Györgyi Lengyel being affiliated as a new member, and in Baán becoming the new chief executive officer. Secondly, throughout the preparations for the project 'personal taste' repeatedly came to play a role. While in 2011 Szőcs's idea to reutilize Andrássy Avenue as a horse road did not gain serious consideration, in 2015 proposals to realize the Museum of Hungarian Photography and the Museum of Hungarian Architecture were rejected by the government, reportedly because Prime Minister Viktor Orbán, along with the already mentioned László L. Simon, did not like the winning plans (e.g. Botos, 2015; Hamvay, 2015; Schultz, 2015). Thirdly, even though—in contrast to the modus operandi of the Embellishment Committee and the Hungarian Millennial Committee—the Liget Budapest Project seemingly separated the commissioner from the decision-making body, a conflict of interest did emerge. Baán who, first as a government commissioner and then as a ministerial commissioner was personally responsible for the direction of the Liget Budapest Project, not only functioned as a member of Városliget announcing the applications, but also served as the head of the various committees deciding the winning applications. In this sense, Baán himself represented the essence of the Liget Budapest Project, in which the distinct role of experts and politicians dissolved and intermingled.

Fences and defences: City Park of Budapest 139

Within these complications, the budget for the Liget Budapest Project had already increased from 3.7 billion (2011) to 230 billion HUF (2017).

While the example of City Park clearly shows that investments of these kinds are always—even if to different extents—political projects, it also demonstrated that politics became ever closer to the state. This move is also unambiguously illustrated by the appropriation of City Park itself: Originally belonging to the city, during the time of the Hungarian Millennial Exhibition, Pest 'loaned' the property to the government; however within the framework of the Liget Budapest Project the Hungarian government decreed the transfer of ownership rights from the local government of the 14th district, the municipality of Budapest, and the Hungarian state to Városliget, Ltd., for 99 years. The state became a primary actor of security.

Ideas of (in)accessibility

The argument according to which gardens can be understood as symbolic projects of urban politics (e.g. Hindagneu-Sotelo, 2010; Callahan, 2017) also entails that, similarly to cities, gardens "reflect decisions about what— and who—should be visible and what should not, on concepts of order and disorder, and on uses of aesthetic power" (Zukin, 1995, p. 7). Examining the various understandings of (in)accessibility, City Park also reveals different ideas of the 'public' in the 19th and 21st centuries.

For a brief moment at the beginning of the 19th century, City Park held the possibility of integrating the various classes of society. In his concept, Nebbien followed the English approach to garden design, which had both stylistic and philosophical consequences. Nebbien's development plan— featuring the entrance of a colonnade, a rondeau, a lake area with two islands, and an amphitheatre—not only rejected the idea of French gardens based on rigid, regular, and symmetrical forms, but also dissociated itself from the dominant park notion of the 18th century, which had emphasized the "contemplative and edifying recreation of the individual" (Nebbien 1981). As English landscape gardens—influenced by the French Revolution—became the proponents of liberal philosophy and Enlightenment, there was a growing concern—articulated most importantly by garden theoretician Hirschfeld (2001)—that parks ought to function as social metaphors, in which every social class would meet and compound. The main goal of Nebbien's design was—as Nehring (1985, p. 270) showed—to build a 'Volkspark', which was not "opened out of magnanimity towards the public by those in power", but which was "to be the immediate possession and creation of the people". Nebbien wanted to create a place that would provide "common recreation in the fresh air" for "all classes of inhabitants" (Nehring, 1985, p. 269).

This concept of an all-inclusive space was also repeated during the time of the Hungarian Millennial Exhibition, when organizers were eager to create an image based on the notion of peace. Not only did the political elite announce *treuga dei*[8] for the period of the exhibition, suspending all

140   *Juli Székely*

political debates between the political parties, but the city of Budapest was also branded as a 'Fairy City' ('Tündérváros'). In this fairy-like city, magic was indeed operational: With a wide range of spectacles, such as Captain Louis Godard's hot-air balloon, the various social classes and nationalities were shown to live in peaceful cohabitation with each other. The gift of a golden watch, presented to the millionth visitor (Róza Gáspár, a Szekler woman married to a joiner) unambiguously described this idea, which assumed common ground between the various social and ethnic groups.

A tell-tale image of this harmony could also be found on "Nationality Street" in the "Ethnographic Village", in which the art and culture of several minority groups (e.g. Saxons, Swabs, Serbs, Romanians, Bulgarians, Slovaks, Wends, and Roma) were displayed alongside those of Hungarians (e.g. Lowlanders, Transdanubians, Highlanders, Szeklers). Contemporary photographs show an imaginary village of 24 houses together with a church, a school, and a parish hall, in which families of various origins posed in national costumes introducing their own traditions and customs. As a visitor proudly observed, the street reflected "the ardent desire of the nation that the different races inhabiting this country may always live in peace and harmony side by side, united in the love of the common fatherland" (Laurencic, cited in Turda, n.d.). The magnitude of this sensation of peace in all probability culminated in the so-called Negersdorf, in which 250 African people were showcased for a 50-penny entrance fee. The weekly *Vasárnapi Újság* (which promoted both the Hungarian language and a national spirit) reported that

> life is going on here, even though it is quite a lively life, because these happy Negros are joking and cheering each other. There is no trace of enmity or dispute. This race is gentle, peace-loving; and the colony is also well organized. There is nowhere a bad odour among so many wild people! This is really amazing. They do not lack anything; they are in a good shape, they are satisfied, and, what a wonder, they do not beg!
> (D.G.A, 30 August 1896, p. 575).

While the image of the different nationalities represented alongside Hungarians suggested conflict-free cohabitation, the sight of African people evoked a colonial imagination tranquilized. The various images of 'others' were domesticated and brought under control.

A certain kind of notion of wonder similarly returns in the case of the Liget Budapest Project. The official blog states: "Equal access—this is one of the basic principles of renewing City Park. It is to be understood regarding the park, as well as the public institutions" (Ilsemann, 2017). When reading further, the text also reveals that the "Goal of the planners is that no-one will be disadvantaged because of living with disabilities" (Ilsemann, 2017). Disability indeed seems to be a central concern. In one post on the Liget Budapest Facebook page (2017) we read about the project's "green,

Fences and defences: City Park of Budapest   141

child-friendly and smart" planning, through which "inclusive playgrounds" will be built:

> Kids with disabilities will have an opportunity to discover the same games, to meet the same stimuli and to share their experiences with their fellow kids typically developing. This not only gives the promise for children with disabilities to equalize their chances, but it also helps healthy children to develop the skills of empathy, social awareness and responsibility as early as possible.

Evoking the Leibnizian mantra of the "best of all possible worlds", we not only learn that dogs visiting City Park will have "the best of their time" with the opening of a 'dog fun park', but we are also assured that coal-tits are 'joyful', and that a European oak, called Balthazar, is pleased with the redevelopment plan of City Park (Liget Budapest, 2017).

> At Balthazar there is an eventful and mysterious life, it hosts many small creatures with whom he has been friends for many generations. This is the case with the grove's jays and squirrels, who think Balthazar has the best acorns in the neighbourhood. His distant relative, the Major Oak in Sherwood, gave shelter to Robin Hood, whereas in the hollow of Balthazar there are happy coal-tits living. Balthazar followed the construction of pavilions with pleasure, and meanwhile he also discussed several issues with the secret fairies and goblins of the grove [...] Balthazar knows that in the renewed City Park we pay special attention to the protection of old trees. Similarly to last year, this year we take care of nearly a hundred ancient trees so that they can have a healthy life for many more years.

It seems there will be unambiguous harmony between humans (with or without disabilities), nature, and animals.

Nebbien's development plan, the Hungarian Millennial Exhibition, and the Liget Budapest Project all regarded City Park as a potential tourist 'bubble' (Urry, 1999). While Nebbien emphasized the "personal attraction that such a park would represent for Hungary" (Nebbien cited in Nehring, 1985, p. 271), Bálint (1897, pp. 8–9) recalled how the Hungarian Millennial Exhibition hoped to "transform Hungary into the centre of Europe for a time", also inviting Budapest into "the league of world cities". The same endeavours were also repeated in the mission statement of the Liget Budapest Project (Liget Budapest Project, n.d.).

> In various countries of the world, there are museum building complexes. Among them are the Museumsquartier in Vienna, the Museumplein in Amsterdam, the Museumsinsel in Berlin, the Kunstareal in Munich, the Museumsufer in Frankfurt, or the National Mall of Washington, which

142 *Juli Székely*

all are world famous museum quarters functioning as major tourist attractions for their cities. The purpose of the Liget Budapest Project is to transform the City Park into an internationally attractive tourist destination with unique complexity and quality in Europe.

In all cases, the plans gave the impression that they were attempting to navigate between local and global demands: Between the vision of a 'public' park accessible for all of its citizens and the dream of attracting a huge number of tourists.

(Dis)playing security

Efforts to rearrange space in a city easily lead to conflicts among groups who concurrently emerge as claiming that particular space (Zukin, 1995, p. 24). One way of approaching this phenomenon—as Molotch and Coe (2015a, 2015b, p. 15) argued—leads exactly through the study of urban security objects that reveal "how different groups and interests seek to appropriate and (re)purpose their environment". No wonder that—in contrast to Nebbien's all-inclusive plan, the idea of peace invented by the Hungarian Millennial Exhibition or the rhetoric of equal access emphasized by the Liget Budapest Project—objects of security in City Park mediate another kind of image.

Focusing on the everyday usages of City Park during the 19th century, a kind of invisible wall emerges. As Gyáni (1994, p. 97) unambiguously showed, daily practices, instead of uniting, enforced the very separation of the various social groups from each other.

> The efforts of the upper classes to separate themselves from the lower classes, even in recreational public spaces, precluded any democratic mingling. To enforce separation, the strategy of appropriation was applied. Other techniques were also employed, especially where exclusive availability could not be established. In such cases, particularly where the Városliget was concerned, a strategy of division or distribution prevailed. Briefly, this entailed a rigid social topography within the confines of the park. A 'recreational segregation' effectively channelled the movements of the park's population.

At the entrance of City Park a fountain functioned as a division line where—as a contemporary witness described (cited in Gyáni, 1994, p. 98)—"the gentlefolk" tended towards Stefánia Drive, "the middle classes" moved towards the tiny islands of the lake, and "the common people in their best clothes" headed to the firework square. This strategy of appropriation and internal division essentially prevented any confluences of the various social groups while also requiring limited intervention by the police authorities.

Fences and defences: City Park of Budapest   143

Similarly to the daily uses of the park, during the actual event of the Hungarian Millennial Exhibition—secured by several hundred police and soldiers—a certain kind of disguised control was operational, also exposing the artificial nature of the image of peace. Similarly to Godard's balloon, which fell victim to a storm during the exhibition, the idea of 'national unity' turned out to be a wishful dream. Preparations for the Hungarian Millennial Exhibition were already preceded by a public outcry prompted by the prospect of removing approximately eight hundred trees, but since the government acquired utilization rights only under the conditions of erecting temporary buildings on the grounds of City Park and also restoring the original conditions afterwards, these worries did not provoke serious demonstrations; instead, protests centred much more on the ideological message of the exhibition.[9]

Contemporary accounts explicitly show that not even the idea of a *treuga dei* was met with unanimous enthusiasm: The opposition within the Parliament, as well as the leadership of the Social Democratic Party gave voice to its criticism (Tarr, 1979):

> In 1896 the millennium [...] will be celebrated with great lustre and splendour by our bourgeoisie. [...] The most influential circles use all their power to prove that Hungary is a cultural state. And while they boast of richness and splendour to the world [...], no-one will ever be reminded that all this became realized by the diligence of the working class [...]. The ruling class claims that people do not feel the need for rights, that they are satisfied with their bondage. Hungarian people, show that they are lying because they are afraid of your strength, show that you are claiming your rights because you will not endure this situation any more, show that you will not rest until your rights have been acquired!

Although the ruling party—even if through some compromises and threats—finally managed to agree terms with its opposition, and the Social Democratic Party was also persuaded out of the above cited intention of affray, mutual agreement could not be reached with the political leaders of the biggest nationalities. In contrast to modern nation-states that often represent themselves as nationally homogeneous, Hungary—being part of the larger union of the Austro-Hungarian Empire—was (internally) multi-national. Representatives of Romanians, Serbs, and Slovaks decided to boycott the Hungarian Millennial Exhibition, which they regarded as the celebration of Hungarian nationalist hegemony:

> We regard the celebration and exhibition [...] as a delusion showcased to Europe. This image wants to prove that the nationalities of Hungary live in peace and agreement with each other, but in fact the majority of Hungary's population is dissatisfied. [...] We, Romanians, Serbs, and

144 *Juli Székely*

Slovaks [...], ceremonially and firmly note that we do actually exist [...] as independent nationalities [...]. Once our desire is fulfilled, and we can see that Hungary is put on a basis in accordance with its natural ethnical and historical conditions, where the equality of nationalities would indeed be taken seriously, [...] where Hungary would not be a country of only one tribe, but the old and respectable "Hungaria", then we would also be gladly celebrating the thousandth year of existence of the Hungarian state. Yet, the way they want to celebrate the Millennium today, we see in it an attack against our national existence, a praise of our repression, thus we protest against such a celebration.

(Protest of the Executive Committee of the Nationalities' Congress Concerning the Millennial Celebrations 1896)

Then again, beyond these articulations of discontent, minority groups did not significantly disturb the festivities either. Still, a certain feeling of being 'out of place' was tangible, which was perfectly articulated during a visit by King Franz Joseph I to the Nationality Street, when a Hungarian peasant answered the question of whether he belonged there, saying: "Luckily, only while the Millennium lasts, then I can go home" (Tarr, 1979).

Even though the simulation of peace certainly resulted in the absence of any kind of visible scandals, the Hungarian Millennial Exhibition did operate with a distorted image of national unity. In this sense, during the 19th century, material politics of securitization manifested itself much more in hidden security objects. Nevertheless, looking at the photograph of the Roma tents exhibited on the Nationality Street, one also catches sight of a chain functioning as a cordon, dividing the Roma and the visitors.

If the Hungarian Millennial Exhibition signalled a time of hidden control, the Liget Budapest Project can be described through very explicit objects of securitization. In 2016, while starting to implement the Liget Budapest Project, Városliget installed new maps throughout City Park that, despite accurately marking the various construction sites in the area, nevertheless failed to express the experience of entering the park, which then closely resembled a labyrinth of fences (Figure 8.2).

Within this maze of cordons various actions are taking place. While builders are working on the gradual realization of the vision of the Liget Budapest Project, runners, strollers, and picnickers still try to maintain the everyday life of City Park. In the case of the installed fences, beyond indicating a borderline between urban rehabilitation and urban recreation, they indeed became visible signs of urban securitization and urban protest.

At the beginning of 2016, City Park was almost simultaneously appropriated both by groups of private security guards and protestors. Private security companies were commissioned first to secure the demolition of the former buildings of the HungExpo and the Museum of Transport (Patrol Group, Ltd., and Infinity Forest, Ltd.), then with securing the general construction site of the Liget Budapest Project (Valton Sec, Ltd.). While Patrol

Fences and defences: City Park of Budapest 145

Figure 8.2 Construction site on the grounds of the Liget Budapest Project. © Juli Szekely.

Group and Infinity Forest are usually hired to provide security at football matches, Valton is well-known for securing events close to the ruling Fidesz political party. These (semi?-)private police forces were involved in various conflicts with the diverse groups of politicians, experts, and civilians who after several offline and online protests actually appeared within City Park.[10] This physical presence not only referred to the figure of an occasional protester, but also to 'grove defenders' who in 2018 celebrated the two-year anniversary of their permanent stay in City Park. These demonstrators are far from united, and the grove defenders group alone is divided into three main groups embracing a wide range of inhabitants, from homeless people to middle-class intellectuals. However, in recent years they managed to cooperate several times, repeatedly calling into question many aspects of the "barbaric development plan" (Bardóczi et al., 2014).

The protestors do not dispute the need to rehabilitate the landscape architecture of City Park; however (in contrast to the Hungarian Millennial Exhibition), concerns about the possible reduction of green space came very much to the forefront. Even though Városliget claims that the percentage of green area will increase from 60 to 65 per cent, demonstrators very much fear the opposite.[11] They express growing concerns regarding not only the

146 *Juli Székely*

"arrogant" leaders of the project who might manipulate the numbers, but also about the concentration of several museums in one place that will further intensify the degradation of recreation space in City Park. Even though, in a 2016 interview (Pálos, 2016), Péter György (at that time still an official consultant to Baán) referred sarcastically to "tree fetishism" by his fellow citizens, the severity of the issue is also expressed in the official symbol of the resistance, in which a tree springing from a fist clearly makes the association between nature and power.

With these various actors around, the new maps produced by Városliget, Ltd. similarly fell short in illustrating a double process that significantly changed the image of City Park. On the one hand, we saw "muscle men" employing physical violence, "protests turning into scuffles", security guards "smashing up demonstrations", "protesters building barricades", "hundreds of police invading the camp of grove defenders", "demonstrators demolishing cordons", "mysterious baldies in action", "grove defenders being charged with hooliganism", and "the camp of grove defenders being set on fire".[12] Depending on the political sympathy of the particular news channel, the same events also appeared as "liberals agitating", "leftists creating a tantrum", "grove defenders exciting tensions", "grove defenders creating a drug farm", "grove defenders menacing", "aggressive grove defenders being charged", or "terminating the illegal camping of the grove defenders".[13] From either perspective, the vision of a museum quarter becomes inscribed in the urban space of City Park alongside measures that are usually described as the 'militarization' of public space (Davis, 1992), "governing through crime" (Simon, 2007) or a 'punitive turn' (Pratt et al., 2005).

On the other hand, we also come across various urban interventions that transformed the public space of City Park into a private living-area and hacked its very geography. Besides the appearance of tents and various home supplies such as shelves or mirrors, various walls in City Park became reutilized as a message board when covered in graffiti; László János Beszédes's sculpture of the *Lasso Man* (1928) was reinterpreted as the public memorial of the heroic *"Liget Man"*; one part of the Winston Churchill promenade became referred to as "László Bán blind alley"; and even the construction site of the Museum of Transport was rebranded as a "Marriage Licence Bureau of Árpád Habony" (referring to the scandal of Baán loaning, free of charge, the Museum of Fine Arts building for the informal advisor to the prime minister's wedding). The various urban interventions not only show a strong critique of the mega project supported by the government, but offer the idea of community-led development as an alternative (e.g., Patti & Polyák, 2017), also evoking the philosophy of community gardens (Smith & Kurtz, 2003; Crossan, Cumbers, McMaster, & Shaw, 2016).

Within the framework of this parallel universe of a militarized and alternative environment, encounters between security guards and protesters repeatedly resulted in crossing the 'lines'. While surging over the barriers, fences became defences or simply disappeared. Within these practices of

Fences and defences: City Park of Budapest 147

redefining boundaries, the understanding of the fence was also given another twist by an illegally installed information board that—similarly to a name board in a zoo—defined "*Homo insipiens nudus*", referring to the group of mainly bald security guards:

> Its outward appearance resembles a man, but its lifestyle and character differ to a great extent. Its height can reach 2 meters. Most of them are male. Its nutrition is not very varied; it is based on meat, which is consumed together with proteins and carbohydrates in the form of powder. Their herd lives a night life; sometimes even until the morning they stand in one place. It is hostile to every living creature; without reason, they attack with aggression! Because of this characteristic, it is bred worldwide.

This small urban intervention by a group of prankster artists from the satirical political party known as the Two-Tailed Dog Party unambiguously blurred the lines between who is inside and outside (with security guards portrayed not as controlling access but as a captive species displayed for the public), and ultimately also raised the question of who is the 'other' to be feared.

Conclusion

In 2011, the Hungarian Parliament, in order to determine directions for protecting universal values, enacted a law that differentiated between the categories of the "world heritage site", the "protective belt of the World Heritage site", the "expectant World Heritage site" and the "protective belt of the expectant World Heritage site".[14] City Park in its entirety was listed as a protective belt of the Andrássy Avenue World Heritage site and its historical surroundings. In this sense, even though particular areas of the park— such as the boating lake or Vajdahunyad Castle—were already protected by heritage law, City Park in a legal sense also became a heritage site of overriding importance. So how can the main topic of this book—securing urban heritage—be understood in the case of City Park, which is a site that supposedly protects and is being protected?

The history of City Park—told through the security objects of Heinrich Nebbien's development plan, the Hungarian Millennial Exhibition, and the Liget Budapest Project—involves several tales. As Molotch and Coe (2015a, p. 6) argued,

> Our security objects [...] are marks of collective anxieties and attempted remediation. In effect, they lend themselves to a kind of reverse engineering to discover the forces, large or small, which went into their creation, deployment, and the impacts their presence continues to exact.

148 *Juli Székely*

It is no surprise that the City Park envisioned by Nebbien was never realized: Regulated by either hidden or explicit control, the first urban 'public' park in Europe was always part of a securitization process that was directed against various political, social, and ethnic classes.

At the same time, besides the narration of the various qualities of control, the objects of security also revealed the story of attempts to reinterpret securitization as protection. As Oevermann and Gantner (2019) discuss in the introduction to this book, regarding the complicated relationship between *securing* and *protecting*: City Park also became a metaphor for attempted civil control, in trying to protect the 200-year-old green area of the park. The resistance to the Liget Budapest Project—which could initially mobilize several hundred people—did an important job in offering a vision of alternatives: They sustained a dream of revitalizing democracy, in which open space would indeed become an open social arena. Here, this opening includes a potential to free access to this specific urban heritage site and its symbolic power. However, the number of grove defenders is radically decreasing, and the very small number of demonstrators who remain encamped in City Park are clearly losing space and power. Is the heritage status of City Park in danger?

During 2017 one of the construction workers fought a heroic battle outside the construction site for the Museum of Ethnography. He stood alone, in front of wooden planking several hundred metres long, and gradually—with very precise movements—spray-painted it black. When this performance had already been going on for weeks, I dared to ask security guards what was actually happening. As it turned out, the man was entrusted with painting over graffiti, which indeed largely covered the fence and primarily criticized Prime Minister Viktor Orbán. I am almost convinced that he used spray-paint identical to that used for graffiti. As of today, the planking remains black, but there are visible signs of repainting—most likely due to the appearance of new graffiti. It is as if the fence became a surface of black humour, in which the forces of power and resistance fight for the right of (re)presentation. However, even though we still cannot be sure about the actual realization of the Liget Budapest Project, the black fence certainly does not foretell a very bright story for City Park: While it unambiguously symbolizes a new episode in the park's history, it also appears to mourn something lost.

Notes

1 In 2013 a wave of demonstrations began in Turkey, initially contesting the urban redevelopment plan of Taksim Gezi Park in Istanbul, and later also protesting the government's authoritarian policies.
2 According to Gyáni (1994), the competition, published in the newspaper *Vereinigte Ofner und Pester Zeitung*, was probably the first competition ever held in the history of landscape architecture.

Fences and defences: City Park of Budapest   149

3 Law 1892, Act II: *About the National Exhibition to be Organized in Budapest in the Year of 1895*; and Law 1893, Act III: *About the Covering of the Costs of the National Exhibition.*

4 Besides the main exhibition area in City Park, the Hungarian Millennial Exhibitions include various public and representative architectural spectacles, such as the Andrássy Boulevard, the Franz Joseph (now Liberty) Bridge, the Museum of Applied Arts, the Comedy Theatre of Budapest, and the dome of the Hungarian Parliament. However, since discussion of those related projects would exceed the space available here, I focus only on the site of City Park.

5 Law 2013, Act CCXLII: *About the Renovation and Redevelopment of the City Park*; And Decree 1397/2013: *About the Comprehensive Concept Utilizing the City Park as the Second Phase of the Concept Considering the New National Ensemble of Buildings Containing Public Collections.*

6 Besides these, within the framework of the Liget Budapest Project the following plans are to be realized: A new Circus building; renovation of the Museum of Transport building; creation of the Kitchen of the Hungarian Regions Gastronomic Garden; construction of the Square of Arts; reconstruction of the colonnade based on Heinrich Nebbien's original development plan; establishment of the Knowledge and Experience Centre for Children and Youth; demolition of the old Hungexpo office buildings; the foundation of a visitor and educational centre ('Green Grove'); (re)construction of green areas and playgrounds; renovation of City Park lake; and reconceptualization of traffic within City Park.

7 Members of the jury mostly comprised architects and landscape architects. See www.szepmuveszeti.hu/muzeumliget_hirek/liget-budapest-projekt-nemzetkozi-epiteszeti-tervpalyazat-ot-uj-muzeumi-epuletre-1308 or www.szepmuveszeti.hu/muzeumliget_hirek/eredmenyhirdetes-nyilt-otletpalyazat-a-muzeumi-negyed-epuleteinek-elhelyezesere-1124

8 *Treuga dei* (Truce of God) was a customary wartime practice of suspending hostilities during religious holidays.

9 With the exception of the Vajdahunyad Castle (originally made from cardboard and wood), which between 1904 and 1908 was rebuilt from stone and brick because of its popularity, the various elements indeed disappeared.

10 Besides the repeated protests of various civil, art historical, architectural, urbanistic or environmental organizations on various forums (e.g., the following petitions: www.peticiok.com/kerjuk_ne_vegyen_reszt_a_budapesti_varosliget_tonkreteteleben, https://artportal.hu/magazin/ertelmisegiek-ujabb-akcioja-a-var-es-a-liget-ugyeben/), an independent group of experts (led by architect István Eltér) even elaborated an alternative master plan called Liget Budapest+.

11 Protesters claim that Városliget greatly manipulated the numbers: Besides disregarding the area of Heroes' Square (along with the Museum of Fine Arts and the Budapest Hall of Art), Városliget's calculations included the surface areas of the lake, the predicted grassed 'green roof' areas of future buildings and parking lots.

12 See, e.g., the headlines of the online news portal 444. https://444.hu/tag/varosliget?page=1

13 See, e.g., the headlines of the online news portal 888. https://888.hu/tag-varosliget=7c00c04e98f7581a1024a938a7b59962

14 Law 2011, Act LXXVII. the surface areas of the lake, the predicted grassed 'green roof' areas of future buildings and parking lots; see, e.g., the headlines of

150 *Juli Székely*

the online news portal 444. https:// 444.hu/ tag/varosliget?page=1; see, e.g., the headlines of the online news portal 888. https:// 888.hu/tag- varosliget=7c00c04 e98f7581a1024a938a7b59962; Law 2011, Act LXXVII.

References

Bardóczi, S. et al. (2014). *Kérjük, ne vegyen részt a budapesti Városliget tönkretételében.* Retrieved from www.peticiok.com/kerjuk_ne_vegyen_reszt_a_ budapesti_varosliget_tonkreteteleben

Bálint, Z. (1897). *Az ezredéves kiállítás architektúrája.* Bécs: Schroll Antal és Tsa. Műkiadása.

Bell, E. (2011). *Criminal justice and neoliberalism.* New York, NY: Palgrave.

Botos, T. (2015). *Liget-projekt: nem épül meg a fotó- és az építészeti múzeum.* Retrieved from https://444.hu/2015/10/26/liget-projekt-nem-epul-meg-a-foto-es-az-epiteszeti-muzeum

Brint, S. (1990). Rethinking the policy influence of experts: From general characterizations to analysis of variation. *Sociological Forum, 5*(3), 361–385.

Callahan, W. A. (2017). Cultivating power: Gardens in the global politics of diplomacy, war and peace. *International Political Sociology, 11*(4), 360–379.

Crossan, J., Cumbers, A., McMaster, R., & Shaw, D. (2016). Contesting neoliberal urbanism in Glasgow's community gardens: The practice of DIY citizenship. *Antipode, 48*(4), 937–955.

D. G. A. (1896, August 30). Egy darab Afrika Budapesten. *Vasárnapi Újság.* Retrieved from http://epa.oszk.hu/00000/00030/02219/pdf/02219.pdf

Davis, M. (1992). Fortress Los Angeles. The militarization of urban space. In M. Sorkin (Ed.), *Variations on a theme lark* (pp. 154–180). New York, NY: Hill and Wang.

Garland, D. (2001). *The culture of control: Crime and social order in contemporary society.* Chicago, IL: University of Chicago Press.

Gyáni, G. (1994). Uses and misuses of public space in Budapest: 1873–1914. In T. Bender & C. E. Schorske (Eds.), *Budapest and New York. Studies in metropolitan transformation: 1870–1930* (pp. 85–107). New York, NY: Russell Sage Foundation.

Hamvay, P. (2015). *Nagy pénz, nagy kavarás – Fideszes beljátszmák: Liget vs. Budavár.* Retrieved from http://magyarnarancs.hu/belpol/nagy-penz-nagy-kavaras-94631

Hindagneu-Sotelo, P. (2010). Cultivating questions for a sociology of gardens. *Journal of Contemporary Ethnography, 39*(5), 498–516.

Hirschfeld, C. C. L. (2001). *Theory of garden art.* Philadelphia, PA: University of Pennsylvania Press.

Horváth, B. (2016). *Illés Zoltán: A budapesti Gezi park is kinőhet a városliget i tiltakozásból.* Retrieved from https://444.hu/2016/03/18/illes-zoltan-a-budapesti-gezi-park-is-kinohet-a-varosligeti-tiltakozasbol

Ilsemann. (2017). *Nincs akadály a Liget Projekt után.* Retrieved from http:// ligetbudapest.reblog.hu/nincs-akadaly-a-liget-projekt-utan

Kaufer, V. (2016). *A fák és mi – A #ligetvédők első nagygyűlésűnek margójára.* Retrieved from http://dinamo.blog.hu/2016/03/28/a_fak_es_mi_a_ligetvedok_ elso_nagy_gyulesenek_margojara

Lefebvre, H. (1996). The right to the city. In E. Kofman & E. Lebas (Eds.), *Writings of cities* (pp. 147–159). Cambridge: Blackwell.

Fences and defences: City Park of Budapest   151

Liget Budapest Project. (n.d.). Retrieved from www.intezmenyek.ligetbudapest.org/hu

Liget Budapest+. (2014). *Független szakértői csoport alternatív javaslata.* Retrieved from https://tervlap.hu/cikk/show/id/2686

Liget Budapest. (2017). Retrieved from www.facebook.com/miligetunk/

Ligetfalvi, G., & Majkó, Z. (2017). *Városliget Lexikon.* Budapest: Városháza Kiadó.

Molotch, H., & Coe, M. (2015a). Objects of urban security, part I. In R. Scott & S. Kosslyn (Eds.), *Emerging trends in the social and behavioral sciences.* Hoboken, NJ: Wiley-Blackwell. Retrieved from https://onlinelibrary.wiley.com/browse/book/10.1002/9781118900772/toc

Molotch, H., & Coe, M. (2015b). Objects of urban security, part II. In R. Scott & S. Kosslyn (Eds.), *Emerging trends in the social and behavioral sciences.* Hoboken, NJ: Wiley-Blackwell. Retrieved from https://onlinelibrary.wiley.com/browse/book/10.1002/9781118900772/toc

Nagy, E. (2015). *Csak nézünk, mi történik a ligettel.* Retrieved from https://vs.hu/magazin/osszes/csak-nezunk-mi-tortenik-a-ligettel-0414#!s2

Nebbien, H. (1981). Ungarns Folks-Garten der Koeniglicnen Freystadt Pesth (1816). In D. Nehring (Ed.), *Veröffentlichungen des Finnisch-Ugrischen Seminars an der Universität München (Reihe C, Bd. 11).* München.

Nehring, D. (1985). The landscape architect, Christian Heinrich Nebbien, and his design for the Municipal Park in Budapest. *Journal of Garden History, 5*(3), 261–279.

Oevermann, H. & Gantner, E. (2019, this volume). Introduction. In H. Oevermann & E. Gantner (Eds), *Securing urban heritage: Agents, access, and securitization.* New York, NY: Routledge.

Pálos, M. (2016, July 14). "Elfogadhatatlan, ha tetszik, válóok"—György Péter a Liget projektről. *Magyar Narancs.* Retrieved from http://magyarnarancs.hu/belpol/elfogadhatatlan-ha-tetszik-valook-100092

Patti, D., & Polyák, L. (2017). *Funding the cooperative city.* Vienna: Cooperative City Books.

Pratt, J., Brown, D., Brown, M., & Hallsworth, S. (Eds.) (2005). *The new punitiveness: Trends, theories, perspectives.* Cullompton: Willan Publishing.

Protest of the executive committee of the Nationalities' Congress concerning the Millennial Celebrations. April 30, 1896. Retrieved from http://adatbank.transindex.ro/html/alcim_pdf12431.pdf

Schultz, A. (2015). *Mégsem lesz építészeti- és fotómúzeum a Városligetben.* Retrieved from https://vs.hu/kozelet/osszes/megsem-lesz-epiteszeti-es-fotomuzeum-a-varosligetben-1026

Siklóssy, L. (1931). *A Fővárosi Közmunkák Tanácsa Története. Hogyan épült Budapest (1870–1930).* Budapest: Atheneum.

Simon, J. (2007). *Governing through crime: How the war on crime transformed American democracy and created a culture of fear.* New York, NY: Oxford University Press.

Smith, C. M. & Kurtz, H. E. (2003). Community gardens and politics of scale in New York City. *Geographical Review, 93*(2), 193–212.

Tarr, L. (1979). *Az ezredév.* Budapest: Magvető.

Turda, M. (n.d.). *The idea of national legitimacy in Fin-de-Siècle Hungary.* Retrieved from http://users.ox.ac.uk/~oaces/conference/papers/Marius_Turda.pdf

152 *Juli Székely*

Urry, J. (1999). Sensing the city. In D. R. Judd & S. S. Fainstein (Eds.), *The tourist city* (pp. 71–86), New Haven: Yale University Press.

Vezsenyi, P. (2011). *Az ezredévi kiállítás 1896-ban*. Retrieved from www.archivnet.hu/kuriozumok/az_ezredevi_kiallitas_1896ban.html

Wacquant, L. (2008). Ordering insecurity: Social polarization and the punitive upsurge. *Radical Philosophy Review*, 11(1), 9–27.

Wacquant, L. (2010). Crafting the neoliberal state: Workfare, prisonfare, and social insecurity. *Sociological Forum*, 25(2), 197–220.

Zukin, S. (1995). *The cultures of cities*. Cambridge: Blackwell.

9 Rewriting history
Interpreting heritage in Saint Petersburg and Istanbul

Ayse N. Erek and Eszter Gantner

Introduction

The definitions of 'heritage' vary, but they have predominantly been determined by experts and professional organizations. However, during the last decade, the number of actors involved in heritage production has multiplied. Different actors with various backgrounds have been instrumental in producing heritage sites or deciding on the use or demolition of heritage sites according to their various perspectives on urban development. By doing so, in many cases these actors not only rewrite the histories of these sites and define the ways by which the present is constructed and imagined through heritage, but also determine and regulate access to these sites.

In this context, the present chapter analyses the paradoxes of reconstructing and reinterpreting architectural heritage, with a focus on the phenomenon of *disappearing history*. Thus, we assume that in the process of more actors becoming involved in the reconstruction and reinterpretation of heritage sites, history and historical facts are playing a dwindling role.

Based on our previous work (Erek & Gantner, 2018), we understand disappearing history as a process whereby various agents of urban heritage production—such as in Saint Petersburg the civic group called 'Pedestrian Zone in the Degtyarnyy Lane (Дегтярный переулок), and in Istanbul the activists of Emek Cinema and Roma Garden—select and use those historical elements which, on the one hand, support and legitimize their action with historic arguments in order to protect a particular site in the urban space and, on the other hand, become involved in the newly produced 'historical' narratives linked to the particular sites. We therefore argue that through careful selection of certain historical and thematic elements, not only is the area recast but its history is also rewritten (Sider & Smith, 1997).[1]

Within this framework, this chapter examines how the multiplication of actors affects:

154   *Ayse N. Erek and Eszter Gantner*

- On the one hand, the production of new histories of the highlighted heritage sites, and how this process leads to the disappearance of history in these cities;
- On the other hand, how 'rewriting' the histories of these sites by heritage production affects the increasing securitization around these sites and so access to them. Which social groups are included, and which are excluded from these newly recreated urban places, the sites there, and their 'historical' narratives?

Thus, this chapter compares these processes in Saint Petersburg and Istanbul, where heritage and its history intermingle with the creation of national identities as well as social membership produced by collective memories and feelings of belonging; and, in parallel, where urban development is regulated and influenced by global neo-liberal economic agency. Within this framework, the chapter addresses the role of regional organizations, as well as the contributions of grassroots heritage and bottom-up approaches.

Saint Petersburg in transition

Saint Petersburg has a lot to offer in the global competition between cities (Hannerz, 1993): Its history and architectural heritage provide a rich cultural capital (Zukin, 1996) that is also strengthened by UNESCO World Heritage status, gained in 1991 (Vorobyev & Shtiglitz, 2014). As the second-largest city in the Russian Federation (population 4.6 million; ibid.), Saint Petersburg has symbolized the new, more Westernized Russia throughout its history. Although Moscow was the medieval capital and regained this status in 1918, and is the "economic powerhouse" of Russia (O'Connor, 2004), Saint Petersburg still retains a role as a cultural centre of the country (ibid.). With more than three thousand historic buildings, world-famous theatres, and cultural institutions such as the Hermitage, Saint Petersburg possesses a uniquely rich classical heritage. This heritage, "branded and marketed" already during Soviet times, became both a challenge and a burden after the collapse of the Soviet Union. The city witnessed a severe economic crisis in the 1990s. Its main industries collapsed after 1991 and, as a result, everyday life became characterized by unemployment, economic decline, and also the partial collapse of the metropolitan infrastructure, such as sewerage and transport (ibid., p. 43). Thus, the transformation of the state along with the city had impact on the cultural sector and with it heritage management.

In the first half of the 1990s, the city's cultural sector faced new types of regulations such as the clarifying of "property ownership and removing perks and privileges, detaching them from the leisure and welfare structures of the cultural unions" (ibid., p. 43). From 1996 onward, the main problem was rapidly declining state funding, which fell by 40 per cent by 2001 (Belova, Cantell, Causey, & O'Connor, 2002). Consequently, wages were barely paid for employees in the cultural sector, and the lack of financial

Interpreting heritage in Petersburg and Istanbul   155

means also presented a threat to heritage sites. This situation forced cultural institutions to seek new funding possibilities, and the power vacuum led many foreign foundations to step in, such as the Open Society Institute and the Ford and Getty foundations. This had the effect that new patterns and models of cultural policy had been transferred, thereby exacerbating the conflict between local traditions in the cultural sector and the newly transferred Western models of marketing strategies of cultural capital. As Justin O'Connor (2004) pointed out:

> The promotion of culture as a regeneration tool [...] abuts on the wider policy domains which have rarely had to conceive of any systematic relationship to culture. For Russians culture was important [...] but as a gift to the patrimony not as economic investment.

This approach by both the state and local authorities led to focusing on the city's classical heritage rather than supporting smaller innovative, bottom-up cultural activities. Also, the reframing of the national historical narratives—locating the czarist period in the centre—strengthened this process, praising the historical city centre and thereby (over)valuing the classical heritage sites. Due to these policies, "the exclusive appeal to classical culture meant the image of the city was lacking in all contemporary profile" (ibid.).

Consequently, the paradoxical situation emerged that, while the promotion of classical heritage was successfully used to attract investors, tourism, and so forth, it also became a burden due to its omnipotence at every level of local urban policymaking, blocking the development of multiple future-oriented, innovative, and sustainable projects in the urban development, cultural, and heritage sectors.

Breaking *frozen heritage*? Degtyarnyy Lane, Saint Petersburg

"We have a specific Saint Petersburg style here, which is kept and protected. This style has an influence on their minds. They don't want to have something new; only their Saint Petersburg style". So claimed a heritage activist in 2017, discussing the general attitude of the municipality towards new initiatives presenting various ideas for redeveloping certain historical areas of Saint Petersburg.[2] According to both the project interviews and the scholarly literature (O'Connor, 2004), this type of heritage protection is understood here as *frozen heritage* (Callanan, 2016) meaning it is *frozen* in its infrastructures and strategies but also in its approaches, following decades-old patterns, not corresponding with the city's changing urban cultural, digital, and societal environment. However, in many cities globally, not only in Saint Petersburg, this type of heritage policy is challenged by the multiplication of urban agents in the field of heritage production (Gantner, Höffken, & Oevermann, 2015). These actors are claiming their 'right' to re-shape and reuse the urban past in the field of heritage production—suggesting, for

156 *Ayse N. Erek and Eszter Gantner*

example, more small-scale neighbourhood-friendly projects instead of costly and prestigious reconstructions.[3] This process is closely linked to the field of public history—from monuments to museums—where the multiplication of actors is breaking the established hegemonic structures.

The state and its various institutions are gradually 'losing' their power to produce hegemonic narratives of the past (Wolfrum, 2010; Tauschek, 2013). According to our interviewees, this process is also taking place in Saint Petersburg. As one of the activists explained: "Two years ago, I found out that there are some projects, associations, […] movements, which are interested in open environment, like 'Archivy Petersburg', 'Beautiful city St. Petersburg' and others".[4]

The mentioned groups that take interest in the city's sites, places, and heritage belong to the phenomenon described by the urban anthropologist Wolfgang Kaschuba (2013, pp. 20–57) as "the multiplication of urban agents". This means that a sort of democratization happens, not only in the field of public history as mentioned previously, but also in other segments of urban society and social life, such as in urban development. This process is clearly marked by the much-praised 'participation', involving urban citizens in urban planning or urban governance (Selle, 2013). In this particular case, these tendencies evidently overlap each other, demonstrating the beginning of the claim for a more actor-driven production of heritage in Saint Petersburg (see Roued-Cunliffe & Copeland, 2017).

Nevertheless, the claim (right) to participate in the selection and reshaping of sites for protection is to be seen in the broader sense, as part of the concept of 'reclaiming the city' (Lefebvre, 1969). Urban heritage as a significant element of the urban context is still understood in certain political settings as being part of the national historical agenda, as in the case of Saint Petersburg; therefore, the hegemonic approaches in the selection and protection of sites manifest themselves top-down (Zhelnina, 2013). Besides the national historic narratives, neo-liberal economic interests also influence the fate of various sites or urban areas, as illustrated by the New Holland Island (Нóвая Голлáндия) development (New Holland, n.d.). This site is located in the centre of Saint Petersburg and had been developed by a private investor into a modern art hub, creating a semi-public space at the island. However, the development plan and the reconstruction of the site were non-transparent and excluded local actors and stakeholders (Gordin, Matetskaya, & Dedova, 2014). The municipality's involvement in the site's redevelopment remains unclear, and the project was characterized by arbitrariness and a lack of historical contextualization (ibid.).

These two examples highlight the municipality's inconsistent approach to heritage: At the New Holland Island site, the private investor (undoubtedly from the 'new economic elite') was able to proceed unimpeded with the reconstruction of a heritage site, whereas the various civic groups mentioned previously are still struggling to preserve Degtyarnyy Lane and face both administrative and political challenges.

Interpreting heritage in Petersburg and Istanbul 157

Figure 9.1 Trams at Nevsky Prospekt. © Eszter Gantner.

The mentioned civic group started its activity in 2016. Their area of interest is a former tram park from where tram rails still extend into the surrounding streets. Their plan, in cooperation with other stakeholders (the civic group, municipality, etc.), is to turn the area into a pedestrian zone, thereby creating not only an urban public space but also a heritage site termed the memory tram park. Degtyarnyy Lane is situated on the outskirts of the central historic district of Saint Petersburg (Figure 9.1). The residents of this historic neighbourhood share communal apartments (so-called *kommunalka*) and mostly have comparatively low incomes. At the same time, the area has great development potential, as it is very close to Nevsky Prospekt, the city's main boulevard. This potential is already evident from the construction of a new political and business centre that will also be occupied by 20 (!) local government committees (TACT, 2018).

Against this property development and potential gentrification of the neighbourhood, the civic activists present a historical narrative, pointing out the significance of this location for the national (and even global) history of technology. This was the location of the world's first experimental tram system powered by electricity, introduced in 1880 by the Russian engineer Fjodor Apollonowitsch Pirozki. Pirozki was educated in Saint Petersburg

158 *Ayse N. Erek and Eszter Gantner*

and, when serving in Kiev with the Fortress Artillery, had met the leading Russian electrical engineer Pavel Yablochkov. Through Yablochkov, Pirozki became a supporter of electrical energy, and began experiments with electrically powered railway cars in Saint Petersburg in 1874. Pirozki modified a double-deck horse-drawn tramway to electrical power, which entered public service in that area of Saint Petersburg on 3 September 1880. The experiments continued until the end of September 1880, as Pirozki experienced financial difficulties that prevented progress with his enterprise. However, his work stirred interest in electric trams around the world, as news about his experiment was reported in September 1880 (Elektrichestvo, no. 5, 22 November 1880). Among the experts interested in Pirozki's research were Werner and Carl Heinrich von Siemens, who opened the world's first permanent electric tramline[5] with their own design of electric tram in Berlin in 1881 (Medveczky, 1979).

While for decades this part of urban history was known mostly to historians and tram enthusiasts, in recent years numerous websites have covered this moment in Russian technical history, emphasizing its "Russianness" (Myenergy, n.d.), thereby placing this event within a national historical framework. This process of recreating the national historical narrative in versatile relation with political interests, *seem to be effective in securing the location* for further generations. In the civic group's strategy for preserving and recreating this area, historic facts provide for the *legitimation* of their activity. As the legal situation for grassroots activities in Russia is complex and not without risk, urban activism or argumentation based on history potentially protect such activist groups against potential threats. However, the focus on a very particular historic moment, picking it out from the complex urban historical context of the area, demonstrates distinctively how history is perceived as a resource. This was emphasized by the historian Cor Wagenaar (2018):

> Monuments, buildings and historical sites play a remarkable role: they visualize history. [...] Things become problematic, however, as soon as buildings and urban ensembles are integrated in contemporary political campaigns that attribute values that may run counter to historical realities, invent fake histories, and even rebuild monuments to support their views.

Nonetheless, the main conflict in this case concerns the two distinct visions for this area and accompanying perceptions of public space. The civic group is pleading for 'greener' and neighbourhood-friendly *inclusive* development, meaning to transform the area into an open and inclusive pedestrian zone. In contrast, the municipality follows both economic and political interests, involving turning this site into a business and political hub and imagining it as a *representative place*. Degtarniy Lane has thereby become a stage for this developing conflict of interests: The city government is planning a parking

Interpreting heritage in Petersburg and Istanbul 159

lot on the site, whereas residents are campaigning for creation of a pedestrian zone (TACT, 2018).

The introduction of various administrative units of the municipality and of business at this site would lead to the destruction of social and economic and cultural structures among the residents, and also to growing securitization, meaning applying surveillance technologies, security guards at entrances, and so forth. Interestingly, using the historical narrative of the civic group, two different dimensions of understanding securitization clash in this case: On the one hand is securitization in the sense discussed by William Morris, as explained in the introduction of this volume, speaking about securing *the site for future generations*. On the other hand is securitization as *the process of state actors transforming subjects into matters of security*, which enables the use of various means (such as smart surveillance technologies) in the name of security (Buzan, Wæver, & de Wilde, 1998).

Turning this residential area with industrial past into a business and political hub would clearly change the use of the area's public spaces, as: "they are in reality spaces which are heavily controlled and monitored via private security guards and banks of CCTV cameras whose function is to control and/or exclude certain 'undesirable' groups—typically low-income youths, the homeless and non-consumers" (Smets & Watt, 2013).

Ultimately, at a broader level, this conflict concerns the various visions of the city's image and future. The civic group argues for a pedestrian zone as part of a city with sustainable, 'green', liveable, inclusive, and accessible public spaces, whereas the municipality's vision is more 'frozen', perceiving the city as a museum and as a place representing both economic and political power and—linked to them—of history.

Given these opposing viewpoints, open public spaces are interpreted as sources of disorder. According to this understanding, spaces such as Degtyarnyy Lane must be protected from citizens and their uncontrolled usage (Zhelnina, 2013). However, the various layers of conflict affecting this area, briefly described above, also raise questions concerning the practices and means for breaking from the idea of 'frozen heritage', and with it the representation and historically fixed 'frozen vision' of the city. According to interviewees, the civic group recognized that in the current political setting the only way to realize the project is, "To talk with administration, authorities".[6] Besides seeking dialogue with the authorities—meaning constantly *negotiating* with the municipality in various forms, such as submitted plans, presentations, and documentation—the group also utilizes social media, such as VKontakte—the main social media platform in Russia—to organize various actions in the neighbourhood. All documentation concerning the group's negotiations is published on its website, thereby creating an archive of bottom-up ideas and documents, which may also help disseminate these practices to other groups. The group sees its own activity as a "mediating platform", supporting dialogue between key stakeholders such as the district

160 *Ayse N. Erek and Eszter Gantner*

authorities, the development company VTB 24 (VTB Group, n.d.), and local residents.

In this dialogue or negotiation, *securing heritage*—or as the civic activists propose it, *securing the residential area as heritage sites*—would prevent the limitation and regulation of accessibility and with it the usage of this space. The only way to achieve this goal is to emphasize the *historical moment or fact*, which may also be powerful enough to: (a) legitimize their activity; (b) to provide arguments for the negotiations with the key stakeholders, and thereby, (c) to find a compromise that provides at least partial protection of this territory and safeguards it from further securitization resulting from neo-liberal urbanization (Theodore, Peck, & Brenner, 2011).

However, the described form of usage of history ultimately entails the loss of the urban historical contexts and with them the chance for careful renewal and transformation of this industrial area into a complex and multi-layered industrial heritage site (Vorobyev & Shtiglitz, 2014).

Istanbul in transition

Since the 1980s, the city of Istanbul has seen the development of plans for intensive renovation and reconstruction in competition with other cities on the global scale. Such changes in the city's physical form have emerged in part due to neo-liberal policies and their management techniques as well to the real estate sector—seen as a remedy to the economic crises of the 1990s and 2000s. These policies induce particular spatial dynamics in the evolution of cities. In Istanbul, it took the form of a complex, uneven dynamism and expansion based on the real estate sector. After the 1990s, Istanbul's construction boom occurred away from the city centre, with the development of a new financial centre and gated communities, whereas after the 2000s the focus shifted to the urban centre, bringing forth debates and conflicts related to urban history and heritage (Aksoy, 2008).

In 2010, when the city was selected by the European Commission as the cultural capital of Europe, the director of Kültür AŞ (the municipal office in the city senate, founded in 1989 to direct policy in the arts and culture) recommended investing in cultural industries, cultural tourism, and cultural heritage as a city branding strategy (Bayhan, 2011). Istanbul became a driver of Turkey's changing economy, including a push to develop an aesthetic of the new and dynamic in what is at the same time an old and historical city (Erek & Köksal, 2014). These events also reflected the current marketing approach to many global cities, emphasizing a historical and yet modern city.

Simultaneously, the emergence of large-scale urban transformation projects, categorized as urban renovation/urban development, legitimized 'demolition' and 'reconstruction' via the more abstract discourses of urban fear, ecology, natural disasters, but also cultural heritage. This changed the physical forms of the city and its architecture. The changes in the city's

Interpreting heritage in Petersburg and Istanbul 161

economy created new spaces for symbolic values such as 'bohemian, lively, dynamic, full of potential, changing, open, world, and global' (ibid., 2014), while heritage had to be redefined within this framework in a city constantly under construction. Furthermore, the abstractions of history are instrumentalized for the justification of urban regeneration. Privatization and nostalgia, as two driving forces of neo-liberal ideology (Herzfeld, 1987), created a complex discussion with regard to the renewal of the city, while at the same time shaping the local political culture, critical towards the rapid transformation of the city's spaces. It is not surprising that cultural practices of this period, including photography and arts, were saturated with historical imagination and the anxieties of disappearing history.

In this regard, one of the main neighbourhoods under focus was Beyoğlu, a medieval district that expanded in 19th century Istanbul as the changing face of the Ottoman Empire under the conditions of the new economic and cultural networks that the world witnessed at that time. The destruction of some of its buildings in the mid-1980s gave rise to a heated discussion about what the neighbourhood symbolized. While today it forms the cultural and entertainment centre of the city, for some it is "neither Ottoman, nor European, but Levantine; while for others it symbolized 19th-century European capitalism as it was the centre for European finance and cultural life" (Bartu, 2000). In yet another interpretation, the neighbourhood recalls a particular past replete with multi-ethnic and multi-religious identities. Indeed, the various interpretations of Beyoğlu all refer to a city that does not exist today, but which remains the space of a disappeared past. While historical consciousness plays a role in the memory of this central area, the questions of what Beyoğlu resembled in the past, which Beyoğlu was to be revived and for whom: What Beyoğlu represented for whom, stirred up related political topics. Beyoğlu is a case in point of heritage having a key role in both reconstruction as well as for the claims of the public. The reconstruction and reinterpretation of history by various actors produced new narratives, rewriting history in unique ways. In this sense the multiplication of actors in this process also involved—increasingly so after the 2010s—the contributions of groups, neighbourhood associations, projects, and various civic organizations, which also brings forth discussion concerning democratization in actor-driven heritage production.

In this sense the discussion represented by the transitions occurring in the neighbourhood opened up questions regarding the wider changes in the city, increasingly tied to questions of access and security. The emergence of such agency served several purposes: Remaining in a place is political, combined with the 'right to the city' movements legitimized by a supposedly simple fact. The historical site belonged to people, and what defined it as heritage also legitimized the political engagement in deciding the future. On the other hand, the same emphasis led the way to differentiate the sites with concerns to keep them secure, which in reality turned into a tool to legitimize the new needs of the new economic structure. This discussion became clearly relevant

162 *Ayse N. Erek and Eszter Gantner*

to various occasions that represented the complex relationships between history, heritage, neo-liberal adjustments, and grassroots activism, where the effects of the control of governance, finance, and commerce provided fertile ground that made such conflicts apparent through the built space.

The Emek Cinema, Istanbul

The examination of the Emek Cinema building demonstrations after 2009 indicates the rise of new kinds of public discussion focusing on heritage as a result of rapid commercialization in which state control is felt alongside the history that was destroyed by the impersonal logic of real estate investment. The discussion started after the municipality of Istanbul announced plans to demolish the Emek Theatre building in Beyoğlu (see Figure 9.2) in order to construct a shopping venue. Built in 1884 and used for various purposes such as a hunting club, athletics gym, circus, and ice-skating rink, it hosted a cinema that opened in 1924. Built in a neoclassical architectural style, the building was one of the oldest cinemas in the city. It was the symbolic movie theatre that for decades hosted the Istanbul Film Festival, and also represented the revival of the Beyoğlu neighbourhood in the 1990s as a place of urban culture, connected to the international production of culture, hosting alternative lifestyles and youth culture, as well the new cosmopolitanism related to the fall of the Soviet Republic. After a lengthy legal battle, a local court approved the developer's plans, and the ownership announced plans to 'move' the theatre to the fourth floor of the new building, retaining only the original façade. Istanbul's mayor justified the reconstruction of the old building, stating:

> the reflections of the past remain in these buildings. People who have watched beautiful movies in the past, want to sit there like in the past and are looking for today's comfort. The problem starts exactly here. Some demand the protection of the original as it was. Some want to keep the traces of the past while maintaining comfort.
>
> (Haber Türk, 2011)

In this statement, regenerating a historical building with conditions of comfort refers to a hegemonic neo-liberal symbolism, in accordance with the rules of the market. More specifically, the intention to redesign Beyoğlu was not surprising, considering its visibility and symbolic importance within the broader public imagination.

During the ongoing demonstrations against the demolition of the building, one of the major mottos associated with the site was "Istanbul is ours, Emek (cinema) is ours" (Uzunçarşılı Baysal, 2011). In this way, the building was associated with the wider city, but especially with the legacy of the neighbourhood's cosmopolitan past. In claims to protect the site as it was, the case showed a more complicated debate of legitimization by

Interpreting heritage in Petersburg and Istanbul 163

Figure 9.2 Emek Cinema building. © 2018 Ayse Erek.

heritage, in conflict with the dominant heritage construction of the state that referred to a previous period, namely the Ottoman Islamic past of the 16th century (Erdem, 2017). During the demonstrations the building was repeatedly defined as a memory space, a modern space for a cosmopolitan past, a global space housing an international film festival, a landmark, and

164 *Ayse N. Erek and Eszter Gantner*

a social site embodying an old patisserie, *İnci*, a place of entertainment and sharing, and a unique example of the heritage and historical lifestyles of Beyoğlu (Bayhan, 2016; Reclaim Istanbul, 2013).[7]

Nonetheless, the grassroots movement generated media attention. As the critic Nil Kural wrote, "People in Istanbul have a very strong bond with the Emek Theatre" (quoted by Letsch, 2013, 15 April).[8] Another wrote: "Protesting cinema lovers did nothing other than protect Istanbul's cultural memory" (ANF Firat, 2013). The protest took different forms, including marches, graffiti in public space, gatherings, public screenings in and around the building, and so on. The Beyoğlu Kent Savunması (Beyoğlu Urban Defence, ca. 2014) initiative regards itself as "the common forum of those who defend the plurality of Beyoğlu with all its public, historical and cultural diversity". This bond is a product of the feelings of belonging, collective memory, nostalgia, and desire to reclaim the public space, as well as losing the city and its history against the current of globalization.

Emek Cinema is a memory space, creating a language of resistance that is composed of the physical and emotional experiences and narratives embedded in this very space (Fırat, 2015). Nevertheless, this type of nostalgia cherishes shattered fragments of memory and temporalizes space (Boym, 2001). It can be ironic and humorous. It reveals that "longing and critical thinking are not opposed to one another, as affective memories do not absolve one from compassion, judgment or critical reflection" (ibid., pp. 49–50). This case demonstrates how a building, a street, or a public space becomes a living object for imaginative and critical thinking. As Laurajane Smith argues in *Uses of Heritage* (2006), "heritage is [...] ultimately a cultural practice, involved in the construction and regulation of a range of values and understandings". Smith discusses how heritage is a cultural process facilitated with the physical place but which, more importantly, engages with acts of remembering that work to create ways to understand and engage with the present (ibid., 44).

The Roma Garden civic initiative expands this discussion of the legitimization of regeneration projects as well as resistance by civil movements through heritage, regarding the constant negotiation for horizontal urban planning in Istanbul. The Roma Garden (see Figure 9.3) is located at an ancient Roman site within the wider Beyoğlu area, and is a green space with a panoramic view of the historical landscape of Istanbul, which once accommodated Byzantine and Ottoman palaces. Accompanying the city's rapid regeneration and the emergence of new laws in accordance with this process in the city centre since the 2000s, the area has attracted interest from various actors. The municipality's plan to erect a social rehabilitation centre, and plans to expand the nearby 16th-century building towards this area, were criticized by local neighbourhood associations. The *Conservation Development Plan* of 2011 intended to open all the green lots in the district for development, including parks, school gardens, and unattended green areas. This included the Roma Garden, which at that time was a disused

Interpreting heritage in Petersburg and Istanbul 165

Figure 9.3 Roma Garden. © 2018 Ayse Erek.

green space in between buildings. In protest against the proposals, neighbourhood groups claimed the space for 'breathing' within the intensely built environment and started to cultivate the area in accordance with the principles of organic permaculture. The plans to regenerate the area were eventually cancelled in 2014, following legal action taken by the neighbourhood associations. The municipality's redevelopment proposals were rejected by the court, on the basis of disturbing the balance of green areas in the intensely urban space.

A participant in the urban gardening activity stated:

> It's very special for me to cultivate this soil of Istanbul. When I started to work in the Roma Garden, in an area where you can see some of the important landmarks of Istanbul, I felt more connected to the land and the reality of this city. It became an element of belonging.
> (Bostan Hikayeleri Dergisi, 1 November, 2017, p. 5)

This expression in the realm of the private and personal is also connected to the formal political field. Furthermore, in imagining the future, the participants problematize accessibility. As one participant said, "This is a space that is open to anybody, with no fences around" (ibid.).

166 *Ayse N. Erek and Eszter Gantner*

Today, for most cities worldwide, designating 'historic' areas of the city and certain built forms as heritage sites, and developing plans for their preservation, are introduced as remedies for the erasure of memory. However, "these measures, historically informed in their claims and enactment, embody the danger of disregarding recent histories of social and communal structures and of reproducing histories and heritage that reflect the demands of contemporary economic and political interests" (Uluoğlu, Baykan, Boynudelik, & Sevingen, 2010). The demolition of the Emek Cinema building and the case of Roma Garden exemplify how the state's current cultural policy and the local cultural industry operate: restoring memories of a certain past while at the same time erasing memories of other pasts that exist in parallel, in attempts to construct the image of the city.

The civic initiatives linked to the Emek Cinema and Roma Garden symbolize the claim to the right to decide the fate of the city, whose cultural and historical heritage are increasingly at stake. Many are critical of the unchecked urban development that is rapidly remaking Istanbul, and of ever-larger projects being forced upon its residents with little public debate (Letsch, 2013, 15 April). Nonetheless, it is these sites that enable the public to identify with the city's past and present as a political, cultural, and social entity.

Conclusion

In recent decades, urbanization has become the major defining element in globalization, a process demanding not only the participation of policymakers, planners, and urban citizens, but also those actors involved in preserving particular cities' pasts and histories. Furthermore, the rapid changes seen in urban space and society have also increased the securitization of urban places all over the world. However, securitization and the issue of security— due to neo-liberal economic policies in the urban sphere—are challenged with regard to heritage sites: On the one hand, the question arises of how *to secure* the long-term existence of heritage sites connected with local urban memory and identity. On the other hand, the ongoing protests organized on the basis of the bottom-up approach of a 'right' not only to the city, but also to the urban past and the usage of heritage sites, serve to increase:

(a) Conflicts in the urban space, and;
(b) *Security measures* in certain heritage areas and neighbourhoods, as many of these conflicts are based on the exclusion of certain groups of urban citizens from accessing heritage sites.

In these developments, history is used as a pool of elements and motifs for the arguments and actions put forward by all parties involved in the restriction of sites or historic neighbourhoods. This leads to the disappearance of the site or neighbourhood's *complex* history, as various actors employ historic narratives according their particular interests and practices. Such

Interpreting heritage in Petersburg and Istanbul 167

approaches often produce conflicting narratives that are simplistic and one-dimensional, rather than arguing, negotiating, and developing solutions on the basis of the complex history of the particular site or area. Elaborating and reflecting the complex history of a heritage site allows the *inclusion* of various groups and their memories, histories, and local identities, thereby securing the *diversity* and *complexity* of urban spaces, places, and urban citizens.

This chapter is based on research conducted for the project 'Claiming the Public Space: Urban Interventions and the Shift from Vertical to Horizontal Urban Planning' (2016–2018). The project was a collaboration between the Georg-Simmel Center for Metropolitan Studies (GSZ), International Research on Art and City (TACT), and the Centre for Independent Social Research (CISR).

The project was supported by the Alexander von Humboldt Foundation (Research Group Linkage Programme) between 2016 and 2018.

Notes

1 Histories versus history: Histories emerge both within and against large social processes, while large systems and processes are described by history.
2 N. N. Interviewed (in English and Russian) at Degtyarnyy Lane, 22 May 2017 as part of the international research project, "Claiming the Public Space".
3 A good example of such practices and activism is presented in the case of Budapest (See: Juli Székely. "Fences and Defences: Matters of Security in the City Park of Budapest"; this volume).
4 N. N. Interviewed (in English and Russian) at Degtyarnyy Lane, 22 May 2017 as part of the international research project, "Claiming the Public Space".
5 The first permanent tram line in the Russian Empire was opened in Kiev in 1892.
6 Interviewed (in English and Russian) at Degtyarnyy Lane, 22 May 2017 as part of the international research project, "Claiming the Public Space".
7 Bayhan (2016); Reclaim Istanbul (2013); A letter by the famous movie director Costa-Gavras stated: "A prominent theatre, a cultural centre must not be destroyed. It's like erasing a part of our memory and removing a significant place for the future".
8 Quotation from Nil Kural, a journalist and member of the FIPRESCI (The International Federation of Film Critics) jury of critics. As quoted by Letsch (2013, April 15).

References

Aksoy, A. (2008). Istanbul's choice. *Third Text*, 22(1), 71–83.
ANF Fırat News Agency. (2013). New protest against demolition of Emek Cinema. Retrieved from https://anfenglish.com/news/new-protest-against-demolition-of-emek-cinema-1-7036
Bartu, A. (2000). Eski Mahallelerin Sahibi Kim? Kurelsel bir Çağda Tarihi Yeniden Yazmak [Who owns the old neighbourhoods? To rewrite the history in an

168   Ayse N. Erek and Eszter Gantner

age of globalisation]. In C. Keyder (Ed.), *Istanbul: Kuresel ile Yerel Arasında (Istanbul: Between global and local)* (pp. 48–49). Istanbul: Metis.

Bayhan, B. (2016, January 11). *Emek Sineması Ruhunu Kaybetti [Emek Cinema lost its soul]*. Retrieved from www.arkitera.com/haber/26143/emek-sinemasi-ruhunu-kaybetti

Bayhan, N. (2011). Istanbul'u marka yapan da, yapacak olan da kültür ve sanattır [What makes and will make Istanbul a brand is culture and arts]. In D. Ünsal (Ed.), *Istanbul Kültür ve Sanat Sektörü [Istanbul's arts and culture sector]* (p. 35). Istanbul: Istanbul Bilgi Üniversitesi Yayınları.

Belova, E., Cantell, T., Causey, S., & O'Connor, J. (2002) *Creative industries in the modern city: Encouraging enterprise and creativity in St. Petersburg*. St. Petersburg: TACIS.

Beyoğlu Kent Savunması (Beyoğlu Urban Defence). (ca. 2014). Beyoğlu'nu kamusal, tarihsel ve kültürel bir alan olarak tüm çeşitliliği ile savunanların ortak forumu olan Beyoğlu Kent Savunması'nın resmi Twitter hesabıdır (Official Twitter account of the Beyoğlu City Defence, which is the common forum of those who defend the plurality of Beyoğlu with all its public, historical and cultural diversity). [Twitter homepage]. Retrieved from https://twitter.com/BeyogluKntSvnms

Bostan Hikayeleri Dergisi. (2017, November 1) *Roma Garden* (p. 5). Retrieved from https://issuu.com/ermantopgul/docs/bostan_hikayeleri_dergi3?embed_cta=read_more&embed_context=embed&embed_domain=bostanhikayeleri.com

Boym, S. (2001). *The future of nostalgia* (p. 81). New York, NY: Basic Books.

Buzan, B., Wæver, O., & de Wilde, J. (1998). *Security: A new framework for analysis*. Boulder, CO: Lynne Rienner.

Callanan, M. (2016). Managing frozen heritage: Some challenges and responses. *Quaternary International, 402*, 72–79.

Elektrichestvo. (1880, November 22). Elektri*ch*estvo, *Nr.5*.

Erdem, C. Y. (2017). Ottomentality: Neoliberal governance of culture and neo-ottoman management of diversity. *Turkish Studies, 18*(4), 710–728. doi: 10.1080/14683849.2017.1354702

Erek, A. N., & Gantner, E. (2018). Disappearing history. Reimagineering of Berlin after 1989. In K. Bauer & J. Hosek (Eds), *Cultural topographies of the new Berlin* (pp. 181–203). New York, NY: Berghahn.

Erek, A. N., & Köksal, A. H. (2014). Relocating the arts in the new Istanbul: Urban imaginary as a contested zone. *Visual Resources, 30*(4), 301–318.

Fırat, B. (2015). Emek Sineması; Eylem Beden, Duygulanımsal Kamusallık [*Emek Movie Theatre; Action, Body, Sensible Public Space*]. In *77–13 Türkiye'de Direnişin Sanatı (77–13 Resistant Art in Turkey)*. Berlin: nGbK.

Gantner, E., Höffken, S., & Oevermann, H. (2015). Urbane Interventionen und die Transformation des öffentlichen Raumes. In W. Kaschuba, D. Kleinert, & C. Kühn (Eds.), *Berliner blätter – Ethnographische und ethnologische Beiträge*, (pp. 69, 35). Berlin, Panama Verlag.

Gordin, V., Matetskaya, M., & Dedova, M. (2014). New life of New Holland in a classical city. In G. Richards & L. Marques (Eds.), *Creative districts around the world* (pp. 93–97). Breda: NHTV.

HaberTürk. (2011). *Emek sineması yıkılacak mı?* Retrieved from www.haberturk.com/kultur-sanat/haber/699632-emek-sinemasi-yikilacak-mi.

Interpreting heritage in Petersburg and Istanbul 169

Hannerz, U. (1993). The cultural role of world cities. In A. P. Cohen & F. Katsuyoshi (Eds.), *Humanising the city? Social contexts of urban life at the turn of the millennium* (pp. 67–84). Edinburgh: Edinburgh University Press.

Herzfeld, M. (1987). *Anthropology through the looking glass: Critical ethnography in the margins of Europe*. Cambridge, MA: Cambridge University Press.

Kaschuba, W. (2013). Vom Tahrir-Platz in Kairo zum Hermannplatz in Berlin. Urbane Räume als "Claims" und "Commons"? In E. Betuzzo, E. Gantner, J. Niewöhner, & H. Oevermann (Eds.), *Kontrolle öffentlicher Räume* (pp. 20–57). Berlin: Lit Verlag.

Lefebvre, H. (1969). *Le droit à la ville*. Paris: Anthropos.

Letsch, C. (2013, April 15). Turkey's historic Emek theatre facing final curtain. *The Guardian*. Retrieved from www.guardian.co.uk/world/2013/apr/15/turkey-historic-emek-theatre-final-curtain

Medveczky, Á. (1979). A Budapesti Villamosvasút megszületésének elözményei. In A. Közlekedési, *Múzeum Évkönyve Bd 4* (365–375). Budapest: Közlekedési Dokumentációs Vállalat.

Myenergy (n.d.). Retrieved from www.myenergy.ru/popular/video/energetics/history/

New Holland (n.d.). Новая Голландия (New Holland: Cultural urbanization). Project website. Retrieved from newhollandsp.ru

O'Connor, J. (2004). Cities, culture and "transitional economies". Developing cultural industries in St. Petersburg. In D. Power & J. A. Scott (Eds.), *Cultural industries and the production of culture* (pp. 34–54). New York, NY: Routledge.

Reclaim Istanbul (2013). *Resisting the demolition of the famous Emek Cinema*. Retrieved from https://reclaimistanbul.com/2013/04/10/resisting-the-demolition-of-the-famous-emek-cinema/

Roued-Cunliffe, H., & Copeland, A. (2017). *Participatory heritage*. London: Facet.

Selle, K. (2013). Über die Zettelwand hinaus. Was planungsbezogene Kommunikation bewirkt und was nicht—Sechs Thesen zum Stand der Forschung. *RaumPlanung*, *170*(5), 8–15.

Sider, G., & Smith, G. (1997). Introduction. In G. Sider & G. Smith (Eds.) *Between history and histories — The making of silences and commemorations* (pp. 3–31), 12. Toronto: University of Toronto Press.

Smets, P., & Watt, P. (2013). Exclusion and belonging in urban public and quasi-public space. *Open Urban Studies Journal*, 6, (Suppl 1: M1) 27–29.

Smith, L. (2006). *Uses of heritage*. London: Routledge.

TACT. (2018). Manifesto of the civic group "Pedestrian zone in the Degtyarnyy lane". Retrieved from https://tactcity.wordpress.com/2018/05/16/bringing-streets-back-to-people-mediating-co-operation-around-degtarniy-lane/

Tauschek, M. (2013). *Kulturerbe. Eine Einführung*. Berlin: Dietrich Reimer Verlag.

Theodore, N., Peck, J., & Brenner, N. (2011). Neoliberal urbanism. Cities and the rule of markets. In G. Bridges & S. Watson (Eds.), *The new Blackwell companion to the city* (pp. 15–25). Hoboken, NJ: Wiley-Blackwell.

Uluoğlu, B., Baykan, A., Boynudelik, Z. I., & Sevingen, B. (2010). Contestations over a living heritage site: The case of Büyük Valide Han. In D. Göktürk, L. Soysal, & I. Tureli. (Eds.), *Orienting Istanbul: Cultural capital of Europe?* (p. 71). London: Taylor and Francis.

Uzunçarşılı Baysal, C. (2011, May 23). *Emek is ours/Istanbul is ours: Reclaiming Emek Cinema*. International Alliance of Inhabitants. Retrieved from www.habitants.org/notizie/abitanti_d_europa/emek_e_nostro_istambul_e_nostra_rivendicando_il_cinema_emek/(language)/eng-GB

170   Ayse N. Erek and Eszter Gantner

Vorobyev, D., & Shtiglitz, M. (2014). Industrial heritage issues in a conflict case: Okhta center in St. Petersburg, Russia. In H. Oevermann & H. A. Mieg (Eds.), *Industrial heritage sites in transformation—Clash of discourses* (pp. 110–126). Cambridge, MA: Routledge.

VTB Group (n.d.). *About VTB Group*. Retrieved from www.vtb.com/o-banke/gruppa-vtb/skhema-gruppy/

Wagenaar, C. (2018). *Public spaces, urban heritage, and politics*. Retrieved from www.europenowjournal.org/2018/04/30/public-spaces-urban-heritage-and-politics/

Wolfrum, E. (2010). Erinnerungskultur und Geschichtspolitik als Forschungsfelder. Konzepte—Methoden—Themen. In J. Scheunemann (Hrsg.), *Reformation und Bauernkrieg* (pp. 13–32). Leipzig: Evangelische Verlagsanstalt.

Zhelnina, A. (2013). Learning to use "public space": Urban space in post-Soviet St. Petersburg, exclusion and belonging in urban public and quasi-public space. *Open Urban Studies Journal*, 6, (Suppl 1: M1), 61.

Zukin, S. (1996). *The culture of the cities*. New York, NY: Wiley.

10 Disregarding youth proposals

Intangible heritage, securitization, and soccer fan groups in México

Ricardo Duarte Bajaña

Introduction

It can be argued that soccer is not only interwoven with national identity in Mexico, but that it is also perceived as a type of heritage of each city that has a soccer team.[1] Another argument may centre on the explanation of the cultural significance that soccer stadiums might have. However, the present chapter leaves those arguments for another time and instead focuses on the social construction created by a group of young soccer fans, whose practices and rituals may be understood as a form of heritage due to the importance they hold for their own performers, and among those whose lifestyle is closely intertwined with their support of a football team. These practices and rituals represent a series of values and ideals that this particular group has sought to promote since its formation in 2004.

The public-security processes that are proposed for monitoring and controlling social practices concerning soccer within the territory where this group of fans takes action suggest that the group's social relations may not be sufficiently recognized or valued by official agents or any part of the general population. Consequently, emphasis here is placed on the need to understand and increase the visibility of the perspective presented by these young soccer fans in Mexico, who live in a complex context.

Heritage as a complex concept

In legal terms, heritage refers to some rights acquired over a series of goods—with some values—by the members of a certain community or social group. In a broad sense, cultural heritage refers to some resources inherited from the past, created in the present, and passed on to future generations for their benefit (UNESCO, 2003).

In addition, heritage refers to "places of memory" (Marcos Arévalo, 2004; Prats, 2005), that is the symbols and representations that have been significant and that generate identity in the cultural history of a social group. From this perspective, heritage understands legacy as a cultural process that includes elements such as experience, identity, memory, and performance

172 *Ricardo Duarte Bajaña*

(Smith, 2006). Heritage assets are, thus, a selection of relevant elements and expressions for a particular culture that have been 'activated' or recognized by a group of people with sufficient social power to do so (Prats, 2005). However, this interpretation seems insufficient to perceive the great diversity of experiences and local cultural hues that are not implicated in the social constructions, territories, or interactions that have been activated or recognized as heritage at a national or international level (Prats, 2005).

In this chapter, heritage will be understood as a fundamental aspect of culture, for it involves assets, customs, values, and so forth that allow individuals belonging to a certain community to live through and organize collective processes in very particular ways that are specific to the heritage of such communities. However, unlike culture, heritage makes reference to certain objects, places, and manifestations—whether officially activated as heritage or not—that are intimately related to the biography of individuals and their interactions. The population thus gives preference to the meaning over the legitimization of principles arising from this cultural externality (Prats, 2005).

That said, as stated by Laurajane Smith (2006), even places considered as heritage have tangible and intangible characteristics: tangible because of their material dimension and geographical settings, and intangible because heritage is a social construction based on cultural connotations.

Cultural heritage—whether it concerns heritage officially recognized as such, or else places and social interactions that are significant for certain social groups—implies the solidarity that brings together those who share a set of assets and practices that identify them, but could also be understood as a complex scenario of social complicity (García Canclini, 1999).

Securitization as a social conflict

In this chapter, security processes are understood as a tension between an ideal interpretation of social relationships versus some practices that value state power and coercion. In this sense, on one hand there are postulates that serve as a foundation for liberalism and modernity, for example, individuality (Mill, [1859], 1997]), autonomy (Kant, [1785], 1995), and the argument that the rights of individuals are more important than the well-being of the community (Rawls, 1971, 1997). This way of seeing reality has, in some societies, involved the imposition of the rule of law and respect for individual rights. These processes have coincided with profound cultural changes related to control of the instincts, the body, disciplining of the population, and the legitimization of individual rights (Caldeira, 2007).

On the other hand, in Latin-American (and Mexican) contexts, it is common to find social practices that fall into what Partha Chatterjee (2004) calls the "political society", referring to the negotiation and conflict zone between the state and the popular world, which frequently occur alongside violent hues and invariably far from any legal framework. From this

Securitization, and soccer fans in México 173

perspective, a cultural pattern is built that identifies—and even accepts and values—order and authority with the use of violence by police and other state agents. Such practices are associated with the delegitimization of civil rights (Caldeira, 2007). Along this route, the police and other state institutions privilege and monitor certain social conditions, such as comfort and security, to which certain sectors of the population (often those with greater economic resources) are granted access; simultaneously, they treat as infants those groups that must be supervised (Koolhaas, 2014), or regard as violent those with alternative proposals and actions, considering that such groups oppose the established order or have not met the indicated negotiation processes. In this sense, Teresa Caldeira (2007) holds that the problem is neither of liberal principles versus violent practices, nor of a constitutional framework versus illegal practices, but instead results from order institutions that are constituted to operate based on exceptions.

As we will see in this chapter, securitization operates by assigning value judgements to intangible heritage processes: securitization values some aspects of heritage as positive, but excludes those that distance themselves from the ideal liberal morality. From this perspective, the use of force is justified in maintaining an ideal social order. This way of looking at heritage—disregarding all the cultural components that constitute it—makes it difficult to access practices that can be considered a form of intangible heritage.

Methodological aspects

The objective of the ethnographic research presented in this chapter is to describe, analyse, and understand the ideas, meanings, and practices (that will be understood as a sort of intangible heritage) of the members of a soccer fan group from the city of Toluca, the state capital of Estado de Mexico, located 66 kilometres from Mexico City. The fieldwork for this research (Duarte Bajaña, 2017) was conducted from August 2013 to April 2015. Essentially, the instruments used in gathering information consisted of participatory observation, life stories of some informants, unstructured interviews, and in-depth interviews with the members of this group, with advisors connected with Toluca's public security system, and with public officials at the Nemesio Díez soccer stadium located in an urban area of Toluca and whose capacity is 30,000 people. Some of the information presented here was obtained from an ethnography involving one of these soccer fans groups, called la Banda del Rojo (The Red's Gang). Specifically, with Los de Villa (The People of Villa), a subgroup of La Banda de Rojo consisting of young residents of Villa Cuauhtémoc, a town located 21 kilometres from downtown Toluca.

This chapter comprises two major sections: The first section, titled "'Mover el Sector' ('Move the sector'): a sort of intangible heritage", presents a youth approach to social organization by members of La Banda del Rojo that can be understood as form of urban heritage. The second

174   *Ricardo Duarte Bajaña*

section, titled "Securitization processes and difficulties in accessing heritage practices", discusses various security processes, including police operations and surveillance systems that seek to provide an apparent sense of comfort and security. The analysis finds that these security processes restrict and hinder access by official actors and the general population to the "Mover el Sector" youth proposal.

"Mover el sector": a sort of intangible heritage

It is common for the members of La Banda del Rojo to use the term "Mover el Sector" to describe their social organization. This group of fans supports the Toluca Sporting Club soccer team, known as Los Diablos Rojos (The Red Devils). La Banda del Rojo currently has more than a thousand members, including men and women, most under 25 years of age. The group has a hierarchical social organization with three main leaders. In addition, the group is built from subgroups called *sectores* (sectors). Each sector is formed by young people residing in different neighbourhoods of Toluca or nearby municipalities, and each has a leader who is in constant communication, by telephone or through social networks, with the three main leaders.

Mover (to move) means to manage and coordinate—in this case on a weekly basis—all the different tasks, such as planning transportation to accompany the soccer team throughout the Mexican Republic; purchasing tickets for the stadiums where Los Diablos Rojos will be playing; composing and teaching the cheering chants for the group members who will interpret them; and designing and producing materials and elements in support of the team. In addition, the term *mover* (to move the fan group and its sectors) is associated with increasing the social visibility of La Banda del Rojo. Moreover, they *mueven* (move) their group with the intention of turning it into a public organization in the sight of an adult society that, in their opinion, lives without enthusiasm and promotes values and rules that trample life and stifle the freedom of the young.

The Mover el Sector concept could be understood as a sort of intangible heritage (Smith, 2006), since it entails a series of goods, customs, and values that the members of La Banda del Rojo assume as their own and which allows them to live, organize, and to be identified with collective and solidarity processes in very specific ways that have been consolidating since the group's formation.

To explain various behaviours associated with Mover el Sector, it is necessary to understand two concepts that are permanently used by the group members: *Tener Aguante* (endurance/be tough) and *Desmadre* (motherlessness). *Tener Aguante*[2] alludes to the possibility of promoting action in others or in oneself. This is frequently promoted by the leaders of the group and the sectors, but it can also be carried out by the musicians (orchestra) that form part of the group, or by the fans themselves. The group members value and promote the idea that, despite facing various obstacles (weather, changes of schedule, lack of money, etc.), they will nevertheless *se mueven* (move; i.e. carry out) the activities that allow, among other things, each sector to be visible within La Banda del Rojo and that also allow the group to be visible within Toluca and in other states of Mexico where they travel to support their team.

The concept of desmadre has a tinge of unbridled behaviour associated with partying, recklessness, consuming alcohol, fighting, and a double entendre, among other characteristics. In general terms, desmadre is linked to behaviours that transgress moral authority, respect, and the control represented by the mother figure (Magazine, 2008). In order to understand the meaning of Mover el Sector as a form of intangible heritage, it is helpful to present some ethnographic examples obtained during a *caravan* (parade) organized by the youth of La Banda del Rojo through one of Toluca's main streets at the start of the Mexican soccer season. This parade and the practices they exercise have been carried out and refined by members since the group's inception in 2004. With these rituals the group attempts to build a particular form of social interaction based on the link between desmadre (motherlessness), aguante (endurance/toughness), and the hierarchical organization. This is the sense of priority of their social constructions gathered under the denomination Mover el Sector. Specifically, they seek visibility and social recognition of their creative form of organization that privileges neither desmadre nor the seriousness and lack of emotion with which they associate adult relationships.

During interviews, members of La Banda del Rojo Villa stated their wish to free themselves from the pressures they experience in their families and schools—contexts in which the fulfilment of duty is paramount, and which attempt to instil models of behaviour marked by seriousness, demureness, and the blocking of emotions. In contrast, La Banda del Rojo provides the possibility of escaping these responsibilities; participating in carnival activities that include music, noise, colour, and alcohol consumption; and the possibility of expressing themselves through profanity, among other characteristics. However, group members also emphasize the need for seriousness in their commitment to fulfilling certain tasks within the sector. One of the problems faced by the group leader is that some individuals want to engage in desmadre continuously, manifested through arriving late at sector meetings, reneging without warning on their promises to attend the stadium, and believing that being part of the sector means partying but not participating in rehearsals or preparing banners and flags, and so forth. In the face of these destructive attitudes, which make it difficult for the sector to move, the leader assumes much more serious behaviour, possibly involving vigorously and publicly reprimanding those who do not balance their actions between desmadre and their duty to the collective organization.

Specifically, on the day of the parade, which will serve as an ethnographic example in this chapter, members of Los de Villa sector were travelling on a bus hired to transport them to the meeting place where the entire La Banda

176   Ricardo Duarte Bajaña

del Rojo group would begin its activities. As the sector entered the city of Toluca, the boys 'moved' quickly inside the vehicle and opened two hatches located on the roof. Three people then climbed through each hatch and sat on the roof, dangling their legs inside the vehicle. Meanwhile, some boys continued to walk down the aisle trying to find a space to climb up and sit on the outside, while those who were unsuccessful looked out of the windows. The leader of the sector, carrying out his task of *moving* Los de Villa, allowed these unpleasant actions by simply shouting, "Watch out kids, remember that I don't pay your insurance!", alluding to the fact that the action of climbing out of the moving vehicle was under everyone's responsibility and therefore had to be carried out with care.

Afterwards, some people in the bus passed flags to those sitting outside and extended more flags out the windows as the chants increased in volume. The members explained that the sudden uplift in mood was because they had already entered Toluca, making it necessary to draw attention to the arrival of the Villa sector. Indeed, it is very common for most passers-by to stare back at this carnival on wheels.

One of the most important outcomes sought by *moving* in this way is social visibility. Firstly, it is very important, for members of the sector, that other sectors and the overall leaders of La Banda del Rojo should notice them engaging in desmadre while at the same time fulfilling the tasks that allow the group to carry out its actions inside and outside the stadium, such as the parade in this case. Secondly (but equally important), members of the sector want their actions to be noticed by the *rucos*, or adults who, in their opinion, pass negative judgement on these emotional and youthful *desmadrosas* behaviours.

During the fieldwork, some members of Los de Villa pointed out several times that they liked to be part of La Banda del Rojo because within the group "nobody judges us". In this sense, actions such as leaving the bus through the skylights while singing with great enthusiasm and waving flags can be understood as their reaction to a demure and conservative way of life in Toluca.

When the bus arrived at the agreed place, the volume of the chants by the sector inside the bus remained very high, and a few members of La Banda del Rojo, who were already at the site, nodded at the arrival of Los de Villa, validating the desmadre and 'movement' of this sector of the group. Once the bus was parked, the leader of La Banda del Rojo Villa raised his hands to stop the chanting, and everyone became silent. He shouted that they should all climb down together and wait beside the vehicle. He next shouted that he did not want the sector to approach the park, where the parade would begin, like ants.[3] *Moving* the group implies that its members see themselves physically united from a distance. Apparently, this is a valuable indicator that allows La Banda del Rojo to know that a sector is *moving* and is valued for its unity and ability to act as a team.

Already present in the park, the members of all the sectors that make up La Banda del Rojo began to rehearse the group's chants to the beat of drums and trumpets played by members of 'los Ridíkulos 26' (Ridiculous 26), the La Banda del Rojo orchestra.[4] Four young people walked quickly through the sector, handing out small song-sheets with lyrics printed in green that read:

> Dale, Dale, Dale Diablos Rojos / suden la camiseta / queremos otra vuelta dar.
> Esta banda ya aguantó 10 años / los malos resultados / y acá estamos de fiesta.
> Siempre alentamos / vayas donde vayas ahí estamos.
> ¡Oooooh! Deportivo / eres lo más grande, rojo querido.[5]

It was a new song, which would be rehearsed to ensure that everyone would sing it at the stadium. The lyrics evidence the tough aguante attitude that should characterize the group. That is to say, even when the results are not positive, La Banda del Rojo will not be discouraged; they will continue accompanying and supporting the team, each time with greater enthusiasm. In reality, the members of the group feel that the Toluca soccer team is theirs, and it is understood as the group's heritage that must be supported to be successful. It is worth noting that the administrators of the Club Deportivo Toluca do not take this interpretation into account, and therefore change the schedules of certain matches without considering any needs and agreements reached with the members of La Banda del Rojo.

The orchestra began to play the new song, and everyone followed the verses printed on the song-sheet. This activity was led by several members, who walked among the attendees, singing louder and observing who sang and who did not and encouraging them to sing by making increased vocalizations. At the same time, they motioned with one arm, motivating the other members to sing with enthusiasm. Evidently, the orchestra was *moving* La Banda del Rojo through a pedagogical organized activity in which the music and orientation of certain people in charge were funda-mental to learning, with emotion, a song that would become emblematic within the group. Later, some people began to make room for the orchestra to pass, leave the park, and position themselves at the front of the parade. The others followed the orchestra, which now played with great force. The walkers sang, waved flags, and threw colourful confetti. A group of about ten boys ran quickly to the front of the orchestra, each holding a cell phone, to record videos from the front of the parade. There were many flags and *trapos* (fabric banners) displaying the name of the group and the emblem of Toluca Sports Club, which is the team's formal name, as well as the names of different sectors of La Banda del Rojo. There were also the trapos of La Banda del Rojo Villa, and a '*RIDÍKULOS 26*' banner placed in front of the orchestra, effectively commanding the parade.

178 *Ricardo Duarte Bajaña*

This spatial arrangement, in addition to evidencing the hierarchy of the group, in which the orchestra occupies a central place, reveals a strategy to promote the social visibility of the group. Repeatedly, after each game or activity carried out by La Banda del Rojo, videos of the fan group and their sectors are posted to YouTube or Facebook. In addition, when mainstream media outlets cover the groups' actions, showing the festive atmosphere that is part of the desmadre (motherlessness), some members search for these recordings online to copy them and upload them to their social networks, mentioning the friends who can be seen in the footage. On some occasions, the leader of Los de Villa sector uploaded some of these videos to Facebook and WhatsApp, on one occasion adding an explanatory message: "Here we are kids; we keep moving". According to the above, *moving* the group is also achieved based on the visibility of the sector on social networks and in the media.

Continuing with this idea of seeking visibility, during the parade passers-by who did not belong to La Banda del Rojo, stopped and observed the loud and colourful youth march that extended for approximately three blocks, occupying the four vehicle lanes of Morelos Avenue, one of the most important routes in the city of Toluca. From houses located along the route, residents leaned out to watch the passage of the fans. The parade stopped the traffic, with vehicles moving slowly behind the marchers, hoping to find a side street that would allow them to avoid the congestion. Meanwhile, young men and women walked, waved flags, sang, and moved their arms to the rhythm of the songs and musical instruments. Once inside the stadium, the orchestra, located behind a goal, in the central part of the area assigned to the group, took charge of directing the chants. The four or five verses of each song were sung for approximately five minutes, accompanied by the drums and trumpets. The leaders of La Banda del Rojo led the orchestra and were very aware of the emotion with which members of the group interpreted the songs. If the mood decreased, either because the song was played for several minutes, or because the game's actions became monotonous, one of the leaders indicated to the *Ridíkulos 26* to sing a different song. At that moment, the rhythm changes and several group members shout the next song for others to follow (Figure 10.1).

The members of La Banda del Rojo present an emphatic challenge to other soccer attendees, who flock to the stadium and sit in the sunny stands (often thanks to negotiations with the club's directors) with the sole intention of experiencing the atmosphere within a group of soccer fans. These people are called '*ocasionales*' (occasional) by members of the fan group; they visit the stadium sporadically, show no respect for the rituals performed by the group, and do not heed the instructions given by the group leaders. For instance, they do not wave the flags that are passed from hand to hand by the fans in the group; they do not sing the songs directed by the orchestra and by some members appointed by the leaders. Some of these ocasionales think they can sit in the La Banda del Rojo area, only to show inappropriate behaviour

Figure 10.1 Members of La Banda del Rojo in the Nemesio Diez stadium. © Ricardo Duarte Bajaña.

such as drinking beer, shouting profanities at the opposing team, and taking photographs of themselves that they immediately upload to social networks. The members of La Banda del Rojo do not tolerate ocasionales attempting to appropriate the symbols (colours, logos, desmadre, etc.) that they have built and that they assume as their property. One of the biggest drawbacks caused by these ocasionales is that they prevent the organized fans from huddling around the musicians in the stands, giving the appearance from the field and from the other stand zones in the stadium, that there are 'hollow areas' in the fan group, thus suggesting that the group is fragmented and poorly organized. In some instances, these ocasionales are rebuffed, shoved, and verbally berated by members of La Banda del Rojo.

Unlike the ocasionales, fans believe in the constant and co-operative participation of their members. They have built (and are still building) friendship, trust, and solidarity networks with the people who regularly participate in their rituals. As we have seen, it can be said that *mover* (moving) the fan group is a rigorous and hierarchical form of youth self-government, and which offers young people opportunities to demonstrate their leadership as well as their organizational and collective co-ordination skills, through lines of communication with the local and overall leaders who *mueven* (move) each sector.

Younger people associated with La Banda del Rojo are required to commit to and perform certain tasks on behalf of the organization and the collective actions of the group. In the same way, this is a type of social organization that values unruly and emotional actions (*motherlessness*) that contrast with

180 Ricardo Duarte Bajaña

the controlled and repressive environments that some of them must endure within their families and at school—but also in their relationships with some government institutions such as the police, as we will see. This unruly behaviour can be seen in their frenzied singing and shouting as they cheer on their team in the jumps, dances, and shouts that accompany their interventions inside and outside the stadium when the Toluca team plays a match; as well as in their consumption of alcohol and occasional use of hallucinogenic substances. *Mover el Sector* represents a form of heritage because its practices and rituals have a huge symbolic value and are assumed as their property. Also, because they allude to a symbolic conjunction that evidences a particular way of representing the world, and which is put into practice by means of a system of symbols and representations that are very significant within La Banda del Rojo and that generate identity in the cultural history of the group.

Securitization and difficulties in accessing heritage practices

When the Club Deportivo Toluca team makes an attack that threatens the opposite team's goal, it is common for some members of La Banda del Rojo to jump and push from the back to the front of the stands. In doing so, some of them fall, in which case police officers—dressed in black and wearing helmets, bulletproof vests, and thick arm and leg protection—enter the crowd to arrest those responsible for pushing other spectators. In those moments, the fan group increase the commotion, trying to confuse the police and make it more difficult for them to make arrests. On some occasions, the group leaders intervene, attempting to talk with the police and make them understand that these persons are not trying to attack anyone. However, the police often arrest two or three individuals, grabbing them by the neck, while other fans whistle and shout insults at the police in an attempt to *aguantar* (endure) those police actions.

The hostility of the police is evidenced by them beating, striking with the knees, kicking, or pushing group members or else detaining them using wrestling holds. In these situations, the orchestra and La Banda del Rojo fans, *move* the sectors even more forcefully; they maintain and increase the volume of their chants, their jumps intensify, and the flags are shaken with greater emphasis. Moreover, it seems that the aggression and adversity fill the fan group with vitality and energy. According to members of Los de Villa, when these young people arrested by the police are taken to jail, their friends—from the collective way of viewing their group—will have to pay '*lana*' (money) to avoid that they be processed (that is, hoping the authorities drop all charges against them). In practice, their peers collect money to unofficially pay[6] the police officers to release their fellows. This is another strategy for *mover* (moving) the group, where it is understood that everyone is part of the group and that it is necessary to protect each other. It is a security process that is part of a "political society" (Chatterjee, 2004) that young people have learned to negotiate, outside the law, with officials from a law enforcement institution that is constituted to operate based on exceptions (Caldeira, 2007).

Young members of La Banda del Rojo frequently complain about punitive measures adopted against them by the police and the club administrators for not being a group of fans who follow the official rules. These official measures aim to restrain the seemingly ungovernable behaviour of La Banda del Rojo, and to promote a climate of comfort and safety in order to attract families to the stadium. Some informants claim that this strategy seeks to increase the consumption of different products, food, and beverages inside the stadium and in neighbouring areas, assuming that families have greater purchasing power than young members of the fan group.

These practices are consistent with the findings of other investigations (Magazine & Fernández González, 2013), in the sense of viewing the unbridled behaviour displayed by the members of fan groups as straying from the 'family' philosophy that apparently must be experienced in soccer stadiums, and pressuring young group leaders to adhere to institutional authority. This view echoes the statement made by a public-security advisor in Toluca during an in-depth interview as part of this investigation. For her, one of the greatest concerns is that attendance by families, women, mothers and children, has shown considerable decline, only to be replaced by the presence of young men. In her words, this is now a problem, since most of these young men "show no respect for any authority, including police authority and adult authority". In one segment of the interview—and in a clear attempt to infantilize (Koolhaas, 2014) the members of La Banda del Rojo—she stated: "Quite frequently these young men lose the scope of all reasoning [...]; when they are in a group they become a violent crowd" (interviewed October 11, 2014).

According to the advisor and others associated with security inside the stadium, in order to deal with the situation, the public security agencies have decided to toughen the control operations to curb the youth rampages in an effort to pacify soccer venues in Toluca. Some of these measures have led to the transformation and control of venues, installing security cameras—some with facial-recognition technology—and restricting access to certain sections inside the stadium and in neighbouring parts of town. In addition, they are still issuing identification credentials to all members of soccer fan groups, which must be carried at all times inside the stadium. Consequently, this official process represents a mechanism by which the fans associated with La Banda del Rojo may be identified. Furthermore, this means that members of this group will be registered in a database that can be accessed by staff entrusted with the security of the Toluca Sporting Club and by the Toluca police force.

It should be noted that in Mexico the issue of security in sports stadiums has been tied to the crime-prevention agenda since the year 2011, in the wake of shootings that occurred in the vicinity of some stadiums

182   *Ricardo Duarte Bajaña*

in the northern part of the country (BBC World, 2011). More recently, in 2014, immediately after a serious clash between police officers and fans of the Chivas de Guadalajara team, the General Act on Physical Culture and Sports in Mexico was amended in less than fifteen days, which sought to impose a state of law and to use the liberal discourse of respect for individual rights. This reform establishes prison sentences from six months to four years for anyone involved in acts that may compromise security inside Mexican stadiums. It further explains that "Anyone who maliciously incites another individual or individuals to participate in brawls or physical attacks on people or their property shall be considered an instigator" (Ley General de Cultura Física y Deporte, 2018, art. 154). It is relevant that one of the representatives who advocated for this legislative reform stated:

> We are not criminalizing sports fans; we are not criminalizing athletes; we are merely exposing the violent people [...] we will hunt the violent ones, the irrational ones; we will track down the vandals who have acted in an extremely violent manner at sports events.
> (Editorial by Carmen Aristegui, 23 November 2017)

The government of Estado de Mexico (the federal state whose capital city is Toluca), in partnership with the management of Toluca Sporting Club, has encouraged the police to safeguard the stadium during sporting events, to prevent violent brawls. Residents of Toluca deem this measure necessary, because in their opinion some young fans disregard the disciplinary measures implemented by the official institutions. Consequently, for nearly two years the police force has been deployed in the stadium during soccer matches in order to ensure safety and prevent violence between opposing fans; but also to avoid violence inside La Banda del Rojo.

The young members of La Banda del Rojo emphatically challenge this law as well as the official measures, arguing that the alleged violence depends exclusively on the subjectivity of the police. On some occasions (although not always) their chanting and jumping in the stadium—behaviour valued as fun by the mainstream media—are interpreted by the police as violent acts and they are arrested. These young people argue that their actions are not violent because they do not try to hurt anyone, and that this is part of their *desmadre* behaviour, an essential element to *move* the sectors within the group.

During the parade of La Banda del Rojo first approaching the stadium, two blocks before they get there a police patrol had already blockaded the route the group had to take. Only pedestrians were allowed through a small space between the police patrol and the sidewalk, where four people at a time could pass, and through which the parade slowly passed. Columns of police officers, lined up on foot and on horseback, monitored the fans' movements. The young people follow the actions of the orchestra members: They did not look at the police, but just kept walking, reorganizing themselves to slowly

Figure 10.2 Patrol police blocking the parade of La Banda del Rojo. © Ricardo Duarte Bajaña.

pass through the space left by the police, meanwhile continuing to sing as if the police were not there (Figure 10.2).

One of the group leaders repeatedly shouted for the La Banda del Rojo members not to be provoked by the police actions. According to La Banda del Rojo, a parade is intended as a party; as such, any confrontation with the police may lead to a pitched battle of great magnitude that would tarnish the group's image. Mover el Sector implies promoting a non-violent public image of the group. La Banda del Rojo do not want Toluca residents or the media to believe that they would initiate any acts of violence. This intention is consistent with that of José Garriga Zucal (2013), in the sense that organized fans in Argentina prefer to be seen as people with aguante (endurance) or as members of a group, but never a violent group (Zucal, 2013).

In the course of the 21 months of fieldwork for this investigation, we observed only three cases of flagrant aggression and attempts to harm people who were already in the stadium, initiated by members of La Banda del Rojo. It is important to mention that these attacks were personal and involved only two or three people, not the entire group. However, it is necessary to remember that fights are a fundamental part of desmadre (motherlessness), a central dynamic of Mover el Sector.

It is noteworthy that some members of the Toluca Sporting Club management who were interviewed in the course of this study said they have no knowledge of what a *sector* is; ergo they know nothing about it, nor do they comprehend the rigorous organizational structure that has enabled the young members of La Banda del Rojo to become an established fan group.

184 *Ricardo Duarte Bajaña*

From their perspective, desmadre behaviour is the single and dominant trait of the young people associated with this group. In their view, there is a very fine line between desmadre and violence, and there is an urgent need to implement controls on the unbridled behaviour promoted within this fan group.

It is worth noting that these officials point out that during the last three years violent acts by members of La Banda del Rojo have decreased. Actually, officials value and endorse the fact that in recent years the group's leaders have attended the official meetings hosted by the club management and police representatives prior to major soccer fixtures held at the stadium. They admit that young members of the fan groups have shown an interest in collaborating with the security procedures during fixtures. On the other hand, these young men explain that their intention when attending these meetings is to inform the official agencies that the fan group is not violent, that it is perfectly organized, and that desmadre behaviour is highly valued in their structure.

Nevertheless, the discourses and practices displayed by the public security agencies disregard the organizational processes La Banda del Rojo has built and fine-tuned since its inception. Moreover, this lack of understanding only leads to increased tension during Toluca Sporting Club matches. The difficulties experienced by members of La Banda del Rojo in accessing their city's stadium reveal securitization processes that include police operating procedures and surveillance systems that provide an apparent sense of comfort and security. These security procedures in fact inhibit and restrict access by official actors and local residents to the youth proposal of Mover el Sector, understood as a sort of intangible heritage.

Although it is true that many people—including the mainstream media—value the colourfulness, chants, and emotion that these young people bring, these practices are often construed by security actors as pure desmadre and therefore as closely resembling acts of violence. Actors linked to securitization processes ignore both the rigorous social organization required to design and manage these acts and also the fact that, beyond the increased comfort and consumption promoted by official acts, the young members of the fan group try to promote values based on collective effort, steadfastness, and perseverance.

Conclusions

Mover el Sector may be understood as a sort of intangible heritage because it is a social construction process with clear characteristics that indicate a conjunction between an organizational structure and emotional and collective actions that are intended to fight for freedom. In addition, their practices and rituals—assumed by the fan group as their property—allude to a symbolic conjunction that demonstrates a particular way of understanding the world through a system of symbols and representations that have been

Securitization, and soccer fans in México   185

significant and that generate identity in the cultural history of La Banda del Rojo. However, there are securitization processes that exclude some aspects of heritage that are far from the ideal liberal morals (alcohol consumption, fighting, etc.). Here, desmadre is perceived only as a behaviour that generates violence, and which deters families from attending the stadium—subsequently reducing consumption of various products sold there. In this perspective, the access to and practice of the (urban) intangible heritage is limited, both physically and symbolically.

In the case of young people associated with La Banda del Rojo, we can observe increasing tension between the official perception that generalizes and criminalizes the activities of young people, and the young people's distrust for the decisions made by those responsible for public security in Toluca. This tension only causes discord between fans and public security officials; each side sees its counterparts as opponents who must be fought. This struggle has led to increased surveillance procedures in and around the stadium and makes it difficult for the Toluca population and those involved in security to comprehend the meaning of the Mover el Sector youth proposal, understood here as a sort of intangible heritage.

In parallel with the state security procedures implemented inside and outside the Toluca Stadium, the young members of La Banda del Rojo have managed to build a social system wherein solidarity and affection are interwoven (Hansen & Verkaaik, 2009). For the young members of this fan group, this is a way to combat the attacks on them typified by the government's security procedures, and to find pathways towards emancipation (Risør, 2016). Some of these roads entail unofficial negotiations. Evidently, this is not about choosing between security schemes in the constitutional framework or apparently illegal youth practices. The example of unofficial payments to release young men arrested by the police only confirms that we are facing official institutions that have been created to operate on the grounds of exceptions (Caldeira, 2007). Although members of the public security forces in Toluca and La Banda del Rojo have made some attempts to reach agreement, it is crucial to build bridges to help the state authority to understand that Mover el Sector can be accepted as a form of intangible heritage, one which would allow co-operating with security procedures inside and outside the Toluca city stadium.

Notes

1 Acknowledgments to Dr. Roger Magazine and the members of the Seminario Itinerante de Estudios Sociales del Deporte (Itinerant Sports Social Studies Seminar, SIESDE) based in Mexico, for their contributions that allowed the development of some arguments presented in this chapter. However, responsibility for the information and arguments set out in this chapter lies entirely with the author.
2 This work does not focus on the complexities of this concept, which does not have an exact translation into English. However, it has warranted a series of

186 Ricardo Duarte Bajaña

academic studies in Argentina (see Alabarces, Zucal, & Moreira, 2008; Archetti, 1985; Cabrera & Zucal, 2014, among others) and in other Latin American countries (Varela, 2012). It is worth noting that members of La Banda del Rojo also mention the idea of *aguante*, specifically in the sense of what Zucal (2013) calls "stoicism of the spectator when facing sports setbacks" (Zucal, 2013, p. 67).

3 Ants are actually highly socially organized, regimented species that manage to precisely co-ordinate the actions and movements of millions of individuals towards completion of a common task. However, in this context the group leader refers to the need for all members to move in the same direction, rather than (as happens with ant colonies) some individuals walking in one direction while others move in the opposite direction.

4 The young people of La Banda del Rojo have formed an orchestra called *Ridíkulos 26* in reference to the first 26 young people who started the project.

5 Song translation: "Go ahead, go ahead, go ahead Red Devils/Sweat the shirt/ We want another round to give [when a team wins a championship, its players run around the field receiving the ovation of the fans]/This band has endured 10 years/Bad results/And here we are partying/We always cheer/Wherever you go, there we are/Oooooh! Deportivo [in reference to the Toluca Sport Club]/You are the greatest thing, dear red [in reference to the team colours]".

6 No person with whom the field work was carried out used the word "bribe" to refer to this type of practice.

References

Alabarces, P., Zucal, J. G., & Moreira, M. V. (2008). "Aguante" y las hinchadas argentinas: Una relación violenta. *Horizontes Antropológicos, 14*(30) 113–136.

Archetti, E. (1985). *Fútbol y ethos*. Buenos Aires: Flacso.

Aristegui, C. (2017, November 23). Cárcel y multa a quien desate la violencia en los estadios, aprueban diputados. *Aristegui Noticias*. Retrieved from https://aristeguinoticias.com/2803/mexico/carcel-y-multa-a-quien-desate-la-violencia-en-los-estadios-aprueban-diputados/

BBC World (2011, August 21). Balacera provoca la suspensión de partido de fútbol en México. *BBC World*. Retrieved from www.bbc.com/mundo/noticias/2011/08/110820_mexico_ tiroteo_futbol_en Ciudad de México.

Cabrera, N., & Zucal, J. G. (2014). *Aguante y transgresión: Organización y lazos sociales en las barras de fútbol Argentino*. Paper presented at the II International Seminar on the History of Violence in Latin America XIX and XX Century, Córdoba.

Caldeira, T. (2007). *Ciudad de muros*. Barcelona: Gedisa.

Chatterjee, P. (2004). *Politics of the governed: Reflections on popular politics in most of the world*. New York, NY: Columbia University Press.

Duarte Bajaña, R. (2017). *"Desmadre organizado" y "mover el sector"*. *Clientelismo, estado corporativista y juventudes en dos barras de futbol en Toluca, Estado de México*. (Doctoral dissertation). Retrieved from Library of the Universidad Iberoamericana Ciudad de México. (X4.A12017 16424)

García Canclini, N. (1999). Los usos sociales del Patrimonio Cultural. In E. Aguilar Criado (Ed.), *Cuadernos patrimonio etnológico: Nuevas perspectivas de estudio* (pp. 16–33). Granada: Instituto Andaluz del Patrimonio Histórico.

Hansen, T. B., & Verkaaik, O. (2009). Introduction—Urban charisma: On everyday mythologies in the city. *Critique of Anthropology* 29(1), 5–26.

Kant, I. (1785 [1995]). *Fundamentación de la metafísica de las costumbres*. Madrid: Editorial Espasa Calpe, SA.

Koolhaas, R. (2014). *Are smart cities condemned to be stupid?* Retrieved from: www.archdaily.com/576480/rem-koolhaas-asks-are-smart-cities-condemned-to-be-stupid

Ley General de Cultura Física y Deporte (2018). Retrieved from: www.ordenjuridico. gob.mx/Documentos/Federal/html/wo82065.html

Magazine, R. (2008). *Azul y oro como mi corazón: Masculinidad, juventud y poder en una porra de los Pumas de la UNAM*. Universidad Iberoamericana, México.

Magazine, R., & Fernández González, S. (2013). La afición futbolística y la violencia en México: 1995 a 2012. In: Zucal, J. G. (Ed.), *Violencia en el fútbol: Investigaciones sociales y fracasos políticos* (pp. 185–208). Buenos Aires: Ediciones Godot.

Marcos Arévalo, J. (2004). La tradición, el patrimonio y la identidad. *Revista de estudios extremeños*, 60(3), 925–956.

Mill, J. S. (1859 [1997]). *Sobre la libertad*. Madrid: Alianza Editorial.

Prats, L. (2005). Concepto y gestión del patrimonio local. *Cuadernos de Antropología Social*, 21, 17–35.

Rawls, J. (1971 [1997]). *Teoría de la Justicia*. Ciudad de México: Fondo de Cultura Económica.

Risør, H. (2016). Closing down bars in the inner city centre: Informal urban planning, civil insecurity and subjectivity in Bolivia. *Singapore Journal of Tropical Geography*, 37, 330–342.

Smith, L. (2006). *Uses of heritage*. New York, NY: Routledge.

UNESCO. (2003). *Convención para la salvaguardia del patrimonio cultural inmaterial*. París: UNESCO.

Varela, S. (2012). Al América se le odia o se le ama Afición futbolera, melodrama, aguante, identidad y clientelismo en México. Doctoral thesis. México: Universidad Iberoamericana.

Zucal, J. G. (2013). Entre aguantadores y picantes. Violencia y Sectores populares en una hinchada de fútbol Argentina. In *Deporte y ciencias sociales: Claves para pensar las sociedades contemporáneas* (pp. 169–200). La Plata: EDULP.

11 (Re)activated heritage
Negotiating socialist history in the urban space of Luanda

Nadine Siegert

Introduction

With its anti-colonial commitment and promise of progress and equality, socialism was an attractive ideology for the first Angolan government within the era of Cold War binaries. Manifestations of socialist realism and alternative modernist practices derived from South–South and South–East cultural exchange and remain visible in Luanda's cityscape today. These range from monuments to commemoration sites and architectural experiments. The impact of socialist aesthetics on these concepts in Angola—and in Africa in general—is yet to be researched. Little is known about the agents and their motivations behind these projects, which were ideologically framed by a politics of solidarity and by the socialist construction of a new nation and the new (wo)man. Research on Luanda, Angola's capital, focuses on the impact of post-Angolan civil war capitalism and the oil boom (Ferraz, 2007; Gastrow, 2017). Bringing this research gap together with questions concerning heritage and the preservation of official memory in forms of visual culture is the key motivation of this chapter. How is this socialist cultural heritage reactivated today, and how does this reactivation impact the accessibility and securitization of this heritage? I focus on these questions by presenting two examples of recently renovated, state-sponsored art and architecture in the public space of Luanda: (a) The mural at the Military Hospital, and (b) the mausoleum of Agostinho Neto, Angola's first president. Both sites lack a profound study of their history and relevance within the historiography of the city. In the socialist years, some Angolan artists were commissioned by the state to conceptualize and construct monuments, murals, and commemoration sites. In retrospect, except for discussion in some newspaper articles, those works are not particularly relevant for the historiography or public heritage value of their respective sites today. This is also true of the two sites presently in focus. As the chapter will show, it is possible to trace some of the agents that were part of their construction, although the sources are rather vague. Nevertheless, both sites have gained new interest in the post-war and post-socialist Luanda of today, and new agents have claimed interest in reactivating this heritage. Practises of

Negotiating socialist history in Luanda 189

accessibility and securitization are also tested in this context—although cultural heritage practises are rather new. The country dealt with an ongoing civil war until 2002, followed by a brief oil boom that manifested in rather brutal real-estate growth. In this context it is difficult to find sites that might be regarded—either officially or unofficially—as public heritage; furthermore, practises of conservation, reactivation, securitization, and accessibility are still very much in the making.

Socialism as alternative aesthetic ideology in the decolonization process

Angola's capital, Luanda, has a population of approximately 2.8 million in the city centre and about 7 million in the greater metropolis. When approaching the city by plane, the convex seashore with its peninsulas are the first characteristics that catch one's view. Getting closer, we see the small city centre with an architectural collage: colonial buildings from the late 19th and early 20th centuries, tropical modernist blocks from the mid-20th century, as well as the hypermodern skyscrapers that have been placed within this fragile urban infrastructure of the inner city. Beyond the centre, huge semi-urban and peripheral areas spread into the space as well as newly built monocultural suburban structures that speak of the oil boom of the early 2000s. In the rather small core of the city centre, one building stands out that does not resemble any other architectural structure in Luanda: a rather tall and slender structure of grey concrete, with a futuristic shape reminiscent of a space rocket. It occupies a vast empty space near the city's seashore, which contrasts with the densely populated inner city. The concrete rocket is a mausoleum for Angola's first president, Agostinho Neto, and is today not only a cultural centre and commemoration site but—in its aesthetic and function—a remnant of a past period in Angola's history. Starting with this bird's-eye perspective on Luanda, I aim at an understanding of these spatial leftovers of the socialist period in Angola by understanding them as heritage that is produced and contested in the context of a negotiation of history in the postcolonial, post-war, and post-socialist context of the country's capital.

In Angola, the first years after independence, from 1975 to the early 1990s, formed a short but nevertheless important period when, due to the Marxist–Leninist political direction of the government, socialist values and aesthetics were also implemented on a cultural level. It is important to relate the emergence of the Military Hospital mural and the Neto mausoleum not only to a broader transnational aesthetics of socialism but also to understand the local context of that time. In the intellectual environment of the newly independent nation of Angola, different cultural strategies emerged. The intellectuals of the late 1960s and 1970s are referred to as the "utopian generation" (Pepetela, 2000), taking up a self-confident stance with their contribution to Angola's independence, through armed guerrilla struggle on the one hand, and on the other hand a cultural struggle initiated by

190 Nadine Siegert

urban writers, musicians, and artists. Many of them had been educated in European universities, like most of the intellectuals of the late colonial era, and instead of turning to arms in their struggle for independence, their weapons were arts and ideology (Rocha, 1997). Out of this intellectually rich atmosphere and the expressions of cosmopolitan culture grew the strong belief in a trans-ethnic, egalitarian, and socialist-universalist modernism in the early post-independence years, at least in the capital. Nevertheless, this ideological project manifested itself in the official programme of the ruling party, the People's Movement for the Liberation of Angola (MPLA), under the leadership of Angola's poet–politician president, Agostinho Neto (Brookshaw, 2002).

Socialist aesthetics as part of a decolonization process

Socialist aesthetics were part of the decolonizing practises in the context of nation-building from the 1950s to 1980s in a number of African states, such as Ghana, Tanzania, Ethiopia, and the former Portuguese colonies of Angola, Guinea-Bissau, Mozambique, and São Tomé and Príncipe. In African states that were leaning towards socialism, nationalism was not only formulated politically but also expressed aesthetically. With its anti-colonial commitment and promise of progress and equality, socialism was an attractive philosophy for a number of African states in the era of Cold War binaries (Babu, 1981; Keller, 1987; Pitcher & Askew, 2006). A formulation of artistic practises was embedded in this specific historical moment and its aesthetic paradigms. In some cases, this decolonization process included the rejection of Western categorizations of art, and a turning towards the local, renovated, and invented senses of tradition for the sake of aesthetic nationalisms; for some artists, such projects were imbued with a strong sense of nostalgia (Collier, 2016; Harney, 2004). During the 1950s and early 1960s the Négritude concept, which had been put into cultural political practise by Léopold Sédar Senghor in Senegal, was also one of the ideological role models in Angola (Egar, 2008; Ekpo, 2010; Harney, 2004). This tendency has been described and criticized by Fanon as "cultural nativism" that includes the danger of self-essentializing Black culture. Fanon (1963) proposed more radical concepts, drawing on ideas of the decolonization of body, mind, and spirit. Some actors strongly supported the idea that the arts were an important means by which to realize a socialist utopia, and their convictions set the stage for an Angolan state that sponsored and supported art production.

I argue that this rather socialist aesthetic ideology provided another, an alternative, register that did not draw from aesthetic resources that were considered as native and therefore 'authentic'. Rather, it derived from a collective archive of revolutionary aesthetics connected to socialism as a global ideology. In this political process of appropriation and adaptation, images have been transformed to adapt to new cultural contexts, when socialist

Negotiating socialist history in Luanda 191

iconography has travelled widely since the early 20th century, in particular through the development of visual propaganda as one of the major forms by which to communicate political agendas. Manifestations of socialist realism and alternative modernist practices thus derived from these South–South and South–East cultural exchanges. African nations could draw from a variety of ideological role models such as Cuba, the Soviet Union, or Maoist China, ideologically and aesthetically combined with often very diverse regional and ethnic cultures that had to be manufactured into a national culture.

In the former Portuguese colonies, this cultural transfer of socialist aesthetics was quite obvious, and—particularly during the initial years—went side by side with other aesthetic tendencies that amplified indigenous forms and media. The comparatively late process of independence among these countries was coined a 'revolutionary' process due to its violent and radical process of political and societal change. A violent liberation struggle against Portugal had preceded this independence and, in the heated global political atmosphere of the late 1960s and 1970s, the anti-colonial wars in what Portugal by then called its 'Overseas Territories' had also been the projection screen for Western leftist solidarity and Eastern communist aspirations. It was part of the imagination of a global anti-imperialist struggle that manifested itself rhetorically and visually in the propaganda produced by solidarity movements on both sides of the Iron Curtain (Frick, 2003; Henrichsen, 2002; Müller, 2014). The independent governmental parties adopted Marxism–Leninism as a political ideology after independence—all acting as single-party systems leaning towards the Soviet Union, the Eastern Bloc, and Cuba as their main international allies. In this context the formulation of a national culture was a key element of nation-building, and the formulation of a universal modernism was directed to a socialist future.

Socialist heritage in the urban space of Luanda

This text focuses on two manifestations of socialism in the urban space of Luanda, questioning how they relate to the dimensions of accessibility and securitization. Even if these manifestations have not been officially declared part of Angolan heritage, they receive a certain form of attention. Both sites have recently been renovated and reconfigured by the state, which hints at a certain importance within the public space. Nevertheless, neither site is listed as official cultural heritage. The Tentative List of the UNESCO World Heritage Centre for Angola lists sites from the precolonial era, such as the archaeological site of Tchitundu-Hulu in the Namib Desert; and the early colonial period, such as a number of fortresses and churches. Recently, the site of Cuito Cuanavale has been added to the Tentative List, a place where one of the biggest battles of the Cold War period occurred during the 1980s. This is a rather unusual decision, since the site is charged with the cultural memory of both the Angolan Civil War and also Cold War memories. The

192 Nadine Siegert

battle of Cuito Cuanavale included Cuban troops, who fought against the South African army—a clear indication of the ideological basis of the war, against both imperialism, generally, and South Africa's brutal apartheid system, in particular. However, beyond Cuito Cuanavale, the list neglects Angola's recent period of socialism. This reflects the current situation on socialist sites and their relationship to the urban heritage discourse—not only in Angola (Leturcq, 2009; Peterson, Gavua, & Rassool, 2015). In Luanda's urban space, socialism might be part of an uncomfortable, yet too-recent past and 'heritage-making' in relation to the idea of heritage. Therefore, the official engagement with the sites reveals this discomfort and inability to position the socialist period in a way that makes this history comprehensible and accessible. The following sections present two very different examples of sites in urban space, both of which relate to the socialist past and have been taken care of by initiatives that are state-sponsored or close to the Angolan government: a mural depicting MPLA history at the Military Hospital, and the mausoleum of Agostinho Neto.

Both sites were created within the framework of a certain aesthetic ideology. They can thus be regarded as visual culture of the socialist period in Angola, manifest in both a historical and contemporary dimension. I am less interested in the social dimension of the two sites as part of the urban space, but rather in their aesthetic content. Therefore, I view them from an artistic perspective, analysing their form and media but also by contextualizing them in their historical and cultural frameworks. Besides analysing the production of the works, I will also describe how they have been transferred into the contemporary urban space as cultural heritage and which forms of transformation this heritage-making has entailed. How is this socialist cultural heritage reactivated today, and how does this reactivation impact the accessibility and securitization of the heritage?

The medium of the mural as heritage in urban space

Murals were a popular genre in the early socialist years, including in Angola, as one of the prime media for communicating socialist values. In the form of political agitation, they depicted socialist values and visions. As part of the classical genres of socialist realism in Eastern Europe and the former Soviet Union, murals had to be "realistic in form and socialist in content", as defined in 1932 by Aleksandr Gerasimov, emphasizing the educational role of art within society (cited in Groys, 2013, p. 141). After the Russian Revolution of 1917, murals became one of the most important genres for agitprop groups, who sought to find a visual manifestation of revolutionary ideas and to agitate the masses. This form travelled globally to other socialist countries such as China and North Korea during the Cold War period after World War II (Portal, 2005, p. 20), and also to a number of socialist countries in Africa such as Mozambique, Angola, Ghana, and Ethiopia between the 1960s and 1980s. Socialist realism media, such as posters, monuments, and murals employed many recurrent motifs reflecting its four principles: (a) The work must be proletarian and thus relevant to the working class; (b) it must be realistic in a representational sense; (c) it must be partisan and support the aims of state and party; and lastly, (d) it must be 'typical' by representing recognizable issues (Groys, 2013, p. 141). More idealistic than realistic, the murals—as diverse as they might be in their local and regional peculiarities—visualized the ideal socialist society or the struggle that brings about such a society. Often, a motivational aspect was embedded in the murals, a direction that made clear where the struggle would lead, through the depiction of a major figure who reassured the righteousness of the cause. Although this leader figure is often shown larger than other figures in such murals, there was sufficient diversity within the portrayed characters to enable identification with one of the idealized socialist archetypes. Aside from the obvious figures of the soldier, the peasant, and the worker, such images also represented the teacher, the technician, and the intellectual, often both male and female. As such, the mural as a medium for agitation depicted not only what the socialist society had already achieved but, moreover, what it aspired to become. It can therefore be regarded as a futurist genre, in the sense that it visually anticipated how the future might look and how it might emerge from the present (Zander, 2004).

The artistic form of mural painting was not only prominent in the socialist countries of the Global North but was also an important factor in socialist and socially engaged art in Latin America, most prominently in Chile, Cuba, Mexico, and Nicaragua. The figurative works reflected society and its immediate concerns and, as a genre, it spread not only within the Americas but also to other parts of the Global South (Kunzle, 1995). Next to Soviet agit-prop art, Latin American muralism is the second most important socialist reference on the African continent. In the 1960s and 1970s it was primarily the work of Chilean artists, who formulated their resistance against the Pinochet dictatorship that influenced mural artists globally. A number of Chileans fled Pinochet's regime to find refuge in Mozambique; together with Mozambican artists they formed muralist collectives in the late 1970s, and skilled artists adapted their knowledge and styles to the local context (Sachs, 1983; Seidman, 2012, p. 19).

It would, therefore, be limiting to consider these transnational influences as unilinear. Specific moments also created refluxes of images; for example, the mosaic that Michail Posochin created in 1967 at Moscow's Oktyabr Cinema was aesthetically inspired by Mexican muralists (Rupprecht, 2015, p. 123). Additionally, the first Wandbildaktionen ('mural actions') of artist collectives in the early years of the German Democratic Republic were also informed by Mexican muralists (Jacoby, 2007, p. 190). On the African continent, two murals stand out when considering Socialist Modernism: those by João J. Craveirinha at the Praça dos Heróis in Maputo (Mozambique), and by Teresa Gama at the Military Hospital in Luanda. In the following, the latter will serve as my first example.

194 *Nadine Siegert*

The mural in Luanda—anticipating the society yet to come

Leaving the birds-eye view and entering the streets of Luanda, one finds a number of other traces of history in the city centre.[1] Monuments and empty pedestals speak of the colonial period that started in the late 15th century with the arrival of the Portuguese. But socialist aesthetics have also inscribed themselves in monuments and other forms within the urban space. Such monuments were mostly state-commissioned projects that activated transnational cultural relations with socialist brother states, such as North Korea, which through the Mansudae Overseas Projects gifted the Angolan government two bronze sculptures. Although these cultural–political relationships have been increasingly researched in recent years, very little is known about the development of the other communicative public art forms, such as murals and posters, in that context.

In the post-independence period, murals, wall paintings, and mosaics appeared that referred to socialist aesthetics. Teresa Gama was one of the artists eager to support the independent state with her artistic skills. She was not only one of the very few female artists in the history of Angolan art, but was also politically active during late colonialism. Her studio in central Luanda was a meeting point for artists with anti-colonial and radical leftist positions. After independence in 1975, she was commissioned to paint the mural together with a group of art students that included Rui Garção and Cilita Martins,[2] who were taught at the then fine art school called Barracão.

Until the early 1980s, the arts were considered an important means of realizing a socialist utopia, and such convictions set the stage for an Angolan state that sponsored and encouraged art production, similarly to the formulations in the socialist realism movements of Russia and Cuba. On the physical level, in the first years after independence, socialist realism was predominately seen in public murals and monuments. During this period, only a few artists, such as Gama and António Ole, worked closely with the MPLA in both art and film. Yet, the movement of 'socialist art' soon ended in the early 1980s, and most of the regional artists focused on painting and sculptural practices, exploring the potential of transforming traditional and indigenous imagery into contemporary aesthetics. Despite this shift, the state did not commission any further works until the end of the civil war in 2002, except for rare examples such as António Ole's iron sculpture, *Mitologias II*, in 1986.

Gama's untitled mural conveys the euphoria of independence, the departure birth of the new nation, and communicates new values and visions in the form of political agitation in the characteristic representation of the history of the MPLA as the leading political party with its socialist direction. In close proximity to the mural, colonial monuments to Portuguese heroes were pulled down and replaced with socialist statues such as bronzes of the Angolan president or the anti-colonial heroine Queen Ginga (Siegert, 2017).

Negotiating socialist history in Luanda 195

The mural was created in 1978, one year after the founding statement of the National Union of Plastic Artists (UNAP) was written in 1977. Like the mural in a visual form, this statement also communicates the cultural discourse of that time, which was both linked to universalist socialist concepts and to tropes such as the "New Man", as well as ideas of a genuine Angolan identity (termed *Angolanidade*) based on notions of collectivity and "Africanity" (Collier, 2013, p. 188). Thus, the subject matter of Gama's mural went beyond what Fanon has criticized as nativism also within the Négritude philosophy, as uncritical references to African traditions without embracing modern values with a critical mind (Fanon, 1963, p. 215). Both history and future are depicted on the wall, which surrounds the entire hospital near a traffic intersection. Applying the classification of socialist realism stated above, the figurative scenes of the mural—though closer to propaganda than to revolutionary art—convey the euphoria of independence and the birth of the new nation.

The mural's images are visible on the outer side of the encircling wall. A good time to observe the mural is while sitting in a traffic jam around the square on a late afternoon: One can read a narration into the mural, in which sequences of panels each tells a singular short story, starting from the key moments in the history of the independence struggle against the Portuguese colonialists, such as the start of Angola's armed struggle in 1961; the exiling of headquarters to Brazzaville (Republic of the Congo) in 1963; or the flying of the new flag in 1975. Content-wise, the artist was drawing from the classical register of socialist typologies, and we find the teacher, the industrial worker, and the peasant among the depicted figures.

Although Gama's panels depicting the anti-colonial struggle have a narrative quality, many panels dedicated to the post-independence period have a more emblematic character, showing, for example, the national emblem or the word "independence". The emblem of the period was—like the flag—designed in a very characteristically socialist form: Different plants, such as corn and cotton, formed a circle with a cogwheel, a machete, and a hoe. In the centre of the circle were the rising sun, an open book, and a golden star. Another panel even depicted the emblem of the National Organization of Women, showing a woman with a child and a rifle—a typical representation of that period. These emblematic representations are surrounded by scenes that depict a set of figures necessary to complete a socialist society, such as a teacher speaking in front of a group of people. Other panels show aspects of communality, representing the mass struggle, and crowds with raised hands and fists. It is striking how impersonally the figures are represented, clearly emphasizing the idea that socialism is an ideology for 'every man and every woman'. Through its socialist aesthetic, the mural provides a transparent message and simplifies the anticolonial struggle and its teleological aim. There are no other known artworks by Gama, so it is not possible to contextualize the mural within her oeuvre, but the mural can nevertheless be regarded as one of the focal points of socialist

196 *Nadine Siegert*

aesthetics within the public space of Luanda. Further research is needed, not only because—unlike most other public artworks of the period—it was produced by a group of Angolan artists rather than commissioned by socialist brother states, but also because it is one of the very few works made by a female artist during Angolan Socialist Modernism. In comparison to the mural in Maputo, called "*em honra dos nossos heróis*" (In Honour of our Heroes), it is also interesting that the one in Luanda does not depict any iconic personalities. The Maputo mural was conceptualized by the Mozambican artist João Craveirinha and finalized in 1980 with many international assistants (Saehrendt, 2017, p. 105). Whereas Craveirinha decided to represent the two revolutionary leaders, Eduardo Mondlane and Samora Machel, in very stylized and recognizable form, Angolan revolutionaries are not personalized on the mural in Luanda. This is also interesting because depictions of the leader Agostinho Neto had been quite common in the first years after independence and appeared in various forms and media. Also, stylistically, the mural at the Military Hospital differs from another rather orthodox socialist mural located at the pedestal of the Memorial of Agostinho Neto. Whereas the pedestal artwork clearly draws stylistically from socialist realism motifs and formal aesthetics, the Gama mural at the Military Hospital is closer to the visual language associated with Latin American muralism. There are three strong formal elements in the mural: the figurative scenes that depict the typical protagonists of a socialist revolution; secondly, rather pictorial elements such as rainbows and waves; and thirdly, a decorative abstract background rendered in bright colours that enhance the non-realist style. This 'pop art' style is also found in other African murals from that period, such as one in Maputo.

Restoration: negotiating different interests

The mural was renovated in 2008 by a group of 15 local artists, among them Sozinho Lopes, Dani Adão, Manuel Ventura, Antoninho, and Sabby. Nevertheless, in terms of style and subject matter, the mural now somehow appears misplaced within the urban landscape of Luanda, which has been dominated by the capitalist post-war construction boom of recent years. The Ministry of Culture commissioned the private arts initiative, Espaço Dizalalu, to renovate the mural under the supervision of the artist António Gonga. This recent restoration may suggest that the ruling party is comfortable being depicted through this nostalgic mode of artwork from the 1970s, the styles and subjects of which one might imagine had long ago been left behind.

From the mural at the Military Hospital, two different sets of images are available. The majority are recent pictures taken by myself or found online after the mural's renovation in 2009. A smaller set of images predate the renovation work and show that the mural has been considerably transformed (Figure 11.1). For example, colours have not only been refreshed

Figure 11.1 Mural at the Military Hospital in Luanda. Original version painted by Teresa Gama in 1978. © Nadine Siegert.

but probably also changed. Today's mural is therefore not only a renovated original but has also been made 'heritage' according to the needs and values of contemporary political interests. The renovation has created a second layer, a form of palimpsest that hides the initial aesthetics but at the same time reveals a certain interpretation of the probably outdated aesthetics. In a way, by erasing a more complex and ambivalent narrative from the past this practise secures a certain narrative of the past that is appropriate for the present. It simplifies, reducing the historiography of the struggle to a digestible form.

The anti-colonial struggle is represented with two different historical scenes: the atrocities of Portuguese colonialism, and the guerrilla war. In this section, a number of panels have been over-painted, for example one that previously depicted a certain degree of violence by the colonialists. Among the older pictures taken prior to the renovation, one scene shows two men in military uniform, one with a machete, one with a rifle, committing violence towards two smaller figures, supposedly children. This might depict colonial violence against the indigenous population and resembles documentary photographic material available from the period of the 1960s. Another panel shows two figures in dark-green military uniforms. They are pursuing two lighter-skinned, bearded figures wearing lighter-coloured uniforms and holding bags in their hands; From one bag, paper is dropping that resembles money. Of the two men in dark-green uniforms, one carries a machete and has darker skin, whereas the other figure has an animal-like head and is depicted leaping headlong towards the other two men. This

198 Nadine Siegert

image may also depict a scene from the anti-colonial struggle—a moment when the Portuguese are chased from the country while attempting to take with them as much wealth as possible. The depiction of the animal-headed figure might hint towards the involvement of magical practices in the guerrilla war, and the narrative of the ultimate military superiority of the anti-colonial movement. Both scenes have been deleted from the contemporary version of the mural. This practise can be understood as a form of heritage-making that neglects particular aspects of Angolan history that remain uncomfortable. Angola considers itself as an economically strong post-colonial state, but only rarely addresses the atrocities of both the anti-colonial and civil war periods. Even more interesting is the silencing of certain aspects of the struggle that go against the dominant doctrine of the secular state. The fact that this panel was not retained is probably due to the level of violence depicted and the relative opaqueness of the scene involving the animal. It is nevertheless one of the most interesting parts of the mural, as it disturbs the orthodox format of socialist aesthetics by introducing the animal-headed figure; the socialist party MPLA tried to not only flatten cultural diversity through its trans-ethnic politics but also rejected animist practices in its anti-religious and anti-spiritual modernist secularism. This motif therefore transgresses the standard cast of 'socialist scenery.' Both examples demand further investigation but might serve here as a first example of the complexities of heritage-making in the post-socialist space of urban Luanda.

As a commemoration of anti-colonial resistance, the mural still serves its function as a unifying symbol of the Angolan state. The country's socialist era and its accompanying aesthetics have not been completely abandoned, however, and can be reactivated. This supports the continuation of the political narrative of the MPLA as the party of the people and is embedded within a commemorative mode of innocuous nostalgia. The murals of the late 1970s may have been reactivated, but the panels with the greatest political potential have been irrevocably destroyed. As such, it is also a form of *authorized heritage discourse* (Smith, 2006, p. 29), since it is irretrievably erased, which thus excluded a certain narrative of the struggle, thereby allowing only for a dominant, authorized version. This can be understood as an authorized form of securitizing and making accessible only a certain interpretation of the past as national memory, flattened to a simplified version. Maybe this also has an effect on attitudes towards the site. Despite being a colourful site that is visible to many people who pass the Military Hospital on their daily routes either by foot, public transport, or car, it receives little attention: Nobody stops to look at the panels, and neither is it a topic of discussion concerning the city and its aesthetics. It is rather ignored and disregarded—perhaps because the mural is not able to tell a story beyond the already worn-out narrative of the anti-colonial struggle, where the dominance of the MPLA's history is unquestioned and does not leave space for other versions nor for small his- and herstories.

The Mausoleum of Agostinho Neto

My second example, the mausoleum of Agostinho Neto, is obviously very different in form, but the practise of making it heritage within the urban space of Luanda also hints at the inconclusive attempts to deal with the socialist past within Angolan society and by the government (Figure 11.2). The mausoleum's construction began in the 1980s with financial support from the Soviet Union.[3] When Angola's first president died in Moscow in 1979, the USSR offered the new republic a monumental mausoleum to host his embalmed body and symbolize his greatness, in line with the socialist tradition. In 1980 a team of Soviet designers from the Design Institute of the Union of Soviet Socialist Republics conceived the building that was to be erected in Luanda. Two years later, in 1982, the laying of the cornerstone

Figure 11.2 Memorial Agostinho Neto, Luanda. © 2015 Nadine Siegert.

200 *Nadine Siegert*

took place, but due to the long-running civil war, the economic and political crisis in Angola, and finally the collapse of the USSR, its completion was delayed for more than 20 years. In 1998, the Angolan government decided to restart the works, transforming the mausoleum into a cultural centre. First, with Brazilian architects, and since 2005 with the North Korean company Mansudae Overseas Projects, the building was completed in 2011. The same company has also been commissioned to construct other memorials and monuments on the African continent, such as in Namibia, Zimbabwe, and recently in Senegal (Becker, 2011; de Jong & Foucher, 2012).

In 2012 the building opened to the public as a heritage site and, today, the 120-metre-high concrete structure of the mausoleum is a public venue and one of the most visible landmarks in the city. Similarly to Lenin's mausoleum in Moscow, the sarcophagus of the former Angolan president is stored in a central block that is also the pyramidal base of the constructivist concrete tower. The contrast between the rough and brutal elegance of the memorial's exterior and the airport-like interiors, or the Dubai-like design of the surrounding area, reveal the long history of the project and the shifting paradigms between the early post-independence government and that of today. Neto's memorial talks about a specific Eastern European tradition of monument building, in line with the purest constructivist tradition. The bright socialist future embedded in Neto's engraved words, and in the beauty of the original design of the monumental building, clashes with the current social issues that are evident in Luanda and which affect the country.

The (in)accessibility of the memorial

The memorial is situated within an empty urban space that was previously rather abandoned and was beautified after its renovation as a park and parking space. Access is limited, since the access arrangements are designed for cars rather than pedestrians. Individual visitors are rare, and visits take place in the rather organized form of guided groups. When approaching the monument, one must be careful not to take pictures of it from outside the memorial space, since this zone is secured by military personnel and photographing them is strictly prohibited. When entering the physical space, visitors are asked to join a guided tour and are not allowed to stroll around at their own pace and direction. Thus, visiting the memorial also always includes receiving the official narrative provided by the guides. The guided tour follows a series of information boards with photographs that narrate the history of independence, focusing on Agostinho Neto. The basement is divided into three wings. At the main, central entrance a gallery displays 12 bronze sculptures representing different professions in an almost Socialist Realistic style, and Neto's signature engraved in bronze is flanked by two of the most famous of his poems: "The way to the Stars" and "Farewell to the Start Time". In the corridor around the room that hosts the body of Agostinho Neto, 48 bronze plates are engraved with the eulogy and with extracts from a speech delivered by the former president on 11 November 1975. That wing also accommodates a library, a digital library, a documentation centre, two VIP rooms, and three shops. In the right wing is located a conference room and other research spaces, while the left wing hosts four art workshops.

At present, the building could be seen as an architectural metaphor for a failed socialist utopia in Angola. As a manifestation of late Socialist Modernist architecture, it was part of a Soviet Modernism that referred aesthetically to space travel and hyperbolic futurity; a monument as a projection of a future that was already threatened when the mausoleum was constructed in the early 1980s. Today, the Memorial of Agostinho Neto is an ambiguous, almost schizophrenic object. Viewing it from a certain distance, the mausoleum is a completely abstract construction, a gigantic, beautiful landmark on the boundary between sculpture and architecture. Its geometric shapes, built of indestructible material, seem to be firmly skewered, yet ready to move. The monument reveals a neutral iconography with no decorations but plastic shapes.

In contrast, the interiors and some elements of the outdoor space—such as the giant statue representing Neto when national independence was declared and the flag was hoisted—are devoted to the cult of the national hero, with relics of the great leader, images and statues representing him, and symbols of his world.

If, on the one hand, the Memorial of Neto talks about a specific Eastern European tradition of monument building, in line with the purest constructivist tradition, on the other hand the redevelopment of the area that hosts the memorial and the newly designed interiors show a visual language that reveals a shifted symbolism and world view. The cultural centre has to be a crowd-pleasing place of static memory that forces one to forget present-day social contradictions in Angola. The bright socialist future, embedded in Neto's engraved words and in the beauty of the original design of the monumental building, clashes with the current social issues that are evident in Luanda and affect the country, caused by the severe economic imbalances and a political journey to the sun—creating access through arts

Whereas the actual accessibility of the Neto memorial is a limited and highly predetermined one, public approaches might offer another alternative, and maybe even a counter-narrative that gives access to the mausoleum in other, more imaginary forms. Not surprisingly, the most popular nickname for the futurist building is the 'space rocket' (*o foguetao*). The Angolan artist Kiluanji Kia Henda built his multimedia work *Icarus 13: The First Journey to the Sun* (2007) around this appropriation of the site by the public. In many works, the artist uses fiction to inscribe alternative narrations into collective memory (Siegert, 2016, 2017). Also, in this work, the artist transforms the mausoleum into a rocket named *Icarus* (Bould, 2012). The work reflects the post-independence utopia, when socialist countries strived to be equally as powerful as their Western antagonists. This 'way

202 *Nadine Siegert*

to the stars' is also a reference to the poem by Agostinho Neto, published in his book, *Sagrada Esperança*, one of the main texts anticipating independence (Neto, 1979).

The engagement by artists such as Kiluanji Kia Henda with sites of the colonial aftermath can be considered as a form of memory work and heritage-making that is fundamentally different from the narrative of the official sites of commemoration. Reference points in the cityscape, such as the ubiquitous mausoleum of Agostinho Neto, are reinterpreted and thus enable alternative readings. Here the mausoleum—a monument and, as such, part of the cityscape—not only becomes a spacecraft but is connected to a (post)socialist and even Afro-futuristic imaginary space—an imaginary city. In this work the artist plays with the heroic past and its political icons. Kiluanji Kia Henda's preferred visual metaphor for the futuristic building is the space shuttle; here, it recalls the story of the African political leader who, in order to prove the progress of decolonization during the Cold War, proposed a manned space journey—to the sun. To avoid being burned like its Greek predecessor, Icarus, the journey was to take place at night. Combining the narrative of the mythical flight with the historical saga of the accident that occurred during the United States's Apollo 13 mission, Kia Henda adds to this the narrative of an anonymous African political leader eager to challenge the space programmes of the great powers. The outrageous reach and hyperbolic attitude comments roundly on attempts to vie for national power, the hypermania of the booming oil business, and indeed the same oversized visions in the context of the universalist, modernist utopia and its failures in Angola and beyond.

By transforming the mausoleum into an artwork, Kia Henda counters its role as a commemorative site, even questioning its seriousness by mocking it as a space shuttle. Nevertheless, this achieves a form of accessibility that the commemorative site is not able to provide. The artist builds on the public reference of the site as a space rocket and denies the relationship to the political history of the first leader. He thus creates a direct link to a popular discourse that is probably much more accessible than the exaggerated, artificial, and highly inaccessible manifestation of the mausoleum as commemoration site.

Conclusion

Practises of restoration and preservation of heritage are rare within the context of post-war, post-socialist Luanda. The dominant ideology of oil-based capitalism also impacts the cultural sector and asks for new buildings that reflect the image of Luanda as Africa's Dubai—with shiny surfaces for the economic elite (Gastrow, 2017; Oliveira, 2015). History in the form of old architecture within the city centre is rather perceived as cumbersome in this context and is either erased or squeezed between the glossy high-rises of postmodern times. Therefore, it is maybe surprising at first glance that the mural of the Military Hospital and the mausoleum of the first president have been renovated and supposedly considered as heritage within the urban space of

Negotiating socialist history in Luanda 203

Luanda. Since this socialist heritage is connected to a political ideology that has been abandoned by the capitalist Angolan state, its relationship with the physical leftovers remains ambivalent. They are included in debates concerning reconciliation after the post-civil-war trauma, and their former political context has been widely neglected by the public discourse. The socialist history embedded in the two sites has been incorporated into the narrative of the post-war nation instead of being unpacked to enable a critical discourse of the past in all its complexities. As we have seen, the historical and socio-political context of the Angolan nation is consciously activated in a form of heritage culture that shows how the Angolan political elite seeks to embed the socialist past in a contemporary memory culture. Socialism in this narrative becomes an unquestioned part of that history, serving to communicate a story of heroism and pacification. It is not used in any way to cast a critical view on contemporary social and economic imbalances or on Angola's savage capitalism. This manifests in the recourse to images from the archive of political revolutions. The images themselves are pacified and bereft of their revolutionary power in the case of the restored mural, and in the case of the mausoleum transformed into a commemorative centre that freezes an ambivalent socialist past in a unified official history—a national heritage.

With regard to securitization, both sites function very differently, although their faith is rooted in the same historical and political decision. The analysis of both sites clearly demonstrate the ambiguity of how this historical and political conceptualization of securitization influences access, both limiting and broadening: one being rather ignored and therefore highly accessible, the other rather inaccessible due to the securitization measurements practised on it. In both cases, we see an attempt by official agents to apply authorized heritage practises: In the case of the mural, by erasing complex and ambivalent parts of history; in the case of the mausoleum, by transforming it into a sealed and over-secured commemorative site for the first president. Both sites lack public engagement or even make that impossible by regulating the public or making the site irrelevant for public discourse. One way to resolve this inaccessibility through streamlining and over-securitization might be an artistic one, as the work *Icarus 13* by Kiluanji Kia Henda has shown. Looking at the creativity of contemporary Angolan artists, we can anticipate such creative engagements with public heritage, which quite soon will transcend the authoritarian forms.

Notes

1 The research is based on my fieldwork in Luanda and other related places since 2006. There, I visited the mural several times and discussed it with artists, cultural producers, and academics. In particular, I want to thank the anthropologist Margarida Paredes, who was a close friend of Teresa Gama. Together, they were part of the female division of the FAPLA (originally the armed wing of the MPLA, the People's Movement for the Liberation of Angola). See also Paredes (2015).

204   Nadine Siegert

2 This information stems from personal communication with Margarida Paredes and e-mail confirmation by Rui Garção.
3 Parts of this subchapter were written together with Favio Vanin of Vrije Universiteit, Brussels.

References

Babu, M. (1981). *African socialism or socialist Africa?* London: Zed Books.

Becker, H. (2011). Commemorating heroes in Windhoek and Eenhana: Memory, culture and nationalism in Namibia, 1990–2010. *Africa, 81*(4), 519–543.

Bould, M. (2012). Superpower: Africa in science fiction. *Science Fiction Studies, 39*(3), 559–561. Retrieved from https://doi.org/10.5621/sciefictstud.39.3.0559

Brookshaw, D. (2002). Voices from Lusophone borderlands: The Angolan identities of António Agostinho Neto, Jorge Arrimar and José Eduardo Agualusa. *NUI Maynooth Papers in Spanish, Portuguese and Latin American Studies, 4.*

Collier, D. (2013). A "new man" for Africa? Some particularities of the Marxist Homem novo within Angolan cultural policy. In J. E. P. Mooney & F. Lanza (Eds.), *De-centering Cold War history: Local and global change* (pp. 187–206). London: Routledge.

Collier, D. (2016). *Repainting the walls of Lunda: Information colonialism and Angolan art*. Minneapolis: University of Minnesota Press.

Egar, E. E. (2008). *The crisis of Negritude: A study of the Black Movement against intellectual oppression in the early 20th century*. Irvine, CA: Universal Publishers.

Ekpo, D. (2010). From Negritude to Post-Africanism. *Third Text, 24*(2), 177–187. Retrieved from https://doi.org/10.1080/09528821003722108

Fanon, F. (1963). *The wretched of the Earth*. New York: Grove Press.

Ferraz, S. (2007). *Compreender o espaço público para requalificae a cidade – Luanda*. Presented at the Seminário Estudos Urbanos. Vazios Úteis, ISCTE Lissabon.

Frick, R. (2003). *Das trikontinentale Solidaritätsplakat. El cartel tricontinental de solidaridat (The tricontinental solidarity poster)*. Bern: Comedia.

Gastrow, C. (2017). Aesthetic dissent: Urban redevelopment and political belonging in Luanda, Angola. *Antipode, 49*(2), 377–396. Retrieved from https://doi.org/10.1111/anti.12276

Groys, B. (2013). *Art power*. Cambridge, MA: MIT Press.

Harney, E. (2004). *In Senghor's shadow*. Durham, NC: Duke University Press.

Henrichsen, D. (2002). *Das Archiv Der Solidaritätsgruppe Medic' Angola, Kämpfendes Afrika (Zürich, 1971–1988): The archive of the solidarity group Medic' Angola/ Kämpfendes Afrika (Zurich, 1971–1988)*. Basel: Basler Afrika Bibliographien.

Jacoby, P. (2007). *Kollektivierung der Phantasie?: Künstlergruppen in der DDR zwischen Vereinnahmung und Erfindungsgabe*. Bielefeld: Transcript Verlag.

Jong, F. de, & Foucher, V. (2012). La tragédie du roi Abdoulaye ? Néomodernisme et Renaissance africaine dans le Sénégal contemporain. *Politique africaine*, (118), 187–204.

Keller, E. J. (1987). *Afro-Marxist regimes: Ideology and public policy* (Auflage: new edition). Boulder, CO: Lynne Rienner.

Kunzle, D. (1995). *The murals of revolutionary Nicaragua, 1979–1992*. Berkeley, CA: University of California Press.

Leturcq, J.-G. (2009). Heritage-making and policies of identity in the "post-conflict reconstruction" of Sudan. *Égypte/Monde Arabe*, (5–6), 295–328. Retrieved from https://doi.org/10.4000/ema.2904

Müller, T. R. (2014). *Legacies of socialist solidarity: East Germany in Mozambique.* Lanham, MD: Lexington Books.

Neto, A. A. (1979). *Sagrada esperança.* Lissabon: Livraria Sá da Costa Editora.

Oliveira, P. R. S. de. (2015). *Magnificent and beggar land: Angola since the civil war.* London: C. Hurst & Co.

Paredes, M. (2015). *Combater Duas Vezes.* Lisbon: Verso da História.

Pepetela. (2000). *A geração da utopia.* Rio de Janeiro: Editora Nova Fronteira.

Peterson, D. R., Gavua, K., & Rassool, C. (2015). *The politics of heritage in Africa: Economies, histories, and infrastructures.* Cambridge, UK: Cambridge University Press.

Pitcher, M. A., & Askew, K. M. (2006). African socialisms and postsocialisms. *Africa*, 76(Special Issue 01), 1–14. Retrieved from https://doi.org/10.3366/afr.2006.0001

Portal, J. (2005). *Art under control in North Korea.* London: Reaktion.

Rocha, E. (1997). A Casa dos Estudantes do Império nos anos de fogo: Depoimento sobre a acção política da juventude africana da CEI no quadro da luta pela libertação nacional das colônias portuguesas. In *Mensagem* (pp. 103–114). Lisboa: Associação Casa dos Estudantes do Império.

Rupprecht, T. (2015). *Soviet internationalism after Stalin: Interaction and exchange between the USSR and Latin America during the Cold War.* Cambridge, UK: Cambridge University Press.

Sachs, A. (1983). *Images of a revolution: The murals of Maputo.* Harare: Zimbabwe Publishing House.

Saehrendt, C. (2017). *Kunst im Kampf für das 34;Sozialistische Weltsystem34: Auswärtige Kulturpolitik der DDR in Afrika und Nahost.* Stuttgart: Franz Steiner Verlag.

Seidman, J. (2012). Revolutionary Mozambican painter Malangatana Valente Nguenha. In J. MacPhee & A. Dunn (Eds.), *Signal 02* (pp. 7–27). Oakland: PM Press.

Siegert, N. (2016). The archive as construction site—Collective memory and trauma in contemporary art from Angola. *World Art*, 6(1), 103–123.

Siegert, N. (2017). Art topples monuments: Artistic practice and colonial/postcolonial relations in the public space of Luanda. *Portuguese Literary and Cultural Studies*, 30/31, 150–173.

Smith, L. (2006). *Uses of heritage.* London: Routledge.

Zander, M. J. (2004). Instructional resources: Murals as documents of social history. *Art Education*, 57(5), 25–31.

Conclusion

Heike Oevermann and Eszter Gantner

Our starting point for this book was genuine accessibility as a premise and prerequisite of urban heritage. We understand urban heritage sites as symbolic places in dense and heterogeneous environments. In the last decade, public urban space has acquired a renewed urgency for the practice and performance of contemporary politics, including securitization of urban public spaces and heritage sites, but this phenomenon raises difficult questions, especially concerning access. The understanding of security, securing, and securitization as a 'regime' that is oppressing and limiting the diversity of the city is already a well-researched assumption in urban studies. As we have introduced, in heritage studies the expression to secure is more connected to the physical protection of artefacts, sites, and landscapes with a temporal dimension of 'securing things for the future'. However, this book goes further, providing a closer examination of these relationships and opening up new understandings of securitization and security and the process of securing. By doing so, we elaborate on the diverse challenges that securitization presents, both for access and urban heritage, including practices to secure heritage, and also through transforming understandings of securitization and security in relation to access and heritage. As a result, we suggest that securitization can be understood as a multifaceted process of regulation for the long-term securing of urban heritage including a multiplicity of different agents, forms of access, and uses of sites.

Using this assumption as its premise, this book discusses not only different concepts of access but also the practices regulating it. It examines the relationships between access and securitization as a special form of regulation and discusses complex questions of particular relevance to urban heritage sites whose historical and symbolic meanings put them at heightened risk of attack, misuse, or other forms of defacement. Perceiving access as one of the immanent elements of the understanding of heritage, we recognize that ongoing processes of securitization that are occurring in urban public spaces worldwide, bring with them new agents and regulations that may limit (or broaden?) access to heritage sites.

We explore the various strategies and practices for saving and securing urban heritage, highlighting on the one hand those new factors and

Conclusion 207

processes that increase vulnerability and, on the other, those which serve as tools by which to secure sites within this challenged urban environment. Documenting, digitizing, and managing heritage sites are critically discussed in terms of whether—and how—securitization might not only limit but also broaden access to, and the uses of, urban heritage.

Human relationships to 'place' are increasingly discussed today, and since the emergence of the concept of 'dissonant heritage' we know that access to heritage for all is not, in itself, a given. This book takes into account innovations and interventions that consider heterogeneous societies and institutions and their demands. Subsequently, fragmented actors—and their dissonant definitions and multiplicity of uses and forms of urban heritage—coexist at the same time and place, changing extant structures. The impacts of this multiplicity of agents on heritage sites require discussion, reaching from the present situation to long-term perspectives. Whereas for decades groups of experts shaped the faith of heritage sites in cities, such decisions are now increasingly made by diverse and numerous agents—mostly according to their economic and/or political interests. We can no longer apply the former template—characterized by dichotomies of top-down versus bottom-up, or of locals versus visitors—but must instead consider a multiplicity of agents, each following specific interests.

The 11 case studies on securing urban heritage presented here, show that agents, access, and securitization are deeply interwoven. The central questions were: How does securitization challenge access—understood as a basic right for all—to urban heritage sites? And to what degree are securitization and security transformed in relation to urban heritage and its management?

The four chapters on "Agents and forms of agency" show the opportunities and limitations of various forms of participation and sharing of heritage. The chapter on St. Denis demonstrates that municipal strategies involving citizens can lead to new territorial identities, but also to processes of inclusion and exclusion. According to its author, Christophe Foultier:

> However, in practical terms, access to rights, and measures of social inclusion are interconnected through a more security-focused experience of the territory. Thus, the development of political community standards raises normative questions, notably in matters of identity and belonging. In times of insecurity, the management of a '*dissonant heritage*' generates considerable misunderstanding and conflict within the local society.

However, the conclusion is not whether we need participation, but how we understand and organize it. Katarzyna Puzon suggests understanding participation as nodes, in a wider network, that contribute to long-lasting processes of involvement and engagement with and between citizens, institutions, and new arrivals such as migrants. As we have seen in

208 *Heike Oevermann and Eszter Gantner*

Olimpia Niglio's chapter on Kyoto and Osaka, sharing heritage from one generation to another, as well as living this heritage through practices and rituals, can be understood as another form of securitization that enables access. Here, securitization becomes quasi-synonymous with knowledge and cultural practices throughout the community. Dennis Rodwell argues for understanding and managing urban heritage through the perspectives of citizens. Here, participation goes beyond engagement: The recognition of academically undervalued urban heritage offers the path to the future when taking sustainability into account.

The second part of the book—"Technology, heritage, and access"—illustrates the potential to broaden access through new technologies of digitalization. Vanished material heritage can be digitally reconstructed and thus reactivate social awareness of politically neglected heritage and broaden possibilities for belonging and identity. On the other hand, discussion and even conflict may arise from diverse interpretations of such heritage, as urban citizens differ in their assumptions, values, objectives, and concepts of defining and using their (own) urban heritage. Consequently, we have to ask how we might enable this cultural diversity without neglecting and excluding certain heritage communities and urban citizens. One approach is discussed by Torben Kiepke and Hans-Rudolf Meier, in which digitally based informal inventories of post-war modern architecture have been compiled by various initiatives and enthusiasts. These inventories influence official listings but also offer low-threshold information, knowledge, and access for those who are interested. As Piotr Kuroczyński states, "the digital turn is changing our access to knowledge and our understanding of cultural heritage". At the same time, looking back to former innovative technologies of the atomic age, we not only recognize a paradoxical interplay between perceived risk and security, but 'get a taste' of innovative technologies that over time have become challenging forms of heritage in term of the various risks they carry. Storm et al. conclude that

> overall, the security theatre displays reversed characteristics if comparing the establishment period with the processes of heritagization, in the way that the calculable risks were initially high but downplayed, while subsequently being low but exaggerated. This tension between calculable risk and perceived risk, we suggest, forms the key to the attraction of contemporary atomic heritage.

Turning back to digitalization as the innovative technology of today, the main question seems to concern not short-term access but the long-term securing of digital heritage.

The third part of the book, titled "Securing urban heritage in time and space", explores the temporal and spatial foundations of—and implications for—urban heritage. However, while heritagization preserves and secures for future generations the urban fabric or objects from the past, it may also

Conclusion 209

encompass ambivalent processes, "on how objects of security are embedded in a wider context of political structures and social relations, as well as on how securitization can be reinterpreted as protection through community empowerment", as Juli Székely states. The case studies of Budapest, Istanbul, and Saint Petersburg illustrate well the lines of conflict and ambiguity. In the context of the urban renaissance and increasing pressure to control and use urban spaces solely for political and economic interests, citizens and communities have to claim not only their right to the city but also their right to urban heritage.

Analysing the tangible and intangible urban heritage constructed by a soccer fan group in Toluca, Mexico, Ricardo Duarte Bajaña discusses the securitization processes implemented by official institutions supposedly to improve perceptions of security at sporting events, but concludes,

> some of these official institutions value the emotional and festive atmosphere that characterizes the heritage proposal of this fan group, but exclude and ignore some of its fundamental practices because they distance themselves from the group's moral ideals concerning liberalism.

Discussing socialist urban heritage in Angola's capital, Luanda, Nadine Siegert presents different approaches to securitization and argues that "it is the level of attention and acknowledgement as public heritage that correlates with its accessibility".

Analysis of the case studies indicates the following developments:

(1) We propose that securitization in relation to urban heritage sites includes a more complex meaning, as suggested by current social–scientific narratives of Balzacq (2015) and Mavelli (2017). By doing so, we state that securitization in relation to urban heritage is multifaceted, incorporating spatial, temporal, and social factors. This would mean, however, that within the matrix, the facets and foci of the concepts and practices of securitization are "fluid"; and that they change according to social, spatial, and temporal influences and understandings. Consequently, the example of providing an impermanent site in Japan involves very different challenges to those of securing a heritage site in Saint Petersburg or Budapest, or limiting the practices of soccer fans in Mexico, where the access and usage of sites are heavily (socially/politically) controlled.

(2) We acknowledge that the ongoing securitization of urban public spaces worldwide introduces new agents and regulations, thereby limiting access to heritage sites (Davis, 1992; DeVerteuil, Marr, & Snow, 2009; Minton, 2009; Macleod & Johnstone, 2011). Several case studies in the book show, in detail, limitations on the access and use of heritage. However, there are also examples in which the securitization of urban public spaces brings new agents and broadens access to sites, as described in both chapters

210 Heike Oevermann and Eszter Gantner

dealing with new techniques of digitalization. New agents and forms of access can particularly benefit the securitization of heritage sites that are not in the focus of official heritage managers and institutions. This might also present future challenges, as already mentioned, for securing digital heritage in the long term. Moreover, digitalization opens up possibilities for further forms of participation, but only if there is access to appropriate digital tools and know-how.

Furthermore, we understand through the case study on nuclear heritage that the socially constructed understanding of risk frames our understanding of the necessity and politics of securitization. Additionally, as we learn from St. Denis, municipal policies of securitization affect processes of inclusion/ exclusion and citizens' identities. The strong relationships between securitization, access, and agents also become obvious in the context of memory politics when securing post-socialist artworks and buildings in Luanda. We argue that these social processes must be taken into consideration when defining risks and framing the understanding and politics of securitization of urban heritage sites.

(3) The presented case studies also recognize that securitization, which corresponds to the assemblage of urban practices of threat design and threat management, might also offer chances for agency and access that take into account both the spatial and temporal dimensions of securitization. Furthermore, the case studies correspond to holistic approaches known in the field of urban heritage (cf. Pendlebury, Townshend, & Gilroy, 2004; Smith, 2006; Labadi & Logan, 2016, and others), and show that in this specific field of securitization it is beneficial to examine the relationships between agents, access, and sites, including the assemblage of social practices. Thus, in the field of heritage studies, securitization is not only about control and management in order to limit diversity but is also about access for multiple agents—especially (in cases where various agents document and manage heritage) where practices of securitization might even enrich understandings and uses of urban heritage. Several contributions, including those by Ayse Erek, Eszter Gantner, and Ricardo Duarte Bajaña show that a multiplicity of various agents and forms of agency have to be taken into account when managing urban heritage sites; balancing these kinds of conflicts surrounding heritage will be a major task for the future.

The contribution by Dennis Rodwell makes some interesting suggestions for how this more complex understanding of securitization can be implemented in urban heritage management worldwide.

This opens up a new perspective according to ongoing research and practices in our cities, regarding securitization and heritage sites. The book's findings therefore serve as a basis for discussion and further research in this direction.

References

Balzacq, T. (2015). *Contesting security. Strategies and logics.* London: Routledge.

Davis, M. (1992). Fortress Los Angeles: The militarization of urban space. In M. Sorkin (Ed.), Variations on a theme park (pp. 154–180). New York: Hill and Wang.

DeVerteuil, G., Marr, M., & Snow, D. (2009). Any space left? Homeless resistance by place-type in Los Angeles County. *Urban Geography, 30*(6), 633–651.

Labadi, S., & Logan, W. (2016). *Urban heritage, development and sustainability: International frameworks, national and local governance.* New York: Routledge.

Macleod, G., & Johnstone, C. (2011). Stretching urban renaissance: Privatizing space, civilizing place, summoning 'community'. *International Journal of Urban and Regional Research, 36*, 1–28.

Mavelli, L. (2017). Governing populations through the humanitarian government of refugees: Biopolitical care and racism in the European refugee crisis. *Review of International Studies, 43*(5), 809–832.

Minton, A. (2009). *Ground control: Fear and happiness in the twenty-first century city.* London: Penguin.

Pendlebury, J., Townshend, T., & Gilroy, R. (2004). The conservation of English cultural built heritage: A force for social inclusion? *International Journal of Heritage Studies, 10*(1), 11–31.

Smith, L. (2006). *Uses of heritage.* New York: Routledge.

Index

activist/grassroots: democracy 15, 21–2, 25; groups 153–4, 164, 166
actors: of securitization (planners) 132; political/expert dominance 137–8; tensions and attempted dialogue 185–6; top-down hegemony 156
anti-terror measures (altering aesthetic/architectural character) 106
approaches to heritage (inconsistency of) 156
appropriation: intangible heritage (Toluca) 179; of public space (Budapest) 139
architecture: constructivist, and ideological shifts 200–1
art: and decolonization 189–90, 202; and socialist aspirations 193, 195, 200–2; as political intervention 147–8, 164; countering official narratives 201–2; ideological revision of 196–8; in regional regeneration (Japan) 56–9; state-commissioned 191–2, 194; tropes and idealized identity 194–6; Kitakagaya Creative Village (Osaka) 56–7, 59; KUNSTASYL (Berlin) 36–7; private funding (Japan) 57–8
atomic: accidents / dark tourism 7, 114, 119, 126; bombings/UNESCO sites 114; disasters 114, 119; heritage temporality 7; utopian/dystopian understandings 126–7; heritagization (dissociation from risks) 113; utopia 113–14
Atomic Piece (Henry Moore sculpture) 116
atomic reactors: heritagization of 116–17, 118–20; urban sites 111–12; urban (criticisms of) 115, 117, 119–20; urban (justifications for) 119–20;

urban (repurposing) 124; urban (uncalibrated risk) 124–5
augmented reality 83, 87, 93
authorized heritage discourses 6, 64–5, 70, 203, 198

citizen associations 8, 16, 19, 21–3, 26, 51–2, 54–8, 156, 161, 164–5
citizen participation (via digital access) 83–4, 92
citizen science 84, 94
citizens' values 68–70, 75
city branding 4; Budapest (past and present) 137, 140–2; Saint Petersburg 154; via culture (Istanbul) 160
civic participation (urban citizenship/right to city) 14–16
civic pride (working class) 72
civic rights 13, 15–16, 21–2, 24, 28
civil activism: as mediating platform (Saint Petersburg) 159; Istanbul 166
civil insecurity: tackling via securitization 14, 16, 19, 21, 24
Cold War 188, 190–2, 202
colonial heritage: lack of recognition (Suriname/Eritrea) 66, 74
community landscape planning (Kyoto) 51, 54–6
community-led development: countering official plans (Budapest) 146, 148–49; Istanbul 164–5
competing claims 3, 142, 158–9; and district identity (Istanbul) 161–3, 166–7; imagined past 13; municipal versus civil (Saint Petersburg) 158–9; neoliberalism (Istanbul) 161–2; and ideological change 197–8
conflict zone (Budapest) 131, 133, 135
conservation criteria: locally defined 48–9

Index   213

continuity (social / cultural / stylistic) 62–3, 65–6
conversion and reuse: and sustainability 74, 68–70, 75; Japan 58
co-operation in promoting public order / shaping public norms 15
cultural landscapes: preservation of (Kyoto) 51, 54–6
cultural policies: in preserving traditions (Kyoto) 50–6; as a source of tension (Saint Petersburg) 155

Degtyarnyy Lane (Saint Petersburg) 157–9
deindustrialization 16–19, 25, 29
demonstration: Budapest (past/present) 8, 131–4, 143–6, 149; Istanbul 148, 162–6; immigrant rights (Berlin O-Platz) 38–9, 44
dialogue: Kyoto 51
digital humanities: shift from digital to participative archives 107
digital models: enabling physical reconstruction 87, 92, 94
digital platforms: citizen engagement and knowledge creation 83–5, 87, 93–4
digitalization and visualization: for barrier-free access and securitization 89–90; for sustainable preservation 83, 91
disconnect: academic definitions versus citizen experience 71
disorder: as perception of public spaces (Saint Petersburg) 159
dissonant heritage 3, 13–4, 24, 26–7
diversity: in securing/transmitting heritage (Japan) 59; of actors (Kyoto) 51
documentation: as an indicator of public interest (see also digitization) 101; as perceived security risk 106; in multi-actor collaboration 107; official versus community-led 99–100, 101–3, 107

Emek Cinema (Istanbul) 8, 162–4, 166
environmental sustainability: heritage in relation to 74–5
European Capital of Culture: broadening definitions of culture 71
exclusion: economic and physical (Saint Petersburg) 156, 159; Toluca 181

exhibition: daHEIM (migrant experiences, Berlin) 31–2, 36–7; Ferngespräche (Distant Conversations, Berlin) 31, 36, 39–40, 43; Hungarian Millennial 137, 140

frozen heritage: impeding innovative/ sustainable schemes 155–6, 159

gentrification: 70, 157, 162, 166
globalization/neoliberalism: resistance to 161–2, 164, 166
group behaviours: criminalization of (Toluca) 182–4

Heimat: concepts of home/belonging 32–3, 43
heritage: as political resource / instrument of public policy 13; as social and political construct 64; contested (Luanda) 189; expert definitions and regulated access 153; human 49, 51, 55, 59; reactivating (Luanda) 188–9, 192, 198; Toluca: as group meaning/ belonging 171–2, 179–80, 185; transformation / differing uses 200;
heritage (intangible): 172–3; as social organization (Toluca) 174, 180
heritage community 65, 73
heritage designation: driving gentrification / economic exclusion 66–7, 76; need to recognize residential vernacular and community values 68; overlooks recent buildings 103–4
heritage movement: origins and definitions 2
heritage orthodoxy: focus on exemplars, ignoring historical uses 76; challenged by European Capital of Culture 62, 71
heritage sites: reconstruction and reinterpretation 153
heritage-making: selective 198
historical facts: as resource for securing sites and legitimating civil activism 157–8, 160
history: erasure of (including by renovation) 158–9, 161–3, 166–7, 202–3

imagined future 26
imagined past 13, 16, 26

214 *Index*

immigrants: social exclusion of 17, 27–28; social inclusion of 34–5, 42, 53–4, 56; history of (Berlin) 36, 38; O-Platz refugee camp and protest (Berlin) 38–40

inaccessibility: restriction by securitization 184, 201; Saint Petersburg 159–60

inclusivity 53–4, 56, 76; pretence of (Budapest) 140–1

informal/provisional listing: as de facto protection for modern buildings 103–4

insecurity: as political leverage 15, 16

intangible heritage: as group behaviours/identity 174–7, 180; Gion Matsuri festival (Kyoto) 6; in combination with tangible heritage 73–4; Mingei movement (Japan) 48; official ignorance of (Toluca) 183; social construction of 174–5

Internet: as the "third cultural memory" 83, 85, 87, 91, 94

local participation / civil involvement: and community divisions 26–7

migrants: as museum heritage guides 33–4

moderation 72

modern architecture: loss of 98–9, 101, 107, 166; mechanisms for protecting 101, 105

modernism: socialist-universalist 190, 191, 193, 196, 201

Morris, William 1–2, 47–8, 62–3, 67, 100, 159

multi-perspectivism: via digital documentation and technologies 84

multiple actors: 153–4; challenging frozen heritage 15–6; diversity and co-operation 51; Istanbul 161

murals: as global socialist propaganda 192–4

museums: as agents of heritage access/participation 31, 35, 43; as conduits for multi-perspectives and local histories 38

narratives: opposing official versions 201–2; difficult (post-colonial) 192, 202; narrow (official) 200

national culture: construction of (Hungary) 140, 143–4; manufacture of (Angola) 191

neoliberalism: conflict with preservation & accessibility 154, 156, 160–2, 166

new actors: in protecting modern architecture 102–3, 105

online documentation: and new heritage actors 100, 102–3; need for quality/permanence 101; new mechanism for access/protection 100; official privacy/security concerns 100, 105–6; versus security design 100, 105–7

open science/open access: and digital content 84–5, 90–2, 94

parade: as intangible heritage/youth culture (Toluca) 175–8, 182–3; as cultural festival (Kyoto) 51–2

participation: and power dynamics 43; as policy in reshaping communities 13–16, 19–22, 26; digital 84; in democratizing heritage 34; in legitimating official securitization narratives 13; narrow/broad forms 34–5; paradoxes of 14; through museum events 32; Saint Petersburg 156

participatory research: possibilities/limitations of 100

post-industrialization (Japan) 58

prelisting: as mediation and public selection of buildings 105

public parks: as national political projects 139, 135–137; inclusion/exclusion 139–41; in projecting national/imperial identity 140

right to city 4, 14, 16–17, 133, 161, 209

rights: individual versus societal (Toluca) 172, 183–4

risk (atomic) official misrepresentation of 112–3

rituals: as intangible heritage 51–2, 171, 175, 178–80, 184

rural depopulation: countering through cultural events (Japan) 58

Ruskin, John 1–2, 47–8

securitization: migration/nationalism 33; as social conflict/control (Toluca) 172, 181, 180, 182–3, 184–5; as subjugation (after Von Borries) 5; as threat design/management 5; differing understandings of 7, 159; exclusion of targeted groups 148, 166, 172, 185; political structures & social

relations 132; presented as protection 148; surveillance technology and ID cards (Toluca) 181, 184
security theatre: constructions of risk 7, 112–13, 124–6
social construction: via group practices (Toluca) 171, 184
social inclusion: false appearance of 142–3; through arts (Japan) 58
social insecurity 13–16, 19–22
social media: in organizing civil action / documenting official negotiations 159; promoting/protecting modernist buildings 102–3
social practices: control over (Toluca) 171, 184, 185
socialism: incongruity with current narratives (Angola) 192, 197;
socialist aesthetic: and transnational post-colonial identities 188, 189–90, 190–1
socialist realism 188, 191–6, 200; principles of 192–3
solidarity: socialist/anti-imperial 188, 191
special-interest groups: in protecting modernist/marginal buildings 101–103
state funding (collapse of): threat to heritage sites 154–5
sustainable development: broadening heritage definitions 3, 68–70, 72–3, 76; planning approaches (Asmara) 73–4

translocal 38, 41–2

UNESCO designation: in worsening insecurity (Suriname) 66; inconsistencies and criticisms 63–66
universalism: failure of (Africa and beyond) 202
urban regeneration/renewal 14–20, 24–6, 68–70, 74–75; as threat to cultural heritage 160–1; exemplar monuments versus local vernacular 68–70, 74–75, 166; through culture (Osaka) 56–7, 59
use value: neglected in heritage designations 68–9; origins (Giovannoni) 2, 69

violence (non-state): disputed perceptions of 182–4; (state): delegitimization of civil rights / intangible heritage practices 172–3, 180
virtual reality: in presenting heritage 83, 86, 90
virtual reconstruction (Königsberg/ Kaliningrad) 85, 87–90; of lost sites 85–7, 92–3
virtual research environments 91–2
voluntarism 15–16, 21–7, 55

youth: culture as intangible heritage 162, 171–85; disaffection 23, 26; engagement 71–2; intentional exclusion of 159; unemployment 20

Printed in the United States
By Bookmasters